Duncan McNab is a former police detective, private investigator, investigative journalist and media adviser. He was in the Gao murder trial courtroom for eighteen weeks and has been following Rogerson's career – on both sides of the law – for over 30 years. Quite simply, he knows more about Roger Rogerson than anyone else – alive.

Also by Duncan McNab

Waterfront
Outlaw Bikers in Australia
Dead Man Running

ROGER ROGERSON

FROM DECORATED POLICEMAN TO CONVICTED CRIMINAL – THE INSIDE STORY

DUNCAN McNAB

hachette
AUSTRALIA

First published in Australia and New Zealand in 2016
by Hachette Australia
(an imprint of Hachette Australia Pty Limited)
Level 17, 207 Kent Street, Sydney NSW 2000
www.hachette.com.au

This edition published in 2017

10 9 8 7 6 5 4 3 2 1

National Library of Australia
Cataloguing-in-Publication data:

McNab, Duncan, author.
Roger Rogerson/Duncan McNab.

ISBN 978 0 7336 3935 7 (paperback)

Rogerson, Roger.
McNamara, Glen.
Gao, Jamie.
Murderers – New South Wales – Biography.
Police – New South Wales – Biography.
Police corruption – New South Wales.
Murder – Investigation – New South Wales.
Drug traffic – Investigation – New South Wales.

364.1523092

Cover design by Luke Causby/Blue Cork Design
Cover photographs courtesy of Newspix and Luke Causby
Text design by Bookhouse, Sydney
Typeset in Simoncini Garamond Std by Bookhouse, Sydney
Printed and bound in Australia by McPherson's Printing Group

For years it was almost heresy to say or think that Roger Rogerson was anything other than a good bloke. This book is dedicated to those who had the guts to disagree.

CONTENTS

PROLOGUE

Jamie Gao was born in 1993. That year, Paul Keating was back in The Lodge after winning the allegedly unwinnable election against the Coalition. In New South Wales, corruption was on the front pages, prompting the Wood Royal Commission that exposed decades of corruption in the police force.

However, there was a brief respite from the state's woes on 24 September, when Juan Antonio Samaranch, then President of the International Olympic Committee, took the podium at the Louis II Stadium in Monaco to announce the city to host the 2000 Olympics. In his thick Spanish accent he told the world, 'The winner is Sydney.' The Emerald City was the focus of the world, with the *New York Times* reporting: 'An estimated 100 000 people flocked to Circular Quay on Sydney Harbour where the first European settlers set foot on Australian soil 205 years ago. They shouted in joy as they watched the announcement from Monte Carlo, Monaco on two giant television screens two hours before dawn. Tens of thousands were still dancing in the streets after the sun rose.'

One of Sydney's notables who wasn't dancing in the street was Roger Rogerson, the former golden boy of the NSW Police and a detective who once believed he was earmarked to head the Criminal Investigation Branch (CIB), and maybe get his feet under the Commissioner's desk in Police headquarters in College Street.

Journalist Neil Mercer opened his 2011 interview series *The Life and Times of Roger Rogerson – Beyond Blue Murder* saying Rogerson was 'smart, pragmatic, a born leader'. While Roger was in 'the job' (the police term for the force), he was venerated by many, but his colleagues' enthusiasm began to wane after Roger's shooting of drug dealer Warren Lanfranchi in Dangar Place, then a grimy side street in Sydney's Chippendale, on the afternoon of Saturday, 27 June 1981. It was an event that started the slide of his career from high-flying detective to 'disgraced former detective'.

By 1993, Rogerson was in Berrima Gaol serving his first year of a sentence for conspiracy to pervert the course of justice. His conviction arose from attempts to hide $110 000 believed to be the proceeds from a heroin deal done back in 1985 with Dennis 'Dr Death' Allen. Allen was a vicious Melbourne criminal deeply involved in drug trafficking and a man who bragged of committing over 10 murders, including the grisly dismemberment of a Hells Angels member with a chainsaw. Unfortunately for Rogerson, his problems concealing the $110k cash were recorded on audiotapes after he'd been chatting over lunch in Sydney's fashionable Bayswater Brasserie with colourful identities Dr Nick Paltos, solicitor Ross Karp and businessman

Maurie Nowytarger over what to do with the money. Paltos and Karp were under investigation by the Australian Federal Police (AFP) for drug trafficking, and picking up their post-lunch conversation alerted the authorities to Roger's shenanigans. To use an old police phrase, 'you can't help bad luck'. Roger added to his problems in May 1985 when caught on the security camera of the National Australia Bank in York Street in Sydney's CBD depositing a large sum of cash into an account he'd opened in a fake name. For a former member of the Armed Hold Up Squad – known around the CIB as 'the stick ups' – it was an elementary and unforgiveable error, and, as recent history has shown, one Rogerson would repeat.

His imprisonment came nearly seven years after being booted out of the NSW Police, and after he'd been convicted then successfully appealed that conviction, only to have the High Court overturn that decision. Aside from his legal troubles, his relationship with the homicidal, drug-dealing Arthur 'Neddy' Smith had also been shattered. The year before, Smith, doing life for murder, gave evidence at the Independent Commission Against Corruption (ICAC) about his and Rogerson's criminal antics. According to Neddy they drank, dined and caroused through a large part of the 1980s, and made a chunk of cash from armed robberies and drug deals. Their relationship was later made infamous by Smith's book and the ABC's acclaimed 1995 miniseries *Blue Murder*.

After years of high-stress court cases, not to mention the high cost of representation by the cream of the nation's barristers, to have it all finally done and dusted, the peace of low-security Berrima Gaol in the Southern Highlands may have well been a relief.

The prison was in the twilight of its career, used for inmates who had a low risk of fleeing but a high risk of being assaulted or killed in other prisons either because of the nature of their crimes, or because of who they were. Or both. It was where politicians, police, lawyers, public figures and paedophiles were sent and had been home to the ex-minister for Corrective Services Rex 'Buckets' Jackson, convicted of taking bribes to give prisoners an early release; Tim Bristow, the former copper, standover man, private investigator, 'colourful Sydney identity', and former first-grade rugby player with a reputation that scared anyone with sense, and a contact book that gave him access to some of the nation's most important figures; and notorious paedophiles like Robert 'Dolly' Dunn. When Rogerson arrived, he saw some familiar faces from his police career and said, 'there are about 16 ex-coppers here, including former deputy commissioner Bill Allen, who is almost 71 years of age and a nice old bloke, so I have plenty of mates to talk to. I have been sitting here writing this letter as well as watching the first State of Origin match at Lang Park. Thank God the Blues won. I bet a chocolate bar on them winning. Believe me – that's a big bet down here.'

Another positive was his developing relationship with Anne Melocco, who, like Rogerson, had grown up in the Bankstown area and now lived only a few hundred metres away from the home at Condell Park that Roger had shared with his wife, Joy, and their two daughters. Joy, after finally realising she'd married two different men sharing the same body – the brave policeman, doting father, kind neighbour; and the calculating, ruthless criminal – had filed for divorce while Roger was in prison pending the outcome of his first appeal. Anne, aware of some of Roger's faults and charms, would eventually become wife number two.

In 2005, when Roger was sentenced for another brush with electronic surveillance – this time lying under oath to the Police Integrity Commission (PIC) in 1999 while unaware the true story had been captured on audiotapes – a District Court judge and a prominent psychiatrist both expressed the view that Roger might be rehabilitated and unlikely to re-offend, which helped, in part, get him a decent discount on his sentence. Around this time, while writing my book *The Dodger*, I wasn't sure about rehabilitation, but I thought with Roger now eligible for a Seniors Card and with dodgy knees and a shoulder ruined when a roof collapsed under him while helping a friend demolish a building, the chance of him dabbling in crime again was unlikely. I was wrong.

When Roger emerged from prison a year later he wasn't heading to a life of sunshine. Instead, he was out and looking for opportunities to use his significant abilities and experience to make a quid as the nation's leading crime consultant. If only he'd resisted the opportunity for that one last fling at the sharp end.

In 1993, former NSW Police detective Glen McNamara was living with his wife, Cheryl, and two young daughters in Austinmer, a peaceful little village perched between the beach and Illawarra escarpment 70 kilometres south of Sydney's CBD. McNamara's career in the police force had ended in 1989 and he'd taken the family out of the city, ostensibly for their safety. Four years later he was planning a return to the city. In his 2010 book *Dirty Work* he said they'd 'decided to move back there. It seemed to me that if someone wanted to get at me and my family they would find me anyway even if I was out of Sydney, so we may as well lead the life we wanted to live.' Who that someone might be was never clear, but in 1993 McNamara was poised and ready to write his own history, casting himself in the role of a crusader with an abiding hatred of drug dealers, paedophiles and corrupt police.

Fast forward to 20 May 2014. Roger Rogerson, the nation's most notorious copper whether ex- or serving, the crusading McNamara and Jamie Gao met in a dark storage unit in Padstow in Sydney's south-west to consummate a drug deal. Gao, then studying business at the University of Technology Sydney, was there to sell Rogerson, then 73 years old, and McNamara, then 55 years old, three kilograms of the destructive, addictive and very fashionable drug ice. What the naive young man didn't know was that there would be a gun instead of the cash. Jamie Gao died that afternoon from two closely grouped gunshots to his chest. He didn't reach the milestone of his twenty-first birthday on 27 November. The new face of Australian crime met the old, and the old prevailed.

1

IN THE BEGINNING THERE WAS A HERO

Roger Rogerson, like many of his police peers, was institutionalised by the NSW Police force by the time he'd hit his mid twenties.

He was born on 3 January 1941 and spent his first six years in Bondi, but then the family moved to Stacey Street, Bankstown, in south-west Sydney. It was a working-class suburb, growing quickly in the years following World War II as Sydney sprawled westward. Paul Keating, another old Bankstown boy, described his peers in a speech in 2000 saying they 'represented all that was good about Australia. The people had no inherited wealth. They effectively sold their labour.' It was an ideal place for Roger's father, Owen, who was 'an old boilermaker, a pommy who'd come out here from Yorkshire' according to his son, and had knocked around in rural Queensland before heading to Sydney. During the war, Owen's skills with metal precluded him being allowed to enlist, and instead he worked building ships.

He was a strong advocate for the working man and a member of the Communist Party of Australia.

Shortly after he arrived in Sydney he met the church-going Mabel Boxley and after their marriage lived with her family in Bondi, until her father's asthma prompted a move west to somewhere drier. The family home in Bankstown was on a few acres of land and, as the decades passed, became a valuable site. The Rogersons were a solid, unimaginative lot, as evidenced by their choice of Christian name for their first-born son and Owen for his younger brother.

Roger joined the police force as a cadet at the age of 17 in January 1958. He said, 'I really don't know why I joined. My father hated the police.' His mother wanted him to take a step up in the class structure that was part of the Australian culture at that time and study engineering. 'I was bright enough,' Roger observed in one of his numerous media outings. One possible reason for putting policing in his mind was a cousin who'd been a cadet and told him the work was 'exciting' – which is youthful enthusiasm because the reality of a police cadet's day at the time was making the tea; operating the station's switchboard which was a baffling mass of cables, switches and lights; cleaning up the mess left by prisoners, an unpleasant task, particularly on the weekend when the cells were full of men sobering up after a big night; and being the general dogsbody. A size nine police boot planted in the bottom of the cadet was a frequent incentive to work hard.

Roger was well qualified for the NSW Police of his time. He could read, write, add, subtract, multiply and divide. For those members of the Criminal Investigation Branch who were corrupt, the ability to divide accurately was considered an important skill when splitting the profits of bribes and when portioning out cash that had come their way either through bribes or a crook's misadventure – like having the proceeds of his crime scooped up by corrupt detectives as 'tax'. Most importantly, Roger was healthy, over the minimum height of 173 centimetres and his weight was in proportion. The police force he entered was one of white males of Anglo-Saxon descent, either Protestant (preferably Church of England or Presbyterian, as Methodists were thought to be a little too moral for the coppers and had a reputation for being abstemious – 'never trust a man who doesn't drink' was one of many police mottos) or Catholic. Women or 'Dickless Tracys' were few and their duties were confined to school lecturing or interviewing sexual assault victims or young children. People from Southeast Asia could be found in Chinatown around Dixon Street in the Haymarket, where Roger spent the early part of his career, but not in the force. Not a great deal had changed when I joined two decades later in September 1977.

Shortly after his nineteenth birthday he was sworn as a police officer and got the dream of most young constables – a station close to home. In Bankstown Roger proved himself to be a diligent and capable uniform copper – 'one to watch' as an old detective told me, which, given the level of corruption in criminal investigation work, may not have been a compliment. He said of the time, 'I loved the work, I loved the camaraderie and I was making great arrests and I worked with a great team of blokes.' The only problem with such a posting is that you have the opportunity to arrest people you'd grown up with, but that didn't bother Roger unduly and he turned his local knowledge into a positive to gather intelligence on the local crooks, which is the lifeblood of any detective. He said, 'I knew a lot of the guys.

I'd been to school with them – the car thieves, the break and enter merchants and I was getting pieces of information about them even back in those days, and passing that on to the local detectives and then they invited me to apply for plainclothes. We were forever locking up blokes for doing break and enters on garages – service stations these days – and on the factories that were springing up around Villawood and Padstow.'

Police were encouraged to contribute some of their free time to the Police Boys Club and Roger, a talented musician who'd toyed with a career in music, was a 'musical instructor' at the St George club's musical theatre society. The St George club was, according to Roger, the only one in the state at that time that had female members and he recalled, 'some very attractive ladies came along and were in the musical society and I was very attracted to them as well'. Roger became the musical director, putting to use the years of piano study his mother had encouraged him to undertake. He recalled the prospect of heading into full-time work in the club 'nearly swayed me'. Detective work won, however, and he successfully applied for criminal investigation duty in 1962.

Induction into the brotherhood of policing – 'it's us versus them, son' as I was told in a variety of ways with monotonous regularity during my training – and particularly the sharp end of criminal investigation, was marked by your willingness to break or bend rather than enforce the law. The process started in uniform where 'freebies' like food from restaurants and booze from pubs were part of the daily routine. A publican who didn't 'kick the tin' with a delivery of free grog for the station at Christmas could be guaranteed a leisurely response to any problems at their hotel. A lesson had to be learned, and if the publican got the message, then service levels would improve. Kickbacks from tow truck operators or funeral directors were common. If an accident came over the air on police radio some police would head directly to the scene, whereas others would divert to either a phone box or a phone in the muster room – where we did our paperwork – to make a quick call to a mate in the towing business to get a spotter's fee. If you were called to a 'dead un', and after deciding there was no foul play, the bereaved were introduced to a caring funeral director who did cash kickbacks if they got the job. It was a game in which you either became a player or didn't, but kept quiet and non-judgemental. Whistleblowing wasn't a realistic option.

This cloak of brotherhood was also an effective tool to keep serious corruption well concealed. In the CIB squads who specialised in specific areas of crime, there were usually the 'A team' or the 'B team' (to borrow Rogerson's oft brag of being head of the A team at the Armed Hold Up Squad). The A teams at the squads had remarkable arrest records but kept their secret of success to themselves. In the squad, they kept to their own clique, which proved to be a handy way to keep others ignorant of the specifics of what they were up to. They considered themselves the elite of an elite organisation, untouchable and a law unto themselves – which was pretty accurate until Roger shot Warren Lanfranchi, in an act that prompted scrutiny at a time when corruption was becoming an issue.

I first met Rogerson in my early days at the CIB. In 1984 I'd been transferred to a new squad tasked to deal with underage kids prostituting themselves around Kings Cross. They congregated around the now heritage-listed El Alamein Fountain – then also the preferred venue for buck's nights if you had a set of handcuffs and planned to secure a very drunk and naked groom to something public and prominent. The kids were causing regular headlines in the tabloids, prompting our political leaders to pay attention. Roger had just been transferred to Darlinghurst Detectives, where he was second in charge. He reckoned his transfer was because he was getting too senior in rank to be on the street. However, the likelihood is that his shooting of Lanfranchi and his willingness to talk to the media about it had drawn attention to an incident which was anything but cut and dried. Senior police loathe criticism and scrutiny, and Roger's actions had ensured just that. He'd let his ego put him on the front page, and made himself too hot. The senior CIB coppers and notion of brotherhood had been so successful in keeping below the line that most of the coppers working outside the CIB – and even the honest cops working with them – had no clue about the level of corruption.

I met Roger at the Darlinghurst Police Station, where we usually took people for interviews or to process after arrest, and my colleague offered him a lift down to the Remington Centre where the squads were based. It was less than one kilometre down Oxford Street, but police don't like walking when a drive is on offer, which may account for the girth that often goes hand in hand with seniority. Roger was memorable because he was utterly charming and lacked the aloofness of many senior coppers. He immediately engaged with me, finding out where I'd been, where I hoped to head – smart, probing questions that also left you feeling part of a greater team of blokes who gave a damn. One detective aptly said Roger was 'mesmerising'. After that initial meeting, if I bumped into him in the building he'd always make a point of stopping for a brief chat – firm handshake, twinkling eyes, smile.

Over 30 years later I'm still astounded by my own level of naiveté when I first arrived at the Juvenile Crime Squad. Captivated to be at the heart of the CIB, charmed by Roger, blissfully ignorant of notable corruption and looking forward to a career in which, like my peers, I wanted to be a detective of the calibre of Roger Rogerson and his ilk. However, working around Kings Cross in those days gave you a fast education in a range of things – how your fellow man looked when they'd hit rock bottom; a parallel universe where some crims did have morals, albeit a little to the left of mainstream; the depths some could plumb for cash or pleasure; and that first strong whiff that something was horribly amiss in the brotherhood in which I aspired to succeed.

When I found myself on the carpet – literally – and told in clear terms that should I persist in either visiting brothels in the Cross to make sure that underage kids weren't working there, or visiting Costello's nightclub – later the focus of lurid allegations at the Wood Royal Commission of it being a gay brothel featuring underaged boys – with the same purpose, then I could look forward to a career pounding the beat back of Bourke. I got the message I was unwelcome at these venues, and took my nosy nature elsewhere in the Cross. There were plenty of targets.

Confirmation of the rotten state of the CIB came in 1983 when I was at the Fraud Squad – a mob that considered itself both gentlemanly and a cut above the rest. The squad had its own 'mess' where politicians, businessmen and ex-senior coppers were invited for Friday drinkies and the unofficial uniform was grey slacks, black moccasins, white shirt and blue blazer. Senior 'fraudies' teamed that with a blue shirt with white cuffs and collar and a yellow tie – they looked a bit like salesmen at a luxury secondhand car dealership on Parramatta Road.

Victims of high-value fraud – over $100000 in those days – were interviewed by senior officers who decided whether to flick the investigation to local detectives; pass it off as a 'grey' area and likely to be a civil rather than criminal case; or take on the investigation if it was unavoidable or potentially profitable. I twigged to the discreet game being played when a victim – a prominent Sydney accountant who'd been allegedly rorted by an employee – expressed his surprise when my partner and I turned up to interview him. He thought the case was dead after he'd declined to 'kick the tin' for $10000 as had been demanded of him. The game was that they'd hit the victim first for cash, and if that didn't work, hit the alleged crook to ensure the case went into the black hole of the grey area. My mate and I thought we had a good case, and ignored the scowls and arrested the employee. Still being rather naive, we thought we'd done the right thing and there were no warning bells when the employee turned up for interview accompanied by a partner from one of the top five law firms, and a lawyer whose knowledge of criminal law was rudimentary.

We battled the case through committal in the lower courts, and had a slick prosecution team running the case for the trial – until the morning of the first day. At the District Court in Darlinghurst, beside the 'wailing wall' where young male prostitutes plied their trade after dark, we found that our lawyers had been replaced. The trial was done in two hours and we were neatly shafted. There were all smirks when we returned. A lesson learned, and one that meant I looked at my brothers in a new, and not pleasant, light.

The CIB squads all had their own approach to profitability. The Motor Squad, where Rogerson spent some time in the '70s, were responsible for policing the state's car dealers, many of whom kept the coppers in cash in return for a blind eye that didn't notice stolen cars being sold through their dealerships, or, in one instance, a dealer who rented his trade-in stock to criminals so they could change cars, regularly making evading surveillance by other police a simpler task. The most popular and lucrative was the car rebirthing business. While stealing an exotic car and motoring down to the porous Sydney waterfront and driving it into a shipping container poised to be loaded onto a ship had a touch of élan and could be profitable, the regular and big bucks were in bog-standard Holdens and Fords.

Stealing cars in the days before alarms and electronic locking was easy: force the door lock using a tool developed for the purpose. For some models, just slide a ruler along the door window and into the door itself, and up comes the locking button. The thief then hot-wired the car or stuck a screwdriver into the ignition lock, a twist to break it, then fire up the engine. Back at the rebirther's factory, usually part of a car wrecking yard, the compliance plates and so on from a wreck bought at a salvage auction were used to 'rebirth' the stolen car.

Roger's career peaked at the Armed Hold Up Squad. The squad considered itself to be the heaviest of all – big crimes, big guns, and plenty of danger given the men they were hunting. Some detectives helped themselves to the spoils of armed robbery when they captured the felon. The crook had a range of options depending on the mood of the detectives and their feelings towards him. One who wasn't prepared to do business could face the coppers helping themselves to a large chunk of his cash, and then charging him with a string of robberies – some of which he hadn't committed. An unsigned record of interview or an 'I said, he said'–style conversation faithfully recorded contemporaneously in longhand was sufficient to get the bloke convicted. Professional witnesses of Rogerson's calibre had no problem swaying a jury or a judge.

The more savvy robbers knew a deal could be done. So for an appropriate cash contribution (detectives quip that one of the great crimes was 'offer insufficient bribe') and perhaps some information – 'the drum' on fellow crooks and what they were planning – they could walk free or get a lesser charge. When Rogerson and Arthur 'Neddy' Smith forged their partnership in the late '70s they took an entrepreneurial leaf from the Motor Squad's playbook and crossed the line into joint criminal enterprise.

The good cops of New South Wales worked hard, honestly and diligently, but the crooks were firmly in control.

2

OPPORTUNITY KNOCKS – LOUDLY

In the late '70s a new world of opportunity opened up for the corrupt copper to make a 'quid' and infinitely more than car scams, and standing over robbers and fraud victims. It was not only incredibly profitable but it was also very low risk. Drugs, heroin in particular.

The catalyst was a series of raids on Sydney's north shore in 1979 on suspected heroin traffickers and their key dealers. The scope of the raids was so great, the Drug Squad needed a hand. They had multiple targets all to be hit hard and at the same time. Before mobile phones, communication was based on trust, planning, and the occasional use of pagers or a stop at a phone box. Use of police radio – VKG – wasn't encouraged because in those days anyone with a scanner could be eavesdropping. The Observation Squad, known as the 'dogs' for their ability to faithfully and unobtrusively follow their target, had been on their quarry in the lead-up, watching where they went, who they met, what they drove and so on, establishing a pattern from which the arrest operation could be developed. Most importantly they could let the detectives know when the right people were at the addresses on the search warrants.

Operations of this scale were few, but when they were on, the Remington Centre in Liverpool Street where the CIB was based hummed with excitement. Down in the basement car park, which was protected by a badly dented security roller shutter – dented by too many detectives' cars when their drivers had either forgotten it was there, or were too pissed to notice – the big Falcon 351 cus and V8s were loaded for war. The scene always had me humming lines from the police pirate song 'With Catlike Tread' from Gilbert and Sullivan's *The Pirates of Penzance* – an analogy that Roger Rogerson, the musical theatre aficionado, would have liked. Into the capacious boots were loaded tools of the trade like bullet-proof vests and the Wingmaster shotguns, known as 'alley cleaners' for the large amount of lead they could spray into a confined space. Nothing more sobering than hearing the slide racked from behind you.

Then came the other essentials of the period, the 'exhibits' that could come in handy. Small bags of drugs like heroin or marijuana were useful along with a selection of old handguns handed down over the generations at the CIB, or borrowed from the piles that should have been melted down. They were useful for planting on someone who'd been shot but was found to have been minus a gun, or slipped into a criminal's pocket or dropped in their house during the search. Detectives hated to walk away without an arrest or a bargaining chip to use against the hapless criminal. Welcome to the art of 'loading'.

The atmosphere inside the cars as they sped across the Harbour Bridge towards their allotted targets would have been a mix of testosterone and tension, tempered by the occasional wisecrack – inevitably the black humour of police – from men like Roger who had both a sense of humour and a sense of timing. This raid was out of the ordinary for other reasons too, as it was timed for late afternoon. Police prefer to do their raiding around dawn. The time brings natural light and most crooks are sleeping deeply. But the coppers planned on catching them red-handed. For drug dealers the afternoon was the time when they'd be busy breaking up their supply into wholesale amounts and deals for the night's business.

Raids like those ran to a format. Local police were seldom in the loop because the CIB squads didn't want anyone getting in their way, and also didn't want the locals tipping off the targets. Corrupt coppers assumed, fortunately incorrectly, that their colleagues in blue were also susceptible to being bent. At the scene, cars were parked out of sight, with a few detectives left to drive if someone did a runner or to use the radio to get urgent assistance if matters got out of hand, or to call ambulances and so on. The property, if possible, was surrounded to prevent the occupants using windows or the back door to escape. Like actors waiting to make their entrance, everyone was on the balls of their feet until the sharp three knocks on the door and 'open up, Police' was shouted. Everyone stayed to either side of the door because drummed into you from your first days of training was that if you stood in front someone might just shoot through the door. Nearly 40 years later, I still stand to one side.

In the old days we didn't have battering rams, and a shoulder to the door could result in a very unpleasant injury and a door that hadn't budged. A sledgehammer to the lock was more effective. When the door opened, the coppers poured in, targeting anyone in the place and searching them for weapons, while one would head to the toilet – usually the first place drug dealers ran to in the hope of flushing away the evidence. Those who made it to the back door with the intention of escaping were greeted with the business end of the aforementioned Remington Wingmaster. With the bad guys suitably subdued, the detectives began their methodical search, starting with the roof and working their way down. There was the occasional mishap. One time, my colleague and I, armed with notebooks and pen, had been either side of the door waiting for the 'trained killers' (detectives with special weapons training) to pour through the door after we'd knocked and it had opened. The killers were so enthusiastic that in the rush my mate and I were accidentally shoved through the door and ended up flat on our backs in a room full of stoned youths, one of whom had murdered an old man using the .22 rifle we later found under the couch.

On the day of the major raids, Rogerson hit pay dirt. One source who was there told me Roger walked into a room at one of the target properties and found bricks of heroin wrapped in plastic, which brought a smile to his face – it would be a high-profile arrest that would add to the Rogerson aura. The smile grew when he looked into a large plastic garbage bag that was propped against the wall and found it stuffed with cash. When Roger saw the faces of Charles Kingsford Smith on red-coloured bundles of $20 bills and Howard Florey on the gold-coloured $50 bills, he turned and said gleefully, 'How good is this?' It was one of those rare career-changing moments. Back at the CIB that night, Roger was still excited. One source reckoned he was so delighted he said something along the lines of 'Bugger armed hold ups – they're for yesterday's blokes. This stuff is where the action is!'

Rogerson was correct. Drugs were the way of the future for both criminals and corrupt coppers and the son of a boilermaker who'd learned his craft as a detective from old-school police saw the opportunities. With the arrival of drugs in the life of Roger Rogerson and other corrupt detectives, the opportunity to prosper was theirs.

The prevailing attitudes were perfect for bent coppers looking at new revenue sources. Cecil 'Cec' Abbott was appointed to the commissioner job in 1981; in the '70s he'd been head of the Drug Squad. When asked by a journalist, 'How seriously do you think we are threatened in the future with large scale drug addiction in this country?' he replied, 'I'm not greatly worried about the position. I feel that Australians are not generally drug conscious.' It was both a remarkably naive and plainly stupid answer.

Australia had been the world's leader in cocaine use per capita in the '30s, with Sydney leading the nation in trafficking and use. It was William McKay, who became commissioner in 1935, who'd led the fight against Kate Leigh and Tilly Devine – the head honchos of the trade. World War II and tough laws, rather than good police work, killed a trade that was reliant on imports. Despite his time in the Drug Squad, Abbott hadn't come to grips with the recent history of heroin as a drug of addiction. In 1967, US soldiers from Vietnam came to Sydney on their R&R. Their focus was a good time and Kings Cross was happy to accommodate them. The drug quickly spread through sex workers then into the broader community – it became a problem that touched us all irrespective of social standing or perceived social standing.

The misery of heroin addiction was a great leveller. In Abbott's world the great drug menace was marijuana and that's where his mind was. It was the time of people with Italian-sounding names living in the 'grass castles' of Griffith corrupting the youth of the nation with their insidious product, and the harder the police chased them the less they looked to the new problem heading their way. It's intriguing to recall that the royal commissions and similar inquiries of the '70s when drugs popped up on the national agenda were entirely focused on marijuana that was mainly grown in Australia.

What police also weren't noticing, perhaps because contemporary policing didn't demand business acumen, was that large-scale drug trafficking required organisation and the networks that pushed marijuana around the country were useful for other substances. The only impediment was getting the heroin into the country from Southeast Asia, which is a relatively simple and low-risk enterprise given our porous borders and the advent of a smuggler's dream – the shipping container.

In 1980, Alfred McCoy – a US academic who was then a professor at the University of New South Wales – wrote in his book *Drug Traffic: Narcotics and Organized Crime in Australia* that 'no city in the world could rival Sydney's tolerance for organised crime. During the eleven years from 1965 to 1976, with the Liberal-Country Party in power, the State endured a period of police and political corruption unparalleled in its modern history.' McCoy was correct, but the decade after 1976 was a turbulent mix of crime organising, corruption and the public's slow awakening to the problem.

May 1976 marked the departure of the old government and the arrival of Labor led by Neville Wran – QC, Balmain boy by birth and Woollahra resident by choice. It took a few difficult years for the police to come to grips with the new power in Macquarie Street. So concerned were senior police for the future under Wran they went on the offensive, tasking a team of handpicked detectives to round-the-clock surveillance on some of Wran's ministers and supporters. Two targets were the law officers who'd have the greatest impact on police – the Attorney-General Frank Walker, and Chief Stipendiary Magistrate Murray Farquhar, who was known to be a Labor supporter. The idea behind the surveillance was to 'get a brief' on the men which could be used to blackmail them. One of the team told me surveillance on Walker was to 'catch him fucking out of school, kick in the door and get some tasty photos, then we'd see what a civil libertarian he really is'.

Causing ructions was the break-up of the Vice Squad and a more liberal and intelligent approach to policing the world's oldest profession and one that had provided regular income for coppers for generations. The likelihood of a legal casino for New South Wales, plus the growth of the TAB for those fancying a punt on the horses or dogs meant there was both a practical reason and political capital in making the entrenched and highly profitable illegal gaming sector a target. Tasked to close down the illicit games, the CIB's 21 Division was a mandatory training squad for all aspiring detectives where we learned to work the street, develop informant networks and learned how and when to apply a blind eye.

Being naive and still in awe of the brotherhood I'd been allowed to join, it did take me a while after arriving at 21 Division in January 1980 to fathom why some of the senior men tasked with our mentoring would disappear into brothels – or massage parlours, to be more polite – for a short time. Like a kid at the pub with our father, we'd sit in the car while he went inside – never long enough for the services on offer, but, in hindsight, long enough to pick up an envelope. Anti-gaming became the focus of the division in New South Wales – terrorising card games above or behind shops, SP bookies taking a few dollars in the bar of a pub, and occasional bigger casinos that were littered around the inner west and inner east. A slight whiff emerged when Deputy Commissioner Bill Allen – handpicked and promoted by Wran and later demoted, charged, convicted and sent to Berrima Gaol where he was on the Rogerson welcoming committee – turned up at our office demanding to see our boss, Merv Beck.

The crackdown was going beautifully it seemed, but Beck had raided Chinatown, which, according to Allen's yelling, easily audible through the closed door of Beck's office, had caused trouble. Raid vigorously, Merv, but just not Chinatown. Beck's response was typical: he raided Chinatown but first stopped for a photo opportunity, standing outside the CIB with a sledgehammer to deal with locked doors.

The Wran Government had something of a honeymoon period before the traditional New South Wales issues of graft and corruption emerged. Senior police were alleged to have a weekly collection of a bag of money to keep them out of Abe Saffron's hair in Kings Cross – an allegation later found to be entertaining but not accurate. Corrective Services Minister Rex Jackson was convicted of taking bribes to speed the release of some prisoners, and in 1983 that pesky TV programme *Four Corners* suggested something whiffy had happened which involved the rugby league, politics and the judiciary. The result was a royal commission headed by the Chief Justice, Sir Laurence Street. Wran, at the centre of the allegations, stood aside as premier.

The consensus in the police at the time was that Wran's temporary departure was a good thing. He and his government had been viewed with suspicion as they had the scent of reform about them and change was something police didn't like. For example, the repeal of the Summary Offences Act – a handy piece of legislation beloved by police because it gave them the right to arrest people who annoyed for the most trivial of offences, like 'unseemly words', which could be as simple as telling the constable to fuck off. The appointment of Bill Allen added to their annoyance and concern that the 'business as usual' approach under Premier Askin was about to come to an end because of the 'do-gooders'.

Allen's attack on Beck over Chinatown spread like wildfire around the CIB and did offer a glimmer that the do-gooders might not be as good as first thought, because to take Chinatown off the agenda meant the likelihood of 'quids' being paid to someone, which prompted the sleuths to start sleuthing. One other hope also emerged a little later when a detective with a deserved reputation for integrity was at a casino in Kings Cross in the labyrinth above the fast food joints where Bayswater Road meets Darlinghurst Road. The old rooms have been offices to players in the Australian film business, seedy lawyers and accountants, and entrepreneurs with short-lived careers – the sort of businesses that don't ask questions about the other tenants.

The detective was doing what detectives of the period did: getting out and looking around to see who was about and who they were mixing with, and being in an illegal casino was common because it was where crooks gathered. The detective got a major surprise when a prominent Labor politician walked in and strode up to the owner, who handed him what the detective believed to be a large bag of cash – the weekly payoff. The politician didn't bother to exchange pleasantries, and left immediately. The detective followed and saw the politician chuck the bag onto the seat of the car he'd double-parked in Kellett Street. The detective noted the personalised number plates on the car and later confirmed it belonged to the politician's wife.

One of the final straws came in 1978 with a change to the way police investigate police, which until then had been the province of the ineffectual Internal Affairs Branch, the branch to which I would be 'shanghaied' (transferred without choice) from the Fraud Squad in late 1983.

The argument about police investigating police still appears regularly but while there are, and certainly in the early '80s were, very real concerns of bias – when I was there you really needed to be caught red-handed committing a crime or be just stupid – the flip side is, who do you get to investigate the investigators? Wran's solution to the issue was to give oversight powers of internal investigations to the NSW Ombudsman. In a very New South Wales quirk, Chief Stipendiary Magistrate Murray Farquhar had been appointed by Wran as Acting Ombudsman for a short time. Murray went to prison in 1985 for conspiracy to pervert the course of justice. Lawyers and bureaucrats oversighting police investigations or doing them if the Ombudsman was dissatisfied wasn't a howling success as the Wood Royal Commission proved.

The police corruption problems were bubbling to the surface in the early 1980s and at the forefront were Roger Rogerson and his association with Neddy Smith, then the nation's biggest heroin dealer.

One of the motivators for a hard look at corruption and police was Liberal parliamentarian John Dowd, who said, 'I was concerned about organised crime and the involvement of police at senior levels. It was both a privilege and duty to expose serious corruption in NSW. It was accepted at some levels, but I didn't accept it.' Dowd took his work outside the safety of Parliament and started doing his own 'raids' on illegal gambling dens, and then published his findings under privilege in a Parliamentary Question Paper. Rogerson and his antics disturbed Dowd. In November 1982 he moved an urgent motion in the Legislative Assembly for a judicial inquiry into the Lanfranchi shooting. Rogerson's response was direct – the next morning he rang Dowd at his home and 'used some foul language to my daughter who'd answered the phone'. When Dowd came to the phone Roger said, 'it is easy to make threats in Parliament' to which Dowd replied, 'it's easy to make threats outside Parliament'. Rogerson then said, 'it is very easy. I've read about your background because you have spoken about your family and how important it is to you. I am worried about my own family.' The threat to Dowd was clear, and delivered by a man who believed he could get away with attempting to intimidate a member of parliament, but it didn't work. Dowd recounted Rogerson's approach in Parliament, but very little happened. Some action to rein in Rogerson at this point might have precluded the messes that followed.

3

IN THE LINE OF DUTY — OR SO HE SAID

Long after he was booted from the force, a friend of Rogerson gave him an unusual gift – a pen set made from bullet casings with the names of the three men he bragged of killing in the 'line of duty'. The three were Lawrence 'Butch' Byrne, Phillip Western and Warren Lanfranchi. Roger was so chuffed by the gift that he commissioned more of them that he sold as part of his memorabilia range when he gave a speech. It was a nice little earner for him as he frequently spoke without commanding a fee; he cleaned up on the sales afterwards, sometimes taking a few thousand dollars.

Phillip Western was his first official kill he bragged of. Western was a career criminal with a long and horrendous record, and on 29 June 1976 he was on the run after escaping from prison. Police had tracked him to a fibro house in Avoca on the New South Wales Central Coast, and the SWOS (Special Weapons and

Operation Squad) was sent to capture him. SWOS was a group of the state's toughest detectives drawn from the CIB squads for outings such as this; hence their 'trained killers' nickname. They headed to Avoca, armed with their .38 calibre Smith & Wesson service revolvers, Armalite rifles which shot a bullet that could slice through the engine of a car with ease, and their favourite weapon, the Remington pump action shotgun. The shotgun was lousy at a distance, but up close it was terrifying.

SWOS surrounded the house and, according to legend, decided to shoot when Western saw them and tried an escape by clambering out of a window. The police opened fire, and kept firing until both the house and Western were decimated. Western's body was found in the bathroom. Rogerson later bragged he'd been the one to fire the fatal shot, but the reality is it's impossible to tell who was responsible. Other members of the SWOS team didn't brag about the killing or contradict Rogerson.

The next notch on Rogerson's gun was the death of Lawrence 'Butch' Byrne. The late Mr Byrne was close to the end of a nine-year sentence for armed robbery and was on work release from prison at Silverwater. Instead of dutifully attending his day job as a panelbeater, Butch was busy planning new criminal capers, one of which was to rob the van taking the cash from South Sydney Juniors at Kingsford to the bank. Unfortunately for Butch, details of his planned robbery were passed on to the Armed Hold Up Squad. It was an intriguing moment in the squad's history. The year before there had been 339 armed robberies in the state but in 1978 that number increased dramatically to 605, and a clear-up rate constant at an unspectacular 36 per cent.

Butch had sensibly decided to do the robbery on 19 February 1978, a Sunday when there weren't a lot of people about, police were having a dozy morning attending to things like washing the cars and planning a roast at the station, and the takings from the club would be at their highest for the week.

However, his plans soon went to hell. His partners in crime were Allen Markham and Robert Hewitt. The trio were in a V8 Valiant they'd stolen earlier – a car that would easily blend into local traffic, and with a powerful engine that might help them get out of trouble. The takings from the club were moved into a VW Kombi van to transport to the bank in Kingsford, less than a kilometre away. When the van pulled up in front of the bank that quiet Sunday morning, and the three robbers slipped up behind, they had no clue the place was surrounded by heavily armed police ready to pounce.

Rogerson told journalist Neil Mercer in 2009 that Byrne 'saw police laying in wait and raised his shotgun'. Roger and his colleagues opened fire, and the Valiant drove off, with police following and shooting at it. Rogerson observed, 'by the time it got to the Doncaster Avenue turn off, it looked like your mother's colander. Butchy fell into the gutter as dead as a door nail.' One police officer who was at the scene had a different story, one he still remembered clearly nearly 40 years later. He said, 'it was an execution. The Valiant stopped with the three crims in it. Rogerson had a shotgun and Aarne Tees had his service revolver. The pair opened fire without any warning before the robbers had even opened the doors of the car, and I think Butch copped it first. The driver was still in one piece and gunned the engine, and pulled out from the kerb to try and escape the flying lead. As the Valiant peeled away, the police kept firing. It was very

Hollywood, but they did hit the Valiant repeatedly and luckily shot a tyre out, probably by good fortune rather than good shooting. The Valiant finally stopped near Doncaster Avenue.' He went on, 'There was a young mother pushing her child in a pram nearby as the shooting started. Lucky they didn't get hit.'

Byrne died shortly after in Prince of Wales Hospital. Surveillance police filmed the whole event, which was a problem for Rogerson. Back at the CIB later that day, Rogerson and Tees walked into the room where the surveillance police had set up a viewing of the footage. One source told me that as the pair arrived they were having a good-natured disagreement about who could take the credit for firing the fatal shot into Butch. Police have a black humour that helps to take the harsh edges off some of the appalling situations in which they're involved, but to the men in that room who'd been at the shooting and had watched the tape, Rogerson and Tees had gone too far – a man was dead. Police are pragmatic and there was also the issue of all the paperwork that would follow a fatal shooting by police, and one that also left two live civilian witnesses in custody and able to give evidence about the shooting. One of the detectives gave the pair a dirty look that stopped them in their tracks. He said, 'I think you two blokes should cut the comedy and look at this.'

After Roger and Aarne watched the film, which didn't fit with their script of the bad guys armed to the teeth and about to cause mayhem on the streets of Kingsford, their earlier banter changed tack, with Rogerson claiming Aarne had fired the fatal shot, and Aarne claiming it was Roger. In the end, everyone knew they'd get away with it. Whether you were appalled, indifferent or in favour of what had happened, you couldn't buck the system, unless you wanted to risk a transfer to a remote part of New

South Wales, be reminded of your past indiscretions or be told 'We know where you and your family live'. The force was a brotherhood and the family politics were brutal.

There were no repercussions from the shooting, and, as is often the case, rather than being chastised, the men were congratulated. Giving them a hand was the fact the robbery and shooting happened six days after the bombing of the Hilton Hotel in which Constable Paul Burmistriw had been killed. No one was going to criticise a grieving police force that week. Instead, some of the men at the scene, including Rogerson and Tees, were commended for their bravery. The Police Annual Report for the year 1978 noted the men received commendations for their actions when 'three offenders were surprised whilst attempting an armed robbery of the South Sydney Juniors Rugby League Club at Kingsford on 19 February 1978. In the ensuing pursuit, shots were fired at police which they returned, fatally wounding one offender before effecting the arrest of the other criminals.' It was one of the cases that led to Rogerson collecting the Peter Mitchell Award for his 'exceptional' work.

Rogerson wasn't as fortunate in his next official shooting and it brought his relationship with Arthur 'Neddy' Smith into the public eye. The two had met on 27 November 1976, when Smith had gone to the Rockdale Police Station as part of his bail reporting conditions, but instead of signing the card held behind the station counter and making small talk with the uniform police, Smith alleged he was surrounded by ten detectives from the Armed Hold Up Squad. The detectives pushed him to the ground, and Rogerson pointed the business end of a shotgun in his face and introduced himself, saying, 'Got you, Neddy.' It's an account that makes for good reading, but the likelihood of a team of detectives with shotguns in the public space of a police station taking down a major criminal is unlikely. The probability is that he was taken quietly to a room and interviewed.

It was the start of a long, deep and exceptionally profitable bromance. Smith later commented of the first meeting that he was frightened of Roger but 'not so much the man but the power he seemed to have over the other police around him. When he spoke, they jumped – all of them.' Neddy was charged for his involvement in the botched Fielders Bakery payroll robbery of 20 October that year in which the crooks – Neddy Smith and Bobby Chapman – had loosed off a few shots at the men from the bakery.

Over the next few years Smith became one of the nation's biggest, if not the biggest, heroin dealers, and said, 'My success depended entirely on the connections I met through The Dodger.' Roger was also busy: in 1978 he led the interrogations of members of the Ananda Marga, arrested for their alleged role in the bombing of the Hilton Hotel in February that year. His successes confirmed him as the ascendant detective at the CIB. The two men regularly celebrated their relationship at some of the city's smartest restaurants like The Coachman in Redfern near the old Police Academy, and the chic Eliza's in Double Bay – favoured by society mavens and the glitterati.

On the afternoon of Saturday, 27 June 1981, Rogerson met Warren Lanfranchi in Dangar Place, Chippendale, then a scruffy laneway in an old suburb that was a mix of light industrial buildings and housing for people just scraping by. In generations before, it was the home to many of Sydney's criminal fraternity. Lanfranchi had been introduced to the Smith/Rogerson team after meeting Neddy in prison. When the two were released in

1980, Lanfranchi, a fit, good-looking and wild young man who was the very black sheep of a good, hardworking family, asked Smith for work in his heroin trafficking empire. Lanfranchi was bright, greedy and fearless so he was an ideal recruit, and within a few weeks, was earning $10 000 per week and generating significantly more for his boss. Lanfranchi's girlfriend was Sallie-Anne Huckstepp.

However, Lanfranchi's greed and ego outweighed his common sense and he started doing two things that would ultimately lead to his death. Like many other drug dealers, including Jamie Gao three-and-a-half decades later, Lanfranchi started skimming the heroin he was given to sell. He'd take a bulk delivery of the drug from Smith, who anticipated he'd distribute it as it was delivered, but instead he'd take an amount which he'd sell and trouser the profit, and dilute the rest of the drugs from Neddy to cover the weight of what he'd taken. What Lanfranchi may not have known was Rogerson was Smith's alleged partner, and when dealers contacted the men to complain about the diminished quality, the avaricious Rogerson was unhappy.

Lanfranchi's next mistake was to take a shot at a police officer, and it was that stupid action which gave Rogerson the opportunity to deal with the problem decisively, and send a clear message to the underworld about who was in charge. Lanfranchi had decided, without telling Smith, that he was going to try his hand at armed robbery – then a fashionable crime of which Smith was a leading exponent. He, along with colleagues Stephen Pauley, a prison escapee at the time, and Aaron Thomas Smith were interrupted in the middle of a bank robbery in Drummoyne on 14 May 1981, by police motorcyclist Senior Constable Paul Walker who'd been patrolling Lyons Road and was the first copper on the scene. It was quite a common occurrence around this time and enthusiastic and brave bike-riding police would zoom to the scene, beating uniform police and detectives who were hacking their way through Sydney traffic. Unfortunately the lone bike rider made an excellent target for any criminal stupid or arrogant enough to think that shooting at a police officer was acceptable.

When Walker pulled the car over and approached the driver's side in the classic police vehicle-stop technique, Lanfranchi, who was lying on the back seat, sat up, pointed an automatic pistol at Walker and pulled the trigger. Automatics, particularly when not well maintained, can be erratic and this one misfired. As Lanfranchi tried to re-cock the pistol for a second attempt, the car sped off. The attempted murder of a police officer promoted him to the top of the NSW Police shit list.

It wasn't the first time Lanfranchi had contemplated shooting a police officer – an indicator of just how off the rails he was. A week before his death, Lanfranchi had been under surveillance and police had followed him and Pauley at what they thought was a safe distance and driving what they thought was an inconspicuous Ford Cortina station wagon. What they didn't know was the pair had twigged to the surveillance and when the Cortina was stopped at a set of lights, Lanfranchi wanted to get out of the car and shoot the detective. Pauley, who was less impetuous and had a modicum of common sense, restrained him. This near-miss came to light when Pauley was arrested and decided to tell the truth. Until that time, the surveillance police and their back-up had been told not to arrest either man and maintain surveillance.

When detectives were given authorisation to get Pauley, he was in a car with his girlfriend, Lyn Woodward – a prostitute and close friend of Sallie-Anne Huckstepp – and her baby was in a bassinette on the back seat.

Rogerson directed Smith to arrange a meeting with Lanfranchi. Huckstepp later said that Rogerson had wanted $30 000 to make Lanfranchi's problems with the armed robbery and cop shooting disappear, and Rogerson had suggested he'd accept $10 000 as a down payment, and get the rest as percentage of the take from armed robberies he'd guide Lanfranchi to. Huckstepp either didn't comment on, or wasn't aware of Warren's problems with the drug skimming. He was also the suspect in around six armed robberies.

Rogerson suggested they meet in a council-owned car park in Redfern, but Lanfranchi wasn't keen on that idea, fearing it would be an easy place for an ambush. Instead, they settled on nearby Dangar Place. It was familiar territory for Smith and Lanfranchi. Neddy drank regularly at the nearby Lansdowne Hotel, and Lanfranchi had wrought havoc when he'd ridden a motorbike through the bar of the Broadway Hotel. On the police side of the meeting, it was meticulously planned. An inner cordon from the Armed Hold Up Squad would watch Rogerson's back, while other detectives from the squad would be the outer cordon, making sure the public didn't stray into the place, but were sufficiently distant from the action poised to unfold. There were 19 detectives in total.

According to one source, Rogerson had brought a spare gun with him, which would come in handy if Lanfranchi was shot but found to be unarmed. Neddy's task was to drive the apprehensive Lanfranchi to the meeting, and the two arrived in his silver-coloured Toyota Celica just before 3 p.m. What actually happened next remains a mystery.

According to Sallie-Anne, Warren was unarmed and wearing trousers so tight – he was proud of his buff physique – that he couldn't have fitted a gun into the waistband without doing himself a mischief.

According to Rogerson, the two men approached each other, and when close, Lanfranchi said, 'You've fucking tricked me, this is a fucking ambush' and pulled out an old silver Harrington & Richardson pistol from the front of his trousers, and Rogerson, believing his life was in grave danger, pulled out his more modern Smith & Wesson .38 service revolver and fired twice – the classic double tap aimed at the centre mass (the biggest target) police are trained to use. Lanfranchi didn't fire a shot and was hit twice in the chest, then stumbled backwards into the gutter. Two witnesses who heard the shots contradicted Rogerson's evidence, recalling the shots were around 12 seconds apart.

In what was Rogerson's first starring role in the media, he bypassed the usual police media flacks who handle the press in events like this, and spoke directly to journalists. Warren Owens of the *Sunday Telegraph* was surprised when he called the squad for a comment and discovered he was talking to Rogerson. The resulting article channelled a Hollywood Western with the headline: 'Police Kill Gunman – High Noon shoot-out in lonely city lane.' The talkative Rogerson, when asked what had happened, said, 'I think he wanted to talk about something and thought we would be alone,' then, spinning his script, he said, 'I think he [Lanfranchi] caught sight of Graham Frazer and panicked.' When Owens asked Rogerson – a fan of the Western genre – if it was like *High Noon*, Rogerson replied, 'Well unfortunately it is a bit like that with these sort of people with guns going around the place.' Even at this early stage of his media career, Roger's talents were obvious.

Ron Ralph headed the Internal Affairs team that investigated the shooting. On 15 July they interviewed Huckstepp, who said at the conclusion of her record of interview, 'I believe Warren was murdered in cold blood by Detective Sergeant Rogerson, and was not carrying a gun.' It was game on. Rogerson had made a fundamental error, likely prompted by his arrogance, that Huckstepp was a sub-class of human because of her addiction and profession. He was wrong – she was smart, eloquent and gutsy, and would take Rogerson on in every forum in which she could find an audience. Ralph's investigation concluded in October 1981 when he was ordered, allegedly under the direction of the Commissioner, to hand over the final stages of the investigation and finishing touches on the brief for the looming coronial inquest, to Roger's old partner Aarne Tees. A baffled Ralph resumed his usual duties.

In the lead-up to the beginning of the inquest, the police public relations machine was in full swing, and targeting Sallie-Anne and her growing band of supporters. The Police Association of NSW (the police union) came out with statements to the effect that Rogerson had been the subject of a continuing attack, well-financed and with clear indications of support by radical, and even anarchistic beliefs. Rogerson was doing his own media work, and his acting skills came to the fore when he claimed of the inference he'd been involved in drug dealing that 'I am not now and never have been involved in the drug trade. That suggestion is as ludicrous as it is vile.' Of Huckstepp, he said she wouldn't be 'satisfied short of me getting twenty years'. The Coroner's jury found Roger had killed Lanfranchi 'while endeavouring to effect an arrest', but declined to find he acted in self-defence.

One story that did the rounds of the CIB afterwards was about the provenance of the weapon found on Lanfranchi. When the forensics were finished at the scene, the gun was taken back to the Ballistics section for examination – a routine procedure, which included test firing it to compare the bullet to bullets recovered from other crime scenes. This is when they found out the gun allegedly supplied to plant on Lanfranchi had a history that was traceable – it was a major error, hastily fixed by replacing it with the Harrington & Richardson pistol, which was a gun without a past.

Had the error not been picked up early on it could have been a disaster for Rogerson. All the other parties to the inquest needed to do was subpoena police ballistics records, which would prove the gun had come from police custody and may have been an exhibit in an earlier court case. An old joke at the detective's course in the early 1980s was a magistrate telling a detective he'd seen the gun used as an exhibit a few times and didn't want to do so again. We all laughed at the brazen 'loading' and the magistrate's tolerance of it – in those days some members of the bench didn't mind a criminal being loaded if the police believed 'they were guilty of something'. It was a tolerance that allowed some of the more noxious elements of police culture to flourish.

Nearly 35 years later, I got a tip that up to three teenage boys had witnessed the shooting. One of the boys, according to my source, had waited until he thought he could escape unseen, and ran to the Redfern RSL club where his parents spent their Saturday afternoons. He was intercepted by the doorman, who asked the clearly terrified boy what had happened. The doorman then took the boy to his parents. The decision was made there and then to keep quiet. Finding the boy so many years later was like putting together a jigsaw puzzle and finding a few pieces missing. The first name given to me proved to be wrong, but with a few snippets about the boy's family and connections I was able, with the help of an old colleague who knew the players of the period better than me, to track the boy's likely family and friends. Through an intermediary, one of the boy's family declined any knowledge of someone of the name we'd been given, but when the intermediary mentioned Dangar Place, the man blurted, 'Oh you mean X, we've known about that for years!'

The problem was attempts to get the man to put us in contact with his relative failed. Phone calls weren't returned, and it was obvious the shutters had been slammed shut. Rogerson's reputation still had clout, even though he was in prison awaiting trial.

However, more nosing around finally got the man's correct name and probable address.

A colleague and I finally spoke to the now middle-aged man one evening in February 2016. After first declining to talk, he followed us up the dark driveway as we walked towards our car. My first thought was, uh oh, we're in for some strife, but I was wrong. The man, a fit-looking bloke with a family, was terrified. He was sweating and shaking, and after we'd calmed him down a little he started talking, telling us that he'd been in a tree and later changing the story and saying he'd been on the roof of a nearby property when he'd heard the shots. He emphasised he hadn't seen a thing, but looked surprised when I told him the story I'd heard and he didn't comment. He denied he'd been threatened into silence by police, but said he'd been interviewed in the days after the shooting, and his parents were present as he was under 18. He said he'd given evidence at the inquest and that police had taken him into the court via a rear door and he couldn't recall if his evidence had been given to a single person or to a jury. We left the poor man alone, and after decades of interviews of people in a range of circumstances, I was a little shaken by the man's reaction.

The problem with his story was Ron Ralph had no knowledge of any interviews of a teenage boy or boys who were allegedly witnesses, and pointed out that as officer in charge of the case if there had been a formal interview it would have been under his orders. What was also intriguing was his recollection that the inquest was one of the few occasions in which a jury sits. At the time of writing, the witness list from the inquest can't be found by the Coroner's staff or at the NSW archive. A few days after our visit, I bumped into a well-known Sydney criminal lawyer who mentioned the son of a former client had just sought his advice and representation. While not ethically in a position to disclose the man's name or details of what he said, he told me the man had been a teenage boy playing in Dangar Place at the time of the Lanfranchi shooting, and it wasn't the man I'd visited.

These alleged witnesses were lucky. Lyn Woodward was on the list to give evidence at the inquest, and her evidence may have been highly damaging to Rogerson's version of the shooting.

Woodward was interviewed by lawyers representing the Lanfranchi family prior to the start of the inquest in November 1981, and in what was purported as a taped 'stream of consciousness' talk made while the solicitor doing the interview was out of the room, she allegedly said: 'Steve [Pauley] had a lot of information and evidence on Rogerson from years ago with dealing he'd done with higher up well-known criminals, you know, this heroin deal, where Steve was . . . was actually like, gone into a motel with thousands of dollars on him, and walked out with pounds of heroin, he just bought it for Roger. Roger knew that he'd . . . he was in that circle, see, and you know, the money was there. He knew I knew, you know. I was in the car one night when they've gone to meet him. Another time they'd come home with the heroin and, that they'd just gotten off Rogerson. I think they paid six thousand dollars for a certain amount that was supposed to be "A" grade, they could cut it twenty times or something you know.'

She speculated that the late Lanfranchi 'might have had something on Roger or these police and was a threat to them', and 'Rogerson had obviously thought Warren was a threat'. But like many of us she had dreams, and said Warren was 'fed up with it all and wanted to go overseas with Sally. Steve and I were going to join him, but that meant getting a bank behind you, you know.' Lyn's dream wasn't fulfilled. She was ready to go to the inquest and tell her story, but she didn't get there. When the court officer called her name three times – the traditional method of calling witnesses – Lyn Woodward didn't answer, she'd disappeared and has not been seen since. In 2000 there was an inquest into her disappearance which resulted in the finding she was presumed dead with the 'place, manner and cause of death' uncertain.

When the *Daily Telegraph* sought the inquest file on Woodward in June 2016, it couldn't be located, with the paper reporting a source in the Attorney-General's office telling them 'it's not in the archives. They [the staff] had an extensive search for it and it seems to have disappeared and no one knows when or how. It's a mystery.' While it's compelling to think there may be something fishy, the old adage of 'fuck-up before conspiracy' remains the most likely. Neddy Smith alleged Rogerson had murdered her and dumped her body at Kurnell, then one of the favourite body-dumping places for Sydney crime who couldn't be bothered to take the body out to sea and dump it. In 2007, workers excavating for the desalination plant at Kurnell found some bones that were examined and found likely to be from two males and one female. A black wig and some foot bones in a black nylon sock were among the finds at the site. In a very Sydney move, the political demand to keep on schedule for the building works trumped a full forensic investigation of the site, and the ensuing police investigation wasn't notably detailed or enthusiastic.

Rumours spread rapidly that the bones might be those of Woodward, Rogerson cohort Christopher Dale Flannery better known as Mr Rent-A-Kill, businessman Peter Mitris who disappeared in 1991, and even Juanita Nielsen got a mention. In 2013, DNA results on the bones were finally available but were inconclusive. The mystery of Lyn's disappearance and probable murder endures. She was the second person, after Lanfranchi, in a chain of deaths and disappearances linked to Roger Rogerson. Ian David, the *Blue Murder* scriptwriter when talking to the ABC about the bones on 4 December 2007, said 'there are others, Lyn Woodward, who was a young woman who was allegedly murdered by an associate of Smith's, Roger Rogerson,' and in fact 'Smith maintained that he buried the body either at the Royal National Park or at the sand dunes down there'.

4

SEE YOU OFF

Luton Chu was alleged to be a member of the Hong Kong–based 14K Triad, working in Sydney as a drug trafficker. He was also a gambler with a penchant for horse racing, but unfortunately for Luton he wasn't successful with his punting and was heavily in debt, a situation that prompted him to start skimming from his employers. Rorting his employer was a minor problem compared to the fact he'd been leant on by police and turned informer. Chu had painted a target on his back, and in late 1982 he was in deep strife.

Chu was involved in large-scale heroin importation in league with two other hard Sydney criminals. According to Neddy Smith, Danny Chubb, a wharfie and one of the men who ensured Smith was well supplied with heroin (and who was later gunned down outside his mother's home in The Rocks in November 1984), told him 'the Chinaman', referring to Chu, was a police informer and had tipped them off about an impending deal. Police sources had tipped off Chubb who felt he should do the right thing and get the message to Chu's partners. Smith drove to the home in Kiama of one of the men and gave him the message that the deal with Chu in which Chu had arranged for the two to collect two pounds of heroin from two Triad men was compromised and there was a fair chance he'd be locked up. However, greed and arrogance interposed and the two criminals thought that rather than miss the deal, they'd get some insurance and allegedly kidnapped Chu's wife.

A detective told me that on the night of the deal he'd bumped into one of the hard men at the Coogee Bay Hotel. The detective was working the night shift of the Consorting Squad and was prowling known criminal haunts to see who was about. He had a chat with the bloke who he recalled, 'was looking more shifty than usual. It was a fair bet he was up to something, so I told him to behave, but as the night wore on it was apparent he'd ignored my warning.' Not long after that encounter, the man was arrested for his part in the heroin deal while his partner looked after Chu's wife. The arrested man was lodged in the cells at Central Police Station when the detective bumped into him again. The two had a chat and the man revealed there was a hostage.

The detective told him 'you'd be a dickhead to add a murder to your current problems, so here's a phone, and get things sorted pronto'. Neddy Smith recalled he'd got a call from Rogerson in the middle of the night, telling him the coppers had got wind of the kidnapping and to get it sorted. Smith said the distraught woman was handed over to him, and he in turn handed her over to a solicitous Rogerson who told his police colleagues he'd secured her release. She was safe but there was an opportunity for a quid.

Rogerson and Smith later met with the kidnapper and Smith recounted that the running sheets (details of the police actions) and a video of the bust were offered to the man for a cost of $20000. According to Smith when told about the meeting, he said to Rogerson, 'I'm not going to be a party to another Dangar Place,' to which Rogerson replied, 'just be dead on time,' and started laughing. The deal for the evidence was done without gunfire this time.

Chu knew he had major problems and shortly after contacted Sydney criminal lawyer Chris Murphy. The two met and Chu paid a retainer by cheque, which bounced. Murphy recalled the meeting was only a few days before Chu was murdered. 'He was terrified,' Murphy said. Police were patrolling around the entrance to Royal National Park in Sutherland when they saw a woman pull her car onto the road, driving erratically so they pulled her over. It was another routine traffic stop until they looked inside and saw what they thought was a large amount of blood on the back seat, and a handgun. The driver was allegedly the girlfriend of the kidnapper, and she declined to talk to the police. They called in reinforcements and quickly found a shallow grave containing Luton Chu. The female still wasn't talking and the likely scenario was Chu had been lured into the car and shot by another person while the female did the driving. The two then buried Chu, and the other person left in his own car. The female remained silent throughout her interviews, charging for complicity in the murder and during her remand without bail at Mulawa Women's Prison in Silverwater. She committed suicide in prison by hanging herself using a bedsheet.

Sallie-Anne Huckstepp was added to the list of the dead in which Roger either pulled the trigger or was complicit, when her body was found floating in a pool in Centennial Park on the morning of 6 February 1986. She was 31 years old and had lived an exceptional life. She'd grown up in a well-to-do Sydney eastern suburbs Jewish family and at 17 had married Brian Huckstepp, moved to Western Australia and ended up supporting her husband's heroin addiction by working as a prostitute in Kalgoorlie. In early 1981 she'd met and fallen in love with Warren Lanfranchi.

Her statement to Internal Affairs of 15 July 1981, just a few weeks after Dangar Place, marked the start of her campaign to expose Roger Rogerson for what she believed was the cold-blooded execution of her lover. It was an intriguing battle between two natural media talents, played out on television and in print – Huckstepp was flawed, passionate and compelling; Rogerson was affable, aggrieved and feigned some compassion for his nemesis, and his was a compelling and manipulative performance.

In the years following Lanfranchi's death, Huckstepp had relationships with notable Sydney criminal David Kelleher, and a federal police officer. On the evening of 5 February 1986, Rogerson, who was then suspended from police duty, was drinking at the Merrylands Bowling Club in Sydney's west with police prosecutor Mal Spence – well known for being stabbed with a steak knife by one-time Neddy Smith colleague Graham 'Abo' Henry during a disagreement at the Lord Wolseley Hotel in Ultimo in 1988.

Spence was born and raised in Millers Point and there were a few jokes when the Rogerson alibi became known that Mal 'hadn't been west of Balmain', stirring rumours the drinking session was cunningly planned by Roger, who was by then suffering pariah status among police. The brotherhood is strong but only in fair weather. While Roger was sipping schooners, Sallie-Anne got a phone call at the unit she was staying at in Edgecliff. She told her friend Gwen Beecroft she had to step out briefly, and Beecroft was probably the last person, other than her murderers, to see her alive. Around 8.45 a.m. the next morning her body was found floating in Busby Pool in Centennial Park by a jogger. Her car was found in nearby Martin Road. The park gates close at sunset so she had to leave the car outside and walk in – a dangerous proposition given the location and her longstanding campaign against the NSW Police.

The cause of her death was finally known on 19 February 1986. She'd been strangled and her 'blood showed signs of associated narcotic intake (morphine)' as heroin is known as 'diamorphine'. There were marks on her back suggesting she'd been dragged to the pool and then dumped in, and a mark on her back that suggested someone had firmly applied their foot.

Roger was questioned by Internal Affairs 11 days later at his home in Gleeson Avenue, Condell Park, with his first wife, Joy, at home at the time. It was another fine performance by Rogerson, who looked a little nonplussed when questioned by Austin 'Ozzie' Prescott, who'd spent most of his career as a police prosecutor. Joy came to her husband's aid, reminding the man who in reality had a superb memory, that she thought he'd been drinking late into the night at the bowling club. When Roger got home at 1.30 a.m. the two had a chat, and Roger recalled with his customary grin and twinkling eyes that Joy 'did most of the talking'.

The inquest into Huckstepp's death was held at the Glebe Coroner's Court in April 1987. On the witness list was Warren

Richards, a former Olympic judo champion who turned to crime and was a drug trafficker and hard man about town. One protected witness at the inquest said of him, 'When [the police] catch you, they lock you up. When Warren catches you, he'll put a bullet in you.' At the Wood Royal Commission nearly a decade later, Richards said of his reputation, 'I don't pretend to be as white as the driven snow.' Richards was called because of evidence that he and Rogerson had arranged to meet with Sallie-Anne the day before her death. Richards was brought in from Parklea prison and declined to answer any questions.

Rogerson was also called, appearing on 4 May without legal representation. He told the court that while he didn't like Sallie-Anne, he certainly wouldn't have killed her and said, 'she rubbished me and caused me a lot of harm. I know what sort of person she was.' He also made extremely disparaging personal remarks about some others involved in the case. It was a taste of how hard Roger played when he was aggrieved, and fortunately the Coroner Greg Glass noted that Rogerson's remarks 'brought discredit on himself and in doing so [he] was guilty of disrespect to this court'. Rogerson was having some fun and doing a bit of payback in an arena in which his remarks could be reported. The inquest found Sallie-Anne's death was caused 'by a person or persons unknown'.

While in prison years later, Neddy Smith allegedly bragged to his cellmate, who was secretly recording their conversations, that he had murdered Sallie-Anne, saying 'strangling somebody is the hardest thing in the world (but) the most satisfying thing I ever did in my life'. The *Sydney Morning Herald* of 22 January 1995 reported Smith's prison-cell bragging in a piece headlined: 'I killed six: Neddy Smith – confessions rock police.' He allegedly confessed to Sallie-Anne's murder, which was motivated 'because Roger Rogerson had said she was taping police who'd supplied heroin to the drug trade'. Smith was charged with her murder, but bragging doesn't amount to proof beyond reasonable doubt, and Neddy was acquitted.

However, there is a back story from underworld sources. One told me that a tale had done the rounds shortly after her death, that a man he wouldn't name had come to him early on the morning Sallie-Anne was found. He was highly agitated and had scratch marks on his face and asked for advice on what might happen to a body dumped in water. The man, who had rather broad experience in some arcane areas, asked if the body had been stabbed or opened in some way so it would reduce post-mortem bloating. When told that it hadn't, the man said words along the lines of 'Well, I reckon it will be floating fairly soon'. The conversation ended abruptly as the questioner left quickly, looking even more agitated. News of the finding of Sallie-Anne's body hit the airwaves later that morning.

Another source claimed three men were responsible for her death, and all three were alive at the time of writing. One of the men had allegedly used an intermediary to approach the NSW Crime Commission with a view to giving a confession in return for a deal to get some leniency for current criminal cases in which he was involved. The commission allegedly declined to do a deal, and the man, not a public-spirited chap, stayed quiet.

5

I NEED A HERO

Glen Patrick McNamara was a boy from the Sutherland Shire who, like Rogerson, joined the NSW Police straight after school. In his 2010 autobiography *Dirty Work* he wrote of his career as a detective in hot spots like the National Crime Authority (NCA) which was set up in 1984 in the wake of Frank Costigan QC's royal commission into the notorious Federated Ship Painters and Dockers Union, and ex-NSW copper and later barrister and judge Justice Donald Stewart's royal commission into drug trafficking. The NCA's main thrust was organised crime and its involvement in major drug trafficking. In the NSW Police the NCA was unkindly referred to as 'Gurkhas' because they seldom took prisoners. Other jokes included offering them advice on where to find a courthouse.

Reviews of *Dirty Work* were glowing. The *Sydney Morning Herald* on 11 October 2010 said, 'Glen McNamara still looks like a cop. Solid. Dependable. He could easily play himself in an episode of *Underbelly*.' McNamara portrayed himself as an incorruptible crusading copper, disillusioned by his experiences with some of the most notorious police of his time, and a man who loathed paedophiles and drug traffickers.

According to sources who've known McNamara since he was a boy, he was born into a family with a kind and caring mother. In the pre-sentence report, McNamara described his childhood as happy, but marred by his father's heavy drinking which could make him a 'monster' of whom Glen was scared. Glen was educated in the local Catholic school system. He was an adequate student but an excellent sportsman who loved surfing, particularly at Cronulla. In McNamara's writings he mentioned his father had served with the Australian Army as a sniper in the Korean War, and during McNamara's difficult years in the late '80s was both friend and mentor.

In 1976 Glen became a police cadet, believing it to be a solid and respectable career path. In those days, as in the generation of Rogerson, ordinary families hoped their kids would get a job for life with the government, and policing brought with it the respect of the community – it went with the quarter acre, three kids and if you were fortunate, an annual holiday somewhere near the water, and a new Holden or Ford every three years if you had the money. He said, 'The notion that a kid from a working-class family could join the cops and have the opportunity of a well-meaning career was very attractive to me.' The police, he reckoned, was a logical step, and the military-style discipline, and strong male figures appealed to him. On his nineteenth birthday he was sworn in as a constable and started work near to home in the

Sutherland and St George areas of Sydney. Glen wasn't a hit with his colleagues.

Just before his twenty-second birthday in 1981, McNamara started his training as a detective. It's an important moment in a young copper's career because it can be a tipping point that depends on your own strength and who you're given as a partner to mentor you in those early days. For some it's the start of the seduction that leads you to accept corruption and become involved in it, or 'keep your head down' and your mouth closed. McNamara was fortunate to have been paired with Detective Sergeant Geoff Schuberg, a capable and scrupulously honest copper.

In *Dirty Work* he wrote of finding himself, albeit briefly, in Rogerson's orbit, which gives impetus to the notion of hero worship that would see him becoming Rogerson's acolyte years later. He said that Warren Lanfranchi, in 1981, was wanted nationally for the attempted murder of a traffic copper and that 'my partner and I had information that Lanfranchi sold heroin on behalf of notorious drug kingpin Neddy Smith'. McNamara said the drugs were sold to 'Aborigines who hung out at the Eveleigh Hotel' which he reckoned was in 'The Block' – close but not quite.

McNamara then moved into a gripping account of he and Schuberg entering the bar of the hotel to shouts and threats from the hostile crowd and then searching the place looking for Lanfranchi. Schuberg wasn't intimidated but Lanfranchi wasn't in the pub. He went on to say that Rogerson at his meeting with Lanfranchi and Neddy Smith in Dangar Place, 'blasted Warren out of this life, express style, with a couple of .38 rounds to his chest at close range'.

It was in 1984, McNamara wrote, that he hit the big time when he worked on the investigations of the Milperra Massacre at the Viking Tavern on Father's Day. Seven people died and 28 were injured when outlaw bikers from the Comancheros and Bandidos gangs attacked each other in the tavern's car park. One of the dead was a teenage girl who had the misfortune to be in the wrong place at the wrong time. Thirty-one men were finally convicted of criminal offences in what was, at the time, Australia's costliest and longest criminal trial.

Two years later McNamara followed Schuberg to the National Crime Authority where his mentor was running major operations. At the NCA, McNamara said he was involved in drug investigations and that police involvement was significant. While he implied there were links to the ALP he didn't name names. He revealed his NCA colleagues drawn from the Australian Federal Police (AFP) and Victoria Police believed many NSW Police were corrupt.

This is a longstanding view that ignores the murky history of the Victoria Police and the numerous commissions of inquiry that have exposed dirty dealings in that state. New South Wales coppers were always frowned on as being bent, and New South Wales frowned on Victoria for being akin to Rogerson's B Team, and the AFP or 'plastics' as they were nicknamed after cheap toys, not worth commenting on. Policing in Australia in the 1980s was notable for the lack of co-operation, communication and often petty bickering between forces, which was of enormous use to those organising crime on a national and transnational scale.

McNamara said that his secondment to the NCA finished near the end of 1986 – a short time as most were usually there for up to around two years – and then it was back to NSW Police where he'd expected an 'intelligence-based position' which meant his likely destination would have been the Bureau of Criminal Intelligence which was where information was collated and analysed, but also had operational detectives. However, Glen didn't get there, and instead was sent back to Cronulla in the Shire.

For McNamara, Cronulla was a pleasant suburban backwater where the daily fodder for detectives was break and enters, the occasional fraud, a smattering of small drug matters, assaults at pubs on the weekend and a murder every year or so. Plus, you could surf at lunchtime. Not a bad spot to mark time while waiting for your transfer to the dream job. He said he had an approach from a senior detective from the Armed Hold Up Squad. While he didn't name the man, McNamara described a man of similar characteristics to Rogerson. McNamara declined the offer, allegedly telling the detective he'd need to have a stroke so he could talk out of the corner of his mouth like the rest of the squad. McNamara reckoned he endeared himself to the man from 'the stick ups' with his forthright nature, apparently assuring him he'd done nothing at the NCA that would harm a NSW copper, and adding that fearing the NCA was pointless as they were 'soft cocks'. The latter expression is a Rogerson favourite.

Shortly after this conversation McNamara did get a transfer but not the one he'd hoped for. Instead of intelligence work alongside some of the most dynamic detectives in the force, McNamara was transferred to Darlinghurst where dynamic could be applied to the drinking style of a chunk of the detective staff. It was August 1987 and he lasted there until the beginning of 1989 when he was given an internal transfer within the same police division, to Kings Cross.

Kings Cross Detectives was run by Graham 'Chook' Fowler who was destined to become an unwilling television star thanks to 'crotch cam' footage shown at the Wood Royal Commission. The camera, pointing up at Chook and his bent colleague turned Commission informant Detective Sergeant Trevor Haken, recorded the two plotting graft and corruption, and was shown on television networks around the country after being tendered in evidence. Chook's downfall wasn't the corruption that he profited from while at the Cross, but because he'd faked an accident in which he'd slipped on a spilled milkshake while at work and hurt his back. The contrived accident, followed by lying to the Royal Commission about it, led to criminal charges and two years in prison. Chook was the figurehead in McNamara's view and Larry Churchill was running the show. Churchill was the second in charge, and deeply involved in protecting drug dealers and paedophiles including Robert 'Dolly' Dunn and Colin Fisk. Like Fowler, Churchill would also end up in prison. McNamara said an old friend had told him that Churchill was 'into everything bar a shit sandwich and that's only because he doesn't like bread'.

I'd had the misfortune to spend time with Churchill twice in my career. When I started my A list – the first step to becoming a detective – at Manly in 1979, Churchill was stationed there as a detective and partnered with a bloke he'd worked with before in Redfern, Ron Fluit, a tall moustachioed Dutchman with a preference for cream linen safari suits and noted for his laziness and arrogance. I encountered Fluit again in 1989 when working on the defence of some people charged with some horrible crimes that simply couldn't have physically happened – the infamous 'Mr Bubbles' case in which ritualistic assaults on small children and in one instance a ritual sacrifice – were allegedly carried out. Fluit was the detective in charge, and the first clue to their innocence for me wasn't the evidence itself, but the fact that Fluit had claimed to work long hours and led his team from the front. Fluit, in my experience, could lead the way to lunch but that was about it. He was a master of delegation.

I bumped into Churchill a few years later when we were both at Internal Affairs. By then he'd collected an award for outstanding police work. Churchill wasn't popular – shifty, scheming and arrogant was the consensus. The sort of person who makes the hairs on the back of your neck stand on end when you first meet. In an organisation where trust was imperative, few trusted Larry and within a few years our dim view would be proven to not have been sufficiently dim.

McNamara told the *Sydney Morning Herald* of 7 April 2010 that he found the daily routine of the Kings Cross detectives to be different from what he'd experienced in his career. He said, 'the hours of duty for a detective on the day shift were between 8.30 a.m. and 5 p.m. Morning coffee commenced about 9 a.m. and continued until about 11.30 a.m., whereupon there was a discussion about a suitable luncheon venue, which lasted until about 12.15, then lunch commenced and usually concluded about 3.30 p.m. It was followed by an ale or dozen at the infamous Macleay Street drinking establishment, the Bourbon and Beefsteak.' He was correct.

At the time, Kings Cross was the jewel in the nation's drug-dealing crown. It was where deals were done, shipments broken up and despatched to wholesalers, and had a brisk retail market on the streets and laneways with minimal interference from the coppers they were paying off. The Wood Royal Commission in its *Final Report – Volume 1* noted 'a number of self-confessed Kings Cross drug suppliers as well as proprietors of various establishments who permitted the sale of drugs out of their premises, gave evidence of making payments to particular detectives either directly or through intermediaries'. The commission had a list of properties paying the bribes, and said in return for the right to operate in the Cross, they'd get tip-offs of imminent raids, 'diversion of Drug Unit activity to unprotected operations' and 'show raids without any thorough search being made'.

Kim Thompson, a detective at the Cross during McNamara's tenure admitted to the commission that 'he had shared in substantial payments from the club operators at Kings Cross from 1987' and had 'assumed it went with the position'. The commission noted of Thompson's comment that it 'neatly encapsulates the culture of the time and the abrogation of any sense of responsibilities of supervisions to ensure the ethical and professional performance of detectives'. The inaction of police in the Cross was one reason the place was on its knees.

As a local resident, and one just out of the police force in 1987, it was a source of constant amazement and irritation to me that deals were being done so blatantly and with such little interest shown by the coppers. A walk along Darlinghurst Road, and particularly near the train station – the Cross was a magnet for anyone needing a fix and a train was the fastest and cheapest way to get there – you could see the haggard, furtive and strung-out mingling with sharp-eyed dealers, sometimes in almost as poor condition as their clients, exchanging cash for product under the eyes of police worn down by the misery of the place and the disinterest of their so-called leaders. The good were crushed by the lazy and the bent.

The detectives were conspicuous in their absence on the streets, but readily found sipping coffee in establishments with unlikely names like Cosmopolitan, which was anything but unless you consider thugs, drug dealers and bent coppers exotic, and in the Cross they weren't. It was owned by Louis Bayeh, the underworld kingpin. Then there was Sweethearts, an establishment favoured by Romanian cocaine dealers built like brick dunnies who muttered into their coffee and gave an evil look to anyone they didn't know. Another *habitué* was Rogerson who was close to both Louis Bayeh and his drug-trafficking younger brother Bill.

Heroin addicts nodded off in doorways of old apartment buildings or tucked away out of sight between parked cars in narrow lanes. The morning began by walking around the car and if you found someone, first check for a pulse and try to get them back into the land of the living, and then call the paramedics, who were on speed dial.

McNamara's induction at his new station included Fowler telling him that, 'Anyone that gives up the cops is a fucking weak fucking dog.' It was a comment that caught the culture of the place. He wrote there was a suspicion among his fellow detectives that he was a plant for the recently formed Internal Security Unit (later known as the Internal Police Security Unit – IPSU) which, unlike Internal Affairs who required a formal complaint before investigating, could start investigations based on suspicion – the first time the NSW Police could call themselves 'proactive' when it came to corruption within.

According to McNamara, Churchill and his colleagues tested him by slipping cash into his locked desk drawer to see how he'd react and on one occasion giving him a message to call a certain phone number which turned out to be a 'private line' at the newly formed Independent Commission Against Corruption (ICAC). McNamara also wrote that he'd declined an offer to work at Internal Security and found himself being questioned by Fowler and Churchill shortly after, which was more to show their reach rather than an inquiry about his career course. McNamara said that his response was to reassure them of his veracity, and utter those magic words at Kings Cross, 'So where's lunch? I'm not paying!' 'Relief,' he wrote, 'swept across both their faces.' Lunch was in the restaurant of the Sebel Townhouse Hotel in Elizabeth Bay Road, and then the preferred address for visiting celebrities.

Lunch was a success with McNamara believing he'd finally been admitted to the inner circle. Not long after the lunch McNamara was drinking through the afternoon at the Bourbon and Beefsteak in Darlinghurst Road with other detectives and Alan Saunders, a drug dealer who lived near Parramatta. It rapidly became clear to him that Saunders was moving drugs, and particularly amphetamines like speed and ecstasy that were the recreational drugs of choice for the party crowd, both gay and straight. With one 'eccy' tablet for about $40 as opposed to a gram of heavily diluted cocaine for around $400, they'd quickly become a hit. Better still, they were low risk to make, distribute and use, with heroin and marijuana still the police focus.

Saunders allegedly told McNamara that Churchill was running a large-scale drug business that had him as the distributor and 'some fag' was responsible for the cooking – the process that separates the pseudoephedrine from over-the-counter cold medications, and forms the basis of the amphetamines. McNamara believed it was 'too risky' to take what he'd been told to other police. At the time, it may have been a fair call, and a situation that had confronted other honest police over the years – when an organisation is as corrupt as the NSW Police, who can you turn to who won't pass on your involvement either deliberately or accidentally? McNamara decided to take himself undercover to gain evidence against Churchill and his drug ring and he hit pay dirt very quickly.

Within days of being accepted into the group, he found Churchill was lunching with paedophiles Robert 'Dolly' Dunn and Colin Fisk who supplied the amphetamines. Their appalling assaults on boys under the age of ten was an opportunity for Churchill, and in return for a blind eye to their activities they kept his crew supplied with drugs, most of which were wholesaled by Saunders.

For McNamara, the surprises kept coming because he was given the responsibility of picking up a boot full of amphetamines from the pair while Churchill, Fowler and company were on a two-week sex and booze jaunt to the Philippines. McNamara drove Churchill to the airport on 15 March 1989 and en route, he was told to 'look in his pigeonhole' – in pre email days these were a rack attached to the wall where every officer had their own space into which correspondence to them was placed – where he'd find the pager that was the key communications device in their drug enterprise.

McNamara had reached the point in his unofficial and solo surveillance operation where he believed official support to gain evidence that would be admissible in court and survive a battering under cross-examination from defence barristers was necessary. On Saturday, 11 March 1989 according to his book *Dirty Work,* or 17 March according to evidence he gave to the House of Representatives Standing Committee on Legal and Constitutional Affairs, chaired by Bronwyn Bishop in Sydney on 19 February 2003, he walked into the Internal Security Unit headquarters based at what had once been the Regent Street Police Station. He was greeted by Detective Sergeant Lola Scott and introduced to her partner Detective Inspector Ken Watson. McNamara outlined his tale of drugs, paedophiles and bent coppers to the two detectives who listened with wide eyes, he recalled. Then he offered his services as an undercover officer.

He said Scott asked him, 'What are you here for Glen? What have they got on you?' Curiously, McNamara found her blunt question to be 'endearing', and from the practical view of an experienced investigator, a predictable question. In policing, few come forward because of the high probability of their being complicit or risking being ostracised and having their career ruined. While there is a high moral ground that some ascend to when judging police in a difficult situation, few consider realistically what they'd do if similarly positioned – and if you're a copper the risk is higher than most professions – and many have the added consideration of a family to support and an out of work copper has a skill set that isn't broadly appealing or useful in the employment market. The added layer is that people with intimate details of a crime seldom come forward unless pushed – and Scott was looking for what gave Glen McNamara his shove.

The next move was to get McNamara legally wired up to record his conversations with the crooks. He told Bishop's committee, 'my inquiries established that Alan Saunders was a professional drug dealer who had previously been arrested by Churchill. He had been robbed of his drug sales proceeds by Churchill and subsequently put to work by Churchill to sell drugs in the Sydney metropolitan area. My inquiries established that Dunn and Fisk were commercial manufacturers and drug suppliers of amphetamine. They also disclosed to me throughout the course of my undercover operations with them – and they were recorded on listening device warrants – that they were actively engaged in paedophilia.'

Over the next week or so, McNamara recorded conversations with the drug dealing paedophiles, with McNamara lending a sympathetic ear to their complaints about Churchill and Saunders. He said dealing with men like Fisk and Dunn made him feel sick, but it was overcome by his sense of duty and the hope of insinuating himself into a bigger group of paedophiles and their protectors in the police and government. However, in spite of rumours circling for years in gossip-crazy Sydney, those bigger fish, if they ever existed never made it to the fryer, but the theme of paedophiles in high places would do the rounds for the next decade and become the lynchpin of McNamara's later media career.

He also met with Saunders on a few occasions between 18 and 22 March. Saunders allegedly gave him four street deals of amphetamines and $6180 in cash.

The pivotal meeting for McNamara was on Sunday, 26 March 1989 at the Doncaster Hotel near the Randwick Racecourse in Sydney's east. McNamara was wearing a wire with the microphone near his neck and wires taped down to the device and a power pack strapped inside his jeans – a potentially perilous location because the batteries had a habit of getting hot and leaking.

McNamara walked into the public bar around 2 p.m. and found Fisk and Dunn drinking their preferred double scotches. Outside the hotel were surveillance police with a fine view of the car park where the handing over of the drugs would take place. McNamara's role was to collect what Dunn had bragged was speed with a street value of one million dollars and then take it to Saunders to sell. Dunn, he said, was terrified of Saunders and thought that if he dealt directly he'd be ripped off. Dunn confessed to him the reason he and Fisk were in the drug business was to finance their paedophile network, with both drugs and money as a lure for their quarry. Fisk said, 'Look, Glen, we need enough money to live with young boys just like decadent Roman emperors.' On the list of those young boys the men preyed upon were vulnerable underage boys from the Redfern Indigenous community just a short walk from Dunn's home in Ivy Street, Chippendale.

The successful drug business and the protection they enjoyed meant Fisk and Dunn weren't likely to be arrested and were 'looking forward to drug dealing and they were looking forward to a life gorging themselves sexually on young boys'. McNamara was repelled. Dunn was also essential to Churchill's drug network, as a qualified and experienced science teacher 'cooking' amphetamines was a straightforward and low-risk task, made more so because Australian law enforcement wasn't alert to what was the foundation of today's ice epidemic. Dunn had a long career in teaching and was at Marist Catholic College, Penshurst NSW from 1971 to 1987 where he'd taught boys up to Year 10 and in addition to science, he'd also been 'discipline master'. When interviewed about Dunn's activities in 1996 by *Sydney Morning Herald* journalists Malcolm Brown and Murray Hogarth, Father Brian Lucas who was the spokesman for the Catholic Archdiocese of Sydney, said 'there is nothing on his file to suggest paedophilia, no record of any police complaint or any other complaint to anyone in authority'.

McNamara did what most detectives do when luring their quarry into admissions. He kept pouring the drinks. He recalled, 'I kept pumping whisky into them, making sure all I had was a middy of light.' A good move, because it is not unknown for operations to go haywire when the detective is as sozzled as the targets, and it also opens an avenue of questioning in a future court case about the detective's capacity to recall the circumstances, some of which might require clarification a tape can't provide. McNamara continued, 'they were making the most extraordinary remarks about police protection of paedophiles. At one stage I excused myself to go to the toilet, just to make sure the tape was still going – I couldn't believe it!'

The three finished up their drinks and headed to the hotel car park to collect the drugs that were stashed in the boot of Dunn's car. According to McNamara, the speed was in a large plastic garbage bag that Dunn took out and dumped on the pavement beside the car. McNamara thought it was freshly made and was still 'fuming and bubbling'. There was 1.5 kilograms of speed according to later police reports.

In the boot he saw a priest's clerical clothing. Fisk was amused and said, 'Oh, Robert, you're still not pulling that one, are you? You dirty little bugger!' McNamara, with his Catholic school system education, was horrified and asked Dunn if he'd been a priest, which Dunn denied. He explained, 'Well, Glen, I put them on when I meet boys' parents. You know, they think the boys are safe with me.' And that he wore them while having sex with the child he'd lured.

With the deal done, McNamara and drugs headed to the Internal Security where he entered with the drugs slung over his shoulder and 'dropped the bag of fizzing, bubbling wet speed onto the concrete floor' of the unit's briefing room. Scott and Watson were 'ecstatic'. He said he handed over the tapes and told them 'if you think that's good, have a listen to these disgusting bastards'.

It was at this point the difference in agendas between the ISU police and McNamara became obvious to him. He wanted Dunn and Fisk arrested immediately for the drugs and their admissions on their paedophile activities – and he knew they lived and operated only a few minutes away in the Ivy Street, Chippendale house. The ISU detectives, however, were obliged to investigate corrupt police first and Dunn and Fisk came in second to Churchill and his Kings Cross cronies. McNamara said of the conflict, 'From that point, my professional relationship with Scott and Watson deteriorated to contempt and disgust,' but he did as he was directed by senior officers. He would later focus on Scott, with more than a touch of malice. It was also the beginning of the end of his police career.

In the days following the drug collection it was business as usual for McNamara at Kings Cross, though with Fowler and Churchill still in the Philippines the lunch schedule was less hectic. He did meet with Saunders at the Bourbon and Beefsteak where he explained the drying up of the speed supplies was a failure by Dunn to deliver – a situation he hoped Saunders wouldn't take into his own hands to resolve. It was fortunate that Churchill was incommunicado.

To borrow an expression often used by police, the 'wheels fell off' when the phone beside McNamara's bed rang at 4.45 a.m. on 29 March 1989. This was in the world before mobile phones and detectives had to be available around the clock. The caller said to McNamara, 'You dog. You're fucking dead meat.' A 'dog' is an informer, so it was plain the operation against Churchill was compromised – or someone who mistrusted McNamara was aggressively probing him to see how he'd react.

According to McNamara, Fowler and Churchill arrived back from the Philippines on the evening of 28 March 1989. McNamara, woken early by the phone call, hit the beach for a run and swim to start what was a day off.

At Kings Cross Police Station, Detective Sergeant Kim Thompson, who was the interim boss, was going through the morning routine of seeing what jobs had come in overnight that needed following up and giving the tasks to his staff, and reading through the synopsis of events that might impact on his patrol – anything from mundane matters of stolen cars up to descriptions of suspects wanted for serious crimes. Thompson received a brief call, and left the police station – which wasn't a move normally part of the morning's routine. Fortunately ISU, already alerted by McNamara to a potential problem, had the station under surveillance, and had phone taps on the home phones of the key players.

Thompson, acting with care as he thought the phones at the police station might be 'off' (monitored) headed to a payphone on nearby Darlinghurst Road, and rang Churchill at his home at Collaroy on the northern beaches. Thompson was filmed as he made the call, and recorded by listening devices on Churchill's phone as he told him he'd got a call from a source at ISU to let him know that 'Little Burger' – a nickname McNamara acquired at the Cross because of his passion for eating – was an 'ISU dog'. Thompson wasn't the only one calling. Fisk also rang Churchill shortly after his return and warned him there was 'trouble afoot' and they'd all been 'given up'.

It wasn't a surprise to any detective that ISU might have been leaky. While most of its members were honest, decent and hardworking coppers, not everyone was. Smart but corrupt coppers who could see the old days were on their last legs had shifted stance and were busy forgetting their former antics and those of their similarly astute colleagues in order to prepare themselves for advancement. They were known as 'born agains' and their elevation also provided men like Roger Rogerson opportunity – with his intimate knowledge of their past useful as a negotiating edge. Coppers call it having a 'brief', and others might call it blackmail, and it did ensure you'd get a tip-off of troubles coming your way.

On learning that McNamara had been exposed, the priority of ISU's Watson and Scott was to guarantee his security. Australian law enforcement has a lousy history of looking after informants – who can be duplicitous, self-absorbed, aggressive, abrasive or just some poor soul caught in an awful spot, or the rare bird that is someone trying to do the right thing. In my experience I've seen them dumped and ignored, exposed to further dangers, left to fend for themselves, and in the case of Kings Cross kingpin James McCartney Anderson who informed on his boss Abe Saffron in the late 1980s, treated like a king with first-class airfares and five-star accommodation. McNamara was one of the lucky ones, and handled by people who gave a damn for his welfare and that of his family.

When Thompson made his call to Churchill, Watson and Scott and their crew headed at speed to Cronulla to protect McNamara and his wife, Cheryl. The abrupt end to their operation meant the arrest of Churchill, his crew and their drug network had to be brought forward and this required both planning and formal steps like the approval of police hierarchy, search warrants and so on. With an investigation as complex and sensitive as this one had become, every step had to be legal, reasonable, justified and defensible – it would cause a hullabaloo in public, and played out and forensically examined months later in court.

Around 11.45 a.m. on 31 March, the ISU search and arrest team, led by Detective Superintendent Allan West, made NSW Police history when they raided the Kings Cross Police Station. The raid was timed in the knowledge that Churchill would be there, along with the other day shift detectives, going through the routine of the start of any detective's day. West led a team of around 40 detectives who swept into the police station where they were greeted with looks of genuine surprise by uniformed staff and the public. They headed straight downstairs to the detectives' office where 22 staff were working, and most of them were equally as surprised.

Churchill was arrested and the detectives' office thoroughly searched including desks and personal lockers where a jacket and tie and your gun and handcuffs were stored. Lockers were also where detectives kept their supplies of drugs, guns, knives and so on that could be used for 'loading' people they were keen to arrest but for which they were lacking legitimate evidence.

Lola Scott wasn't on the raid, and told me she'd felt 'sick to the stomach' about its impact on the honest coppers at the station. The place was locked down for around 12 hours as the searches and interviews were done.

While West and his team were raiding Kings Cross, Fisk's home at Helensburgh was hit and Fisk arrested, and as McNamara later said, they found a Filipino boy around 13 years old in the house who was later reunited with his parents. They also raided

Dunn's home in Ivy Street, Chippendale but found the place deserted. He either had an exquisite sense of timing or had been tipped off, which was quite possible as a raid the size ISU were mounting not only involved police from ISU but administrators aware of what was about to happen plus people in the justice system who were aware of search warrants being issued. Trying to keep a lid on something like this was unlikely. The other raid of the morning was on Alan Saunders who was dragged from his bed at the unit he shared with his partner in Parramatta.

Back at ISU in Regent Street, both Saunders and Churchill went on the attack, pointing at McNamara as the mastermind of the drug deals. McNamara said they described him as 'Mr Everywhere', but ISU didn't wear that line of defence and the pair were charged with drug crimes. Fisk was more compliant and started talking – he was also charged with drug crimes. McNamara remained at home under guard. When Churchill appeared at the old Central Court in Liverpool Street Sydney on 1 April 1989, the prosecutor was Robert Hulme, who told the magistrate that bail should be refused because of the danger to 'the informant' – McNamara – and his family who were 'known personally and fondly' to Churchill. Churchill was affluent – as investigations had found the detective sergeant was partner in two retail businesses and owned two BMW cars – and therefore a potential flight risk. John Spencer, representing Churchill, suggested that if they were concerned about the informant's safety, then as a serving police officer he should be placed in witness protection and cast the first bit of mud in public at McNamara, saying 'perhaps this is another one of those "supergrass" type cases where a person is himself caught up in it and then says others are involved'.

The *Sun-Herald* a few days later dedicated four pages to the raids, and labelled McNamara as a 'supergrass'. He believed the story also implied that he'd been complicit and that 'no one came to my defence or championed my honourable behaviour in difficult circumstances, and apart from my family there was no one I could trust or turn to. The police talk about a blue brotherhood and of looking after each other, but this is a fallacy in reality.'

He spent the following days answering questions about the allegations levelled against him by Churchill and Saunders. To add to his woes, the silent number at his home was compromised by an advertisement in the *Police News* that purported to be McNamara selling an unwanted raffle prize and that he should be contacted either at Kings Cross Detectives or via his new and silent home number. Police have a malicious sense of humour and stunts like this weren't uncommon. Police pranksters were capable of something simple like a message to 'Ring Mr Lyons' and leave a number that was for Taronga Park Zoo, up to having your lawn top-dressed with gravel, or lobbing a paper bag of potassium permanganate (Condy's crystals that dissolve in water and turn it purple – and stain) into your swimming pool. It also meant 'we know where you live'.

Of the many allegations made against McNamara by the crooks one was that he'd tried to stand over Saunders for $10 000. The conversation he alleged, had been illegally recorded by Saunders and instead of asking for dollars, he'd used the term 'ten shirts'. For some curious reason, both police and criminals of the period thought that if you used a pseudonym then you couldn't get into trouble – too much Monty Python's Doug and Dinsdale Piranha where they use rhyming slang; 'the

Chinese watch' when referring to stolen whisky. It's a ploy that doesn't work.

Despite the furore caused by the raid, Kings Cross detectives went back to business as usual – minus Churchill's presence at the lunch table. Fowler was departmentally charged with misconduct and neglect of duty; however, Judge Harvey Cooper of the Police Tribunal criticised the internal investigators, with the *Sydney Morning Herald* of 9 February 1990 reporting 'internal police investigators appeared to conduct a witch hunt and try to make a detective [Fowler] the scapegoat for offences by another detective'. Fowler pleaded guilty for 'failing to make correct entries in his official duty book' – likely to place him at work rather than at lunch – and recommended he be fined $100 for each of the four of these charges.

Some of those men, including Fowler, would have to wait a few years for the Police Royal Commission where they'd wind up in strife.

Churchill was denied bail and sent to prison to await his trial. Rumours circulated that a contract had been put out on McNamara, then the key witness in the case. Glen and Cheryl McNamara joined the Witness Protection Program, then in its infancy. Looking after them was John 'Boom Boom' O'Neil – a straight talking, competent and dedicated detective I'd worked with years before in the Juvenile Crime Squad.

Both men were mindful of an unpleasant precedent in 1984 when Michael Drury, an undercover detective and key witness in a drug supply case, was shot while he was doing the washing up in the kitchen of his Chatswood home. Topping the suspect list was Christopher Dale Flannery, the Melbourne assassin who'd moved to Sydney and was dubbed 'Mr Rent-A-Kill'. Flannery disappeared in May 1985, and Roger Rogerson was later charged and acquitted for conspiring to murder Drury.

McNamara said of his protection that police budgets precluded relocation – something he'd have to do at his own cost – and he recognised detectives from Kings Cross lurking near Cheryl's travel agency in Sydney's southern suburbs.

In the months following the arrests, McNamara had little to do. The publicity of his arrest and the relentless police rumour mongering meant that returning to police work, aside from pushing a pen in a headquarters backwater or at Internal Security, was out of the question, and added was the still unfinished investigation into the allegations about him. He was still being paid and not formally suspended or on leave – just left in a twilight by a police force unsure of what to do in these extraordinary circumstances. He described it as 'persona non grata'. There was little in the way of precedent because informing on your fellow officers was rare – pariah status and/or threats of retribution were the common response by the brotherhood and an effective deterrent. One copper I'd served with blew the whistle on the local detectives on the northern beaches. They'd been spotted regularly enjoying hospitality at a brothel – then illegal – and turning a blind eye to its operation. The honest constable reported it. The result was an investigation that saw the detectives disciplined lightly and the constable left at the same police station where his life was made miserable.

Then there was case of Detective Sergeant Philip Arantz who, in 1971, found crime statistics had been dramatically underreported, and after being fobbed off by his superiors, became a whistleblower. When his superiors read the story in the *Sydney Morning Herald* there was only one suspect for the source. Arantz was smart but not politically astute. Premier Askin – a great fan of heavy-handed law and order measures – was publicly embarrassed and his commissioner, Norman Allan, furious. The reaction to Arantz's breaching the code of the brotherhood was swift and brutal. The day of the article, he was taken to the Police Medical Officer, Dr Amoury 'Morrie' Vane, at one point a specialist in women's health, which was handy in a male-dominated police force, who certified him as having a mental illness and he was then carted off to a psychiatric hospital. The perfectly well Arantz was kept for three days in the hospital where after being examined the doctors found 'no evidence of psychosis' and that he was 'an intelligent man with some obsessional traits, but they are not out of control and in the interview he was at all times alert, rational and showed appropriate effort'.

Arantz was released, then charged with misconduct because he refused to answer questions during his interview with senior police. The charge was proved and on 20 January 1972 he was dishonourably discharged and his pension rights forfeited. In 1985, he was finally acknowledged for his integrity and received a payout of $250 000. It was a story still in the minds of the police of the late 1980s. John O'Neil summed it up, as McNamara told the *Sydney Morning Herald* on 11 April 2010, saying '"you're a pariah," he said, "no one will work with you. One of two things will happen. You will be lured to an isolated location by the bullshit report of a job and then shot or your locker will be loaded up with heroin and you'll be locked up. Either way, there is no future for you."'

On 27 July 1989, McNamara and his wife headed to Los Angeles – the same city that Michael Drury had headed to after the attempt on his life. Prior to departing, McNamara had left his itinerary and contact details with Internal Security, and a few days into the trip, John O'Neil called him from Sydney – a plot to murder him while he was in Los Angeles had been uncovered.

Four coppers had been drinking in the bar of the North Cronulla Hotel on 28 July when a local chap had joined their 'shout' and heard them talking about a plot to murder McNamara while he was travelling. Later that day the man told a copper who was with another group drinking at the pub what had been said. Two days later the copper contacted O'Neil at ISU and told him of the plot. He said the local man approached him as he knew him and trusted him; they went outside for a discreet conversation. The local asked him if he knew a copper called Greg McNamara, and that McNamara was going to have a 'job done on him' and that he'd be 'knocked off'. It dawned on the coppper that it was Glen, someone he knew but 'I don't have much time for him'. The copper questioned the local on the conversation and later contacted O'Neil.

After McNamara broke the news to his wife, he went into the bathroom of their hotel suite where he spent 15 minutes gathering his thoughts, and then he emerged to find Cheryl bent over and racked by abdominal cramps. The bed was covered in blood. Cheryl had only recently been told she was pregnant and believed the stress had caused a miscarriage. 'Cheryl blamed me for the loss of the child,' he said, 'and I blamed myself as well. I lost my first child and my soul.' Instead of heading straight to a doctor, the rattled pair decided to head home to Australia, via a circuitous route through the US to try to throw off any surveillance. It was a long and uneventful trip home and Cheryl finally received medical attention. The local man, according to McNamara, was interviewed by Ken Watson from ISU but couldn't identify the plotters from photographs. McNamara allegedly spoke to him and the man said he didn't want to get involved. The conspirators have never been arrested.

McNamara commented to an audience in Camden NSW during the 2010 launch tour of his book *Dirty Work* that with his experiences culminating in the death threat and loss of his child, 'if I could have walked away I would have but it wasn't a matter of going away to hide because if you do that you're an easier mark and it was probably genetics too. McNamaras aren't like that.'

Glen and Cheryl decided it was time to move out of the Shire where they had spent their lives, and, planning on trying again to have a family, they headed down to Austinmer just north of Wollongong. It was close to Cheryl's family and a short drive back to the Sutherland Shire to Glen's family.

McNamara's career was over and on 7 June 1990 he resigned. In 2002 he told the story of his undercover work to the House of Representatives Select Committee, and in 2010 he released *Dirty Work*. However, the story he crafted for the public was more a convenient truth.

6

THE SECRET LIFE OF GLEN McNAMARA

When McNamara was arrested and charged for his role in the murder of Jamie Gao my first thought, shared by a large number of those who'd either known him as a copper, read of his exploits back in 1989 and then seen his ample media appearances from 2002 onwards, was, what the hell is a bloke like McNamara doing with someone like Rogerson? Here was a man who is a crusader against police corruption, drug traffickers and paedophiles now charged for murder and drug trafficking jointly with the man who is known publicly as the most corrupt police officer in the nation. The strangest of bedfellows and a combination that gives you goosebumps. One friend said that after Glen got close to Roger he cut himself off, no calls, no catch-ups, not even a birthday card. Another mentioned how small and old Roger was, and Glen replied, 'That little old guy is still as dangerous now as ever.'

The McNamara public story started to wobble in the early moments of my research shortly after Jamie Gao died. Rogerson has always had an almost cult-like following, with one former colleague telling me that he had a 'mesmerising' quality – a combination of the smile, the twinkling eyes, and a charm that made you feel special when you were acknowledged by him. He was like the actor on stage who makes you feel you're the only person in the audience they're talking to. The charm offensive was so slick few questioned whether it was genuine. On the flip side, it meant that Roger was centre stage, which was precisely where he wanted to be.

Aside from amazement that a bloke like McNamara would be operating with Rogerson, my suspicions kicked into overdrive when McNamara placed himself in Redfern in the lead-up to the Dangar Place shooting. McNamara was on A list at Cronulla working with Geoff Schuberg, and while he was correct about Schuberg's undoubted integrity and ability, that's where it ended. Two detectives stationed at the far southern end of the city simply didn't go rollicking around Redfern chasing a drug dealer. Redfern detectives worked their own area, or detectives from the CIB squads were also there if required. Cronulla detectives worked their own area.

Geoff Schuberg hadn't read McNamara's writing but confirmed the two had worked together when Glen had just started his criminal investigation training. When I showed him the allegation about the Lanfranchi chase he smiled and told me it hadn't happened. Schuberg found his new partner to be very eager to the point of being 'gung ho' – not an uncommon issue with younger detectives keen to impress their superiors during the early days of their criminal investigation career. What

Schuberg also noticed was McNamara was 'susceptible'. He also confirmed he'd been a senior detective at the NCA but Glen had been keen to follow him there, but not the must-have he'd purported to be.

Before heading to the NCA, McNamara did a stint at Sutherland Police Station – the head station for the area – working as one of their specialist drug detectives. It was a common practice of the time to have young local detectives who didn't look too much like police, work the local area tracking activity. Marijuana and heroin were the targets and the men looked for street dealers to arrest then hassle for information in the hope of working their way up the distribution chain. One of McNamara's arrests was a young local car salesman called Jim Byrnes who McNamara and his colleague had found with 3.9 grams of heroin on him. In drug crimes, the amount is critical, and above a certain weight you're deemed to be supplying it rather than having it for personal use. The penalty goes up dramatically. Byrnes had sufficient to be charged and convicted for supplying the drug, and ended up spending 17 months in prison.

It was his first time behind bars and a career-changing time for Byrnes. Within a few years of his release he was advising the then allegedly broke and definitely on the nose America's Cup hero Alan Bond on bankruptcy matters, and later was bankrupted himself. Magistrate Paul Lyons described him as a 'violent standover thug' after Byrnes had taken to a Sydney solicitor's office with a baseball bat for which he got four months prison, reduced on appeal to a good behaviour bond and a fine. Jim Byrnes had long claimed his innocence on the old drug charge and the incident would make a return to the McNamara story a few decades later.

McNamara's tenure at the NCA was, by his own calendar, rather short at less than a year. Secondments are normally for a few years, but his was cut short not because of any operational or administrative reasons, but because he'd referred to a colleague as a 'false pretender', usually a term of derision implying the person is a fraud as a detective – lazy, a braggart, not overly competent. While this sort of conversation isn't uncommon in the robust world of police officers, McNamara had foolishly used the term in front of the NCA head Justice Don Stewart who wasn't impressed. McNamara's departure was swift, back to where he'd come from and explains why he didn't get the job in intelligence he was allegedly promised.

McNamara had also bragged of his work in the investigation of the Milperra Massacre. Old contacts of mine who had been part of the investigation, arrests and trials didn't recall McNamara on their teams and one quipped that 'he wasn't even about to make the tea'. The probable scenario is that, as with his assertion of chasing Lanfranchi, he was gilding the lily and it was unlikely anyone would check.

Back at Cronulla, McNamara wasn't making any friends or a reputation for being an ace sleuth. He was competent but arrogant and not the team player that you're expected to be. One detective said Glen had 'tickets on himself' that weren't justified by the results he achieved, and was a 'smart arse who pissed people off', made worse by his constant refrain that he was destined for great things at the CIB or Bureau of Criminal Intelligence. In August 1987 he got part of his wish, with a transfer into the city, but to Darlinghurst and not to the lofty levels he bragged of. Darlinghurst was a tough, hardworking station policing some of the toughest parts of Sydney, and on the flip side the gay community. In policing at the time, a transfer like this was viewed as payback rather than acknowledgement of ability.

He'd been at Darlinghurst for around 16 months before his internal transfer to Kings Cross – part of the same policing area. His arrival there was, according to his story, the beginning of an eye-opening experience of firsthand corruption. That shouldn't have come as a surprise to anyone who'd been working at Darlinghurst for over a year, and if you were a detective senior constable, as McNamara was, you weren't sent to the Cross if you were still a boy scout.

For a brief moment, McNamara and Rogerson both operated in the murky world of Kings Cross, though McNamara was silent on this during his numerous later media outings. In Rogerson's case, with two killings to his name and a fearsome reputation, it was to further his career as Sydney's go-to man for advice on crime or to fix a problem that conventional means, like litigation, would be too costly, slow and uncertain to use. He was also developing a tidy business in standover.

What McNamara didn't know was that Kings Cross was a hotbed of police operations that were focused on drug trafficking and corruption. While joint operations are common these days, back in the 1980s police usually operated with a silo mentality. Police from different squads, taskforces or the Drug Enforcement Agency (DEA) would operate without telling colleagues in other areas even if they overlapped. Piling on top of that potential for confusion were some joint federal/state taskforces and the NCA and Federal Police running their own operations, neither of which had much faith in the honesty of their New South Wales colleagues.

At the time of McNamara's arrival in the Cross, some or all of these were operating there. To add to the complex situation, a team from Internal Security were also in the Cross following up whispers of major corruption. Added to the mix was Rogerson, just booted out of the force and starting his new career as adviser to the underworld. There were a lot of panel vans with blacked-out windows parked for lengthy times in the streets of Kings Cross, and fit-looking men trying with varying degrees of success to blend into the mix of locals – from the homeless and drug addicted, through hospitality workers to the young gay professionals who now mingled with dowagers in the stately apartment buildings.

Around the time of his arrival in the Cross, McNamara was having lunch with a mix of allegedly corrupt police officers and some major crime figures at a restaurant in Rose Bay. The lunchers were caught on film by the NCA who'd been following the crooks and recognised their former colleague McNamara among the coppers who joined the table. These events probably didn't come as a surprise to an experienced investigator. One of the stories that formed the lore of the CIB was when Federal Police filmed a group of men lunching on the Gold Coast. When lunch was over, one part of the surveillance team followed the known drug dealers as they left the restaurant and the other part of the team followed the men they hadn't been able to identify. They followed them as far as the Gold Coast airport and watched as the men boarded a plane to Sydney. After local investigations failed to offer any leads on who the visitors might be, photos were sent down to the Drug Squad at the CIB. In one of those delicious moments, the squad boss was reading the file, then moved to the photos, and, peering across the top of his half glasses, saw the men in the photos in front of him, sitting at their desks. As usual, nothing happened aside from a quiet word to be more discreet about the crooks you dined with.

That Saturday morning in March 1989 when Glen McNamara turned up at ISU without any prior notification, Detective Sergeant Scott reckoned that McNamara considered himself to be a 'super sleuth' as he went through his litany of allegations against Churchill, his colleagues, Saunders, Fisk and Dunn, and quickly came to the conclusion that he was an arrogant man who 'thought no one else rated'.

Detective Inspector Ken Watson was a highly experienced operator and knew that he had to put McNamara in his place immediately. Scott believed that McNamara hadn't come to tell all for any high moral purpose, but instead, thought he'd noted surveillance in the Cross – possibly one of his former NCA colleagues – and guessed incorrectly that he and Churchill and company were the targets.

Other sources agree with Scott. In the days prior to CCTV keeping an eye on the streets and video cameras still needing a robust physique to lift, surveillance was mainly 35 mm SLR cameras fitted with bulky lenses to get clear shots at a discreet distance. One NSW Police surveillance team was in the Cross and checked in to a seedy hotel offering rooms by the hour, as well as the night. They spotted someone they thought was McNamara and a colleague turning over a room in the same hotel that was used by a sex worker. One of the problems with surveillance of the time was you needed to part the curtains and poke the lens through. My source recalled that as the two men walked along Darlinghurst Road, they paused and looked up to where the team had their camera. As my source said, 'it was time to leave – we might not have been blown, but there was a fair chance we had'. Their departure was timely. Not long after, Tactical Response Group officers arrived at the hotel following reports of some sort of dangerous incident in the room the two had been staying in.

Instead of toughing it out, McNamara decided to pre-empt any problems for himself, and went to Internal Security to strike first with a story contrived to keep him in the clear. To the detectives, his tale of a one-man unauthorised surveillance operation against corrupt police and a drug ring staffed by paedophiles was more Hollywood than reality. They believed he was only telling what he needed to get them on the hook, and ultimately he was successful, though both remained sceptical throughout. In spite of the unreality of the situation, Scott recalled McNamara 'expected everything he said to be taken as gospel,' which in the detective business is the exact opposite of what happens. The cracks in McNamara's story would soon appear.

One scenario that may be reasonable is McNamara was inducted into the luncheon club at Kings Cross and went willingly. As trust developed, he found himself getting in over his head. Sanctioning drug deals in return for cash wouldn't be a major surprise, and even taking an active role in the deals wouldn't stretch credibility either, but to be involved with and profit from men like Dunn and Fisk was too much. For all McNamara's weaknesses, no one doubted his revulsion for blokes like these. To find them key players in the drug ring would have been a staggering moment.

McNamara was disinterested, at that time, in Scott, as she was only one rank higher and female but he took notice of Watson, who told him his future concisely. The operation to put him undercover at Kings Cross was to be done formally and legally – no rogue operations, nothing to compromise the integrity of the case, and all evidence to be gathered legally so it would be admissible in evidence. With the ground rules laid, and Watson making clear that McNamara's future would be bleak if he had any other ideas about how the operation was to run, McNamara was set to task and did a fine job, wired up and dutifully recording meetings, making detailed contemporaneous notes of time, date, place, who and the conversations – also admissible in evidence and the basis of statements that would come later.

The ISU detectives and McNamara concur that picking up the large bag of speed at the Doncaster Hotel was the crowning glory of the operation. However McNamara's assertion that it was bubbling and spitting was theatrical. One source of mine who'd worked as an undercover agent in the Bandidos is an expert on making speed and he told me that when the process is completed 'it's as dangerous as a bag of flour'. The danger time is during the 'cooking' process and if the product was behaving the way McNamara asserted, 'I'd have a decent set of skid marks – it means the stuff might go bang!' and more politely, 'It just doesn't work that way – his story is bullshit.'

ISU's priority for the Doncaster operation was, as Lola Scott said, 'to make sure the drugs never hit the streets'. In the days following, the plan was to put all the links together, then swoop on all the targets – to capture not only the men but evidence of meth labs and anything else that could be scooped up as evidence for when the entire ring was caught. Putting together evidence of a paedophile network is a far more complex task and the bragging of two horrid men on tape to an undercover officer is a good start but not a guarantee of success – particularly if they didn't know who the victims might be. A brag is one thing, but admissible evidence to prove a case to the standard of 'beyond reasonable doubt' is far more demanding.

Scott and Watson were never able to find the source of the leak that prompted Thompson's call to Churchill. Scott was on the team that raced to Cronulla to secure Glen and Cheryl and she recalled how the bravado and arrogance he'd displayed before was gone. The two had a conversation in the police car outside his home and she recalled he was devastated and crying so she gave him a hug to comfort him. On the day of the raids, Churchill and Fisk were arrested by ISU and the DEA was tasked to capture Dunn and Saunders.

Churchill's allegations about McNamara were investigated and found wanting. Had the men not pleaded guilty, McNamara would have been the key prosecution witness, until he delivered a king hit to his own credibility. The revelation of his lunch with some dubious characters at Rose Bay was potentially damaging but could be handled. It was his phone call to Saunders' partner that rendered him useless.

McNamara said that while investigations into allegations about him made by both Churchill and Saunders were still running, he'd received an anonymous message to call a woman. He didn't mention how the message had been delivered to him, but noted it was around the time Saunders was trying to 'implicate me in his drug dealing activities' and thought he was failing, so came up with another plan to get McNamara. For reasons McNamara didn't elaborate upon, he decided to call the woman from a public phone 'miles away from my home'. The woman, he discovered, was Saunders' partner and she had a proposal: Saunders wanted her out of the city and McNamara should pay for her travel. 'Tell Alan to fuck off' was his response.

The problem for McNamara was his later telling of the story differed from what ISU found. Where McNamara's credibility took a hit, was when Saunders' partner took a tape to ISU. The tape was from their home answering machine, one of those devices common at the time that had a tape with the greeting, then another tape that recorded your message and if you liked a chat there was plenty of tape. It was quite common that after the 'speak after the beep' that you picked up the phone and your conversation was recorded by the machine. This is what happened when McNamara rang the number. The machine recorded a conversation where, according to ISU sources, McNamara was 'standing over' the woman for cash. By that time ISU had plenty of examples of McNamara's voice on tape so when she handed it over, comparison was easy and damage control followed. Saunders' lawyers could have used the tape to destroy the high moral ground McNamara had spent so much time building. As a credible witness, he was useless.

For ISU, it was damage control time. On the one hand they had evidence of police corruption and drug dealing with a side order of an entrenched and longstanding paedophile ring. On the other they had their star witness, now mauled by his own voice. The only major positive is they had the arrested men dead to rights – plenty of first-rate evidence and little room to successfully plead not guilty. The prospect of cutting a deal to get useful intelligence from some of those charged in return for a reduced sentence or immunity from some parts of the prosecution seemed sensible. An argument for the greater good. If they'd pleaded not guilty and forced McNamara to give evidence, the prosecution could have some problems. The police and their legal advisers decided to take the common sense line and at the same time cut McNamara loose.

The good news for the police came in October 1989 when Churchill was sentenced to 12 years in prison with a non-parole period of seven years, for his masterminding of the drug syndicate. The Crown prosecutor on the case was Chris Maxwell QC.

Fisk also pleaded guilty and was sentenced to three years and out on parole in February 1991. Saunders received six years with a non-parole period of four years.

While police were arresting Churchill, Dolly Dunn had done a runner and gone to Melbourne. Short of money, and with his paedophile friends believing him too hot to be close to, Dunn was an outcast, and so he left Melbourne for a less costly life in Mallacoota, a small coastal village in East Gippsland, halfway between Melbourne and Sydney. During holiday seasons the town population swelled from a little under a thousand people to around 8000, making it a good spot for a man like Dunn to hide out. On 18 October 1989 he was arrested by police from the NSW Drug Enforcement Agency and their Victorian colleagues at his nondescript little house in Bruce Street, and extradited to New South Wales. Among his possessions they found cartons of videotapes of young boys and some starring Dunn involved in sex acts with them. In a subsequent interview and faced with overwhelming evidence, Dunn admitted some of the tapes 'actually did show myself and other people involved in sexual intercourse with children'.

Dunn joined his compatriots and pleaded guilty to the drug charges, and got the smallest sentence of all, just two years in prison. One reason for the light sentence was Dunn had talked about Churchill and the $40000 he'd extorted from Dolly years before. In return for his testimony, Dunn received an indemnity for prosecution on his crimes against boys. It was this contentious document that would drive McNamara for years and lead him to focus his anger on Lola Scott who'd filled out the application form.

To add to his rising annoyance, McNamara wasn't on the witness list for the prosecution. He said, 'I volunteered to give evidence in relation to the obtaining of the tape in which Dolly Dunn and Colin Fisk set out details of the extortion, their drug dealing activities and their commercial arrangement for protection with members of the New South Wales Police Force including Churchill. In my opinion, my evidence would have placed the evidence of Dolly Dunn and Colin Fisk into its correct context and added much needed credibility to their evidence. Additionally, the jury in the trial may have been afforded the opportunity to listen to the audiotape that I made on this undercover operation, which amounted to Dolly Dunn's initial complaint of the extortion. My offer was declined by Lola Scott and Ken Watson.'

The extortion case failed, but Churchill remained in prison to serve out his sentence. The other detectives returned to work. After Dunn's release from prison he applied for and was given an Australian passport, and headed to Indonesia first, then to Tegucigalpa in Honduras where he was found in 1997 by a team from the Nine Network's *60 Minutes*. Dunn returned to Sydney the following year, and in 2001 was sentenced for sexual assaults between 1985 and 1995 on boys between the ages of seven and 15. His original sentence of 30 years with a non-parole period of 22-and-a-half years was reduced on appeal to 20 years with a non-parole of 18. He died in prison in 2009.

Police can be adept at politics and issues management, so letting McNamara honourably slip away was the prudent choice. In 2002 he wrote in a submission to Bishop's committee that his departure from the police was due to the 'unfounded allegations made against me and the destructive behaviour exhibited by Lola Scott and Ken Watson against me which culminated in me being advised by my Witness Protection Officer John O'Neil that I had no future in the New South Wales Police, no one wanted to work with me, if I did go back to work someone would break into my work locker and load me up with heroin, or I would be lured to an isolated location on a false job call and shot'.

He was a deeply flawed man, but at the same time, he'd also been pivotal in bringing down a major criminal enterprise. He was not charged with any crimes. The Director of Public Prosecutions (DPP), particularly in murky cases such as this one, like to back a winner. Though Scott and Watson wanted him charged, he wasn't. As was often the case, the cops decided to let him quietly depart, and they kept quiet throughout. Oxygen adds heat to a fire, and on the McNamara story they've remained silent for decades. McNamara didn't.

Following his departure from the police he took up a few jobs that would have been quite mundane following his time at Kings Cross. He worked with his wife in her travel business, then as an investigator for the Tow Truck Council, a job he'd been helped in getting with a favourable reference from the NSW Police, but his tenure didn't last. And after a mix of short-term jobs including selling real estate in the Sutherland Shire – a job he left after complaints to his employer that he was far too aggressive even for a real-estate salesman – and a stint as a prison officer, he ended up in the dull world in which many ex-coppers find themselves: investigating claims for insurance companies. The money was lousy, the hours long, and you had the soul-destroying task of sorting the genuine from the bogus claims, and for the genuine, trying to find an 'out' for the insurance company or an edge to reduce the payout.

What rankled him even more was both Scott and Watson were promoted, with Scott having a notably rapid rise. A key to his attitudes and ego can be found in his book *Dirty Work* in which he wrote of his departure, dismissing his Certificate of Service as 'how nice. Not really,' but omitted to note this is all anyone gets, along with superannuation contributions, long service and so on, and if you're popular, a send-off at the pub or RSL, and if you're not, the joke will be 'we've hired a phone booth for his send off'.

As for the police force in general, they forgot about him until a decade later when McNamara, who'd spent a chunk of that time stewing over his fate, decided to paint himself as a victim of injustice – a line he may have borrowed from Roger Rogerson – and went on the attack. He joined a few other disgruntled ex-police, including Rogerson, who'd turned to the media to air their views.

7

MY BRILLIANT NEW CAREER

Roger's transfer in 1981 from the Armed Hold Up Squad to Darlinghurst in the wake of the Lanfranchi shooting had proven providential. He had less work and less responsibility and more time to devote to entrepreneurial activities and long lunches. One asset of now being a Darlinghurst local was he could do more networking at the Tradesman's Arms Hotel on the corner of Palmer and Liverpool streets. For decades it had been the watering hole of Sydney crime figures and their visitors from interstate. It was the sort of hotel a strange face walked into and the conversation stopped. You could get anything from a pistol to a brick of heroin at the pub, and Roger was a regular. Sources who knew him in the day reckoned this is where he first began to work his way into Melbourne's crime scene, chatting to visitors up in Sydney to plan deals or cooling off from torrid times down south.

Roger became a trusted Sydney representative to the point that his services were called on to negotiate a deal with undercover drug detective Michael Drury. In the wake of the Drury incident one source told me that after Commissioner Avery had broken up the CIB into regional units one senior detective told his staff, 'Roger is out. No more contact.' However, Roger was busy cultivating a new career.

Roger's next move has been referred to as a 'three-page script' crafted by him in collusion with the wily Lennie McPherson, and was the blueprint for what was touted in the media as the 'Sydney Gang War' of 1985.

On 27 February 1985, Rogerson, then suspended from duty, hosted a meeting at his home in Condell Park. On the guest list was Aarne Tees, one of the few police still loyal to him, and a few other police keen to hear what Roger's 'confidential' informant had told him about the strife in the underworld, which included the murder of Danny Chubb the previous year, and Mick Sayers – the drug dealer, illegal bookmaker and allegedly occasional fixer of horse races – on 16 February 1985. Roger followed up with a lunch the next day at Poletti's restaurant in Victoria Street, Potts Point where the guest list included Aarne Tees, Bill Duff, Christopher Flannery and Neddy Smith. The potential for conflict between Tees and Smith, who alleged Tees had loaded him in 1976 when the detective had 'planted' a gun on him, was overcome by good food and plenty of wine.

There were a couple of further meetings, hosted by drug kingpin Louis Bayeh at his home near Parramatta, and at these, Lennie McPherson appeared. Tom Domican reckoned the purpose of all these meetings and Roger's weaving tales was to pit Domican against Flannery to sort McPherson's longstanding dislike of Tom, and more broadly to pit other crooks against each other, have them brawl it out, then take over the Sydney underworld. Drugs with their huge profits and need for complex supply networks had changed the underworld dramatically from the old days when McPherson had thought of himself as Mr Big. With Roger's counsel, charisma and contacts, McPherson hoped he could be restored to his former lofty position. It didn't work.

Instead, Sydney crime had a cultural and generational change, with outlaw bikers, Middle Eastern and Southeast Asian crime gangs stepping up their activities and often working in collusion with local criminals like Michael Hurley.

However in 1985 it was still business as usual. On 14 May 1985 Rogerson was allegedly at Sydney's domestic airport to hand over 2.5 kilograms of heroin to a now-protected witness known variously as Miss Jones and Miss X, who claimed to be the girlfriend of Melbourne's Dennis 'Dr Death' Allen. In exchange for the heroin, she gave Roger a bag full of cash, which she estimated was around $100 000.

The likely source of the alleged heroin was a mate of Rogerson's who ran a hotel in Sydney's inner west as his legitimate business, and brothels staffed mainly by young Thai women lured to Australia on the promise of a rosy and profitable future, whose passports were then seized by the man. They were put to work until worn out, after which they were sent home. The girls were often couriers, undertaking the highly risky smuggling of heroin either in their luggage, or on or in their bodies. It was a loathsome business and Rogerson knew precisely what it entailed.

The arrival of this heroin supply chain was timely. The death of Danny Chubb, whose international connections and Australian docklands contacts made getting the drug into the country in large amounts easy and safe, had caused a hiccup in supply to a demanding market. All the modern-day slave trader had to do was increase his importing. Rogerson allegedly helped the trader at Sydney airport because he had 'a brief' on a customs officer who could be pressured into making sure the girls escaped scrutiny.

Miss Jones's evidence under oath was that Dennis gave her a black travel bag containing the cash, and two airline tickets under different fake names – one to get her to Sydney, and the other to get her back. She arrived in Sydney around 11.30 a.m. and found Rogerson near the women's toilets in the terminal. She recalled 'he sort of said g'day, threw the bag at me, and ripped the other one [containing the $100 000] off me and ran away'. She later looked into the bag he'd thrown at her and found clothing, books and plastic sandwich bags of heroin. She then flew back to Melbourne where she handed over the heroin, and the next day $7000 in cash was put into her letterbox for services rendered. She didn't talk of any other similar deals.

Rogerson was a capable and experienced detective but his skills didn't run to laundering the proceeds of crime. The financial institution favoured by police was their credit union, but wandering in with a large bag of money would have been problematic. With Maurie Nowytarger, Roger went to the National Australia Bank in York Street, and with the aid of a helpful bank officer, he opened accounts in the name of 'Mike Roberts' and 'Robert Tracey'. Roger, then a detective on a salary of $32 000 per year, deposited $14 000 in cash, and $60 000 in cash three days later.

A few weeks later he returned to the bank and emptied the accounts, an act caught on CCTV footage. Roger got a tip-off that Internal Security and the Australian Tax Office might be looking at his dodgy bank accounts and had the CCTV footage. Roger was good with guns, crims and courtrooms, but in financial matters he was a novice and so he turned to his more sophisticated mates.

On 21 July he met with Dr Nick Paltos, solicitor Ross Karp and Maurie Nowytarger at the Bayswater Brasserie in Kings Cross. Over lunch, a plan was hatched to give Roger a reason for having a large pile of cash. What none of the men knew was Paltos and Karp, both big and unsuccessful gamblers, were under electronic surveillance by the AFP for cooking up a $40 million cannabis importation scheme.

After deciding the money came from a confected deal involving a Bentley S2 Continental – quite a valuable motor car – which would be allegedly restored to glory by Roger, then onsold to Karp, the solicitor and doctor were recorded by a bug in Paltos's car, telling their fellow drug entrepreneur Graham 'Croc' Palmer they'd done Roger 'the best fucking turn'. Karp said, 'and they think now the money is from ill-gotten gains,' at which point Paltos interjected and said, 'drugs. From drugs. Tell the truth.' Karp said, 'Well he [Rogerson] said drugs. Right? OK?' Three weeks after the lunch, Palmer, Paltos and Karp were arrested for their roles in the bungled drug importation with Karp and Palmer getting 14 years in prison, and Paltos 20 years.

On 29 September 1987, Roger was charged with conspiracy to pervert the course of justice over the cooked-up car plot and on 28 April 1988 for conspiring with the by then late Dennis Allen – he died of congestive heart failure – to supply heroin he supplied to Miss Jones. The heroin charge was withdrawn on 4 April 1990 by the DPP in the wake of Roger's conviction on the conspiracy charge. Roger had gone into the trial for the conspiracy to pervert the course of justice charge in early 1990 on a bit of a roll. In October 1989, he'd faced the Supreme

Court, charged with conspiring to murder Michael Drury back in 1984. His co-accused beside him in the dock should have been Christopher Flannery.

The trial was the first clash between Crown Prosecutor Chris Maxwell QC and Rogerson. Unlike the result in June 2016, Rogerson was triumphant. Rogerson's performance in the witness box was the pivot in the trial. He described Michael Drury, who had been exceptionally emotional while giving his evidence, as 'befuddled', and in the first outing of an angle he'd use in his trial in 2016, he painted himself as a compassionate man, thinking only of helping friends and colleagues, and he said he was only involved in the Drury case, where he'd allegedly tried to bribe Drury to change his evidence, because he wanted 'to help'. Roger, according to Roger, was a victim too, not of an armed assassin, but of senior police of lesser ability than his, who wanted him out of the way. It was a theme that was repeated throughout Roger's numerous subsequent court appearances as both witness and defendant.

Maxwell's assertion that Roger had spun a tale 'with the artful pretence of a skilled witness', and prosecution witness Alan Williams, who asserted Roger was 'a cunning man who will not only stoop to foist off his own guilt on others but a man who will not scruple from doing so', didn't persuade the jury. On 20 November after a three-week trial, it took the jury three hours to come back with a 'not guilty' verdict.

When he returned to court only months later to fight the charge of perverting the course of justice, the evidence against him, including the CCTV from the bank, the Federal Police tapes, and testimony of Miss Jones, made the prosecution case compelling. The jury retired to consider its verdict just before lunch on 2 March and returned with a guilty verdict at 8.15 p.m. Judge Shillington gave him eight-and-a-half years.

Joy Rogerson wasn't in court – her husband's real character had become obvious and they were officially estranged with divorce to follow. In court for Roger that day was his mother, Mabel, and the next Mrs Rogerson, Anne Melocco.

8

MAKE NEW FRIENDS

Rogerson spent nine months in prison, mainly in the hospital unit at Long Bay where high-risk prisoners were housed, before his appeal against the sentence was successful in December 1989. Roger, as usual, courted the media and told them, 'I've always been innocent. Finally justice has been done.' On Nine's *A Current Affair* he said 'justice has been done' and Judge Shillington, who'd said Roger's behaviour had undermined 'the police force and the moral of its members,' should 'eat his words'. Roger, who as a detective had feigned respect for the legal system, had pulled the gloves off. However, his pleasure at being free again didn't last long.

The DPP appealed the case to the High Court and won in June 1992. The case went back to the NSW Court of Criminal Appeal and on 16 December 1992, he received a discount on his original sentence, going to prison for a maximum of four years and three months. Roger's view on the sentence was,

'I have never had any faith in the justice system and this is a good example of it.'

In the period between his departure from the NSW Police and his incarceration, Roger had been busy. His day job, when not in court, was setting up and working in small metalworking businesses Bullion Engineering Pty Ltd and Statewide Security Systems Pty Ltd. Roger was good with his hands, and his father, the skilled boilermaker, had taught him how to weld and work with metal. He'd also started a lawn-mowing business, pushing the Victa around local yards. I encountered a public servant at a conference a couple of years ago, who'd grown up in Condell Park, and she said, 'I came home from school and there's the most famous copper in Australia doing our lawns. He was friendly and did a great job. Meticulous work.' However, lawns and iron bars were just his day jobs, and as usual, there were two Roger Rogersons.

Up in Kings Cross, the Bayeh brothers Louis and Bill had taken over the strip and nightclub businesses following the retirement of Abe Saffron. Saffron had been a stabilising influence up there for decades, but with the rise of the drug trade and the new breed of criminals arriving on the scene, he'd withdrawn and was slowly selling off some of the properties and leases he owned. The Bayeh brothers were the new kingpins, along with a collection of Romanian coke dealers and outlaw bikers, particularly the Bandidos, rebuilding after the Milperra Massacre and the prison stints that followed. In the drug business, in which the Bayehs were both deeply involved, you needed discipline for your dealers and buyers to whom you extended credit – not an uncommon occurrence in the underworld – and failure to pay in full and on time could be fatal at worst or painful at best.

Rogerson, with his reputation for fatal endings and ruthlessness, was ideal. Mention of his name usually worked, but if a visit was needed Roger would be accompanied by a couple of large thugs who'd attend to the physical side of the intimidation. Roger was a man who played the psychological game rather than the physical – his stature was average rather than intimidating – but he wasn't averse to putting in the boot if his heavies pinned down the victim.

One other Rogerson client was Michael Hurley, who allegedly had him on retainer. Hurley was a rogue. Like Roger he was charismatic, entertaining, loved a drink, a long lunch and a yarn. He'd grown up in Housing Commission flats on Sydney's waterfront, before deciding crime paid better than back-breaking labour. Behind the working-class facade he'd cultivated, Hurley liked fine Italian tailoring and a BMW. He pulled stylish burglaries and frauds before moving into the big-time drugs crime – an ideal business for a man with impeccable waterfront connections. At his peak in the early 2000s, he was the nation's leading cocaine trafficker. Hurley could keep his hands clean and other men did the dirty work. It proved to be an enduring relationship.

Roger offered something precious to the underworld. For a set fee or a percentage of a big deal, Roger mentored the crooks on how police gathered intelligence on major drug shipments, surveillance techniques, investigative planning and habits. He could be relied on for getting 'the drum' – operational intelligence – from police he either knew directly or could network. In return for cash or a favour, they would pass on details, with Roger as the conduit. Roger, they knew, could be discreet as well as greedy. In the event of an arrest, other opportunities opened up – a negotiation with arresting police who were known to be malleable, a copy of the brief of evidence, a detective encouraged to 'run dead' with their evidence, or evidence getting lost. In drug cases, it didn't come as a great surprise to have a request by the defence for the drug exhibit to be re-analysed shortly before the court case, and then find what you knew was cocaine or heroin was an innocuous and legal powder. Without the right exhibit, the case was dead in the water. These were the insights the consummate detective could provide. He could also keep one step back from the action and thus be sheltered from the fallout of an operation gone wrong. All care, no responsibility.

During 1991, Roger was busy in the media, building relationships with print journalists who were seduced by his affable nature, great yarns and exclusive insights, and appearing on television programmes as diverse as *A Current Affair* and *Four Corners*. In November 1992, Roger, while protesting his innocence on a range of issues, told *A Current Affair* he was on the dole and living with his mother – a convenient lie as he was involved with Anne Melocco by that time and spending much of his time at her unit in Mitchell Street, Condell Park, less than a kilometre from the family home he'd shared with Joy and the children in Gleeson Avenue. It was in this interview with Jana Wendt he introduced what would become a long-running joke, saying that there had been a number of comments about him that included 'disgraced' and 'one is notorious. I get that all the time, too.'

His media outings were prompted by appearances at ICAC and his looming return to the Court of Criminal Appeal. Roy Thurgar and fellow criminal Neddy Smith had been telling all about bent police and Roger was on their list. During these hearings the infamous 'green light' Smith alleged Rogerson had given him to commit crimes, had come out.

Amid the hullabaloo, Roger was sent back to prison, and this time he went to Berrima, home to corrupt coppers, bent lawyers, dodgy politicians, child molesters and anyone else who didn't quite fit in with the broader prison population. Among the residents were Bill Allen the former deputy commissioner, and ex–Kings Cross detective Larry Churchill. In the village-like atmosphere of the old prison Roger was the centre of attention, offering legal advice, learning potting skills, using his metalworking skills to help with the maintenance of the place, and networking. One of his newfound friends was Arthur Loveday, known as 'Mr T' for his penchant for excessive bling, who became a patched member of the Bandidos after his release.

A Bandidos source said, 'Artie was a piece of shit. A lower form of life would be hard to imagine.' Loveday had grown up in the Bankstown area and had an appalling criminal career that included rape, kidnapping, robbery and escaping from custody. His dismal career and this less than glowing character reference didn't impede their friendship – the two found each other useful – and Roger, with his history of acolytes, had a new one in Arthur and one that would come in handy when both were released. Bandidos sources said that because of the Loveday/ Rogerson relationship, the outlaw gang 'welcomed Roger in any clubhouse across the country'.

Michael Hurley invested in his future relationship by maintaining Rogerson's retainer, albeit reduced to $500 per week because of his temporary unavailability. Roger did have a few trips outside the walls of Berrima to attend the inquest into the May 1985 disappearance of Christopher Dale Flannery, which started on 1 October 1993. The witness list looked like the cast of a crime drama, and some who hadn't made it onto the list, like Stan 'The Man' Smith, were in the public gallery and enjoying the spectacle. With jokes, banter and the occasional hard look, it was like being in a pub during happy hour, minus the drinks. Rogerson's evidence wasn't of much use, with him denying any involvement, and at one point saying 'I don't care at all'.

When Coroner Glass finally handed down his report on 5 June 1997, he had 'a strong suspicion that Roger Rogerson was involved in Flannery's disappearance and his death, or at least knew what happened to him'. Rogerson had the motive and opportunity to cause him harm, 'but there wasn't sufficient prima facie evidence against Rogerson'. Roger told the media Coroner Glass was a 'jerk' and his findings 'bullshit' and the following day had his maiden outing with Alan Jones, the reigning king of breakfast radio.

Roger talked about the hard life of a policeman back in the '60s, '70s and '80s. Named in the inquest as the key to unlocking the mystery, he told Jones he'd known people such as Sallie-Anne Huckstepp and Barry McCann – both dead – and Flannery, but he had nothing to do with their demise. On the evidence given by Louis Bayeh who'd 'rolled over' to the Wood Royal Commission in December 1995 and said that Rogerson was one of the police who'd murdered Flannery, he said, 'Well I know Louis Bayeh well enough to know that Louis Bayeh would not have included my name.' Jones also brought up Roger's other lingering problem – shooting Warren Lanfranchi. Rogerson told Jones 'it was a set-up. That meeting was arranged by Ned Smith. I mean, this again, I mean we had a massive inquest, we had a Supreme Court hearing!' His compelling performance prompted his mother, Mabel, an ABC 702 (then 2BL) listener, to tell the *Sydney Morning Herald* who'd tapped on her door at the old family home in Stacey Street, Bankstown, 'I am normally a 2BL listener, you know, but I listened to Mr Jones and I think that Roger gave a frank and honest account. Roger said all he wanted to say and I don't think he'll be interviewed again. Besides, he's a very busy man you know. He's never been lazy. I can only say good things about Roger. I'm his mum you know.'

The underworld was full of rumours on Flannery's death and the men likely to have caused it, but those who did know the facts weren't talking. Rogerson wasn't someone you crossed.

9

IN VICTORY, VENGEANCE

Glen McNamara suffered the humiliating end of his career in silence for a few years, mainly because no one was interested enough to listen to him, and also because of rumours circulating in the police that he was too tarnished to be a white knight. For their part, the police management hoped that Glen would slide away into obscurity. However, in the 1990s paedophiles were popular media fodder, stirred on by Deirdre Grusovin and Franca Arena, two high-profile, Catholic, Labor members of the New South Wales Legislative Council. Just as Robert Menzies made significant political capital out of the notion we had reds under our beds, the two ladies would have us believe the state had paedophiles crammed into every closet. While their passionate cause was for laudable reasons, what was missing was evidence, and in the great political tradition, never let the facts get in the way of a salacious story.

One of the motivators for their enthusiasm and a public attuned to the issue was the 'Mr Bubbles' case in 1988. The Seabeach kindergarten at Mona Vale on Sydney's northern beaches had been a successful and popular business until one parent, later described by her psychologist as being a 'florid psychotic' believed that comments made by her small child were indicative of the child being sexually assaulted. She told her story to relatives and friends who also had children at the kindergarten, and also took her story to the Mona Vale detectives. Enter Ron Fluit, once Larry Churchill's police workmate.

As the police delved into allegations of ritual abuse, human sacrifice and lurid tales of appalling depravity – including a male dressing up as a clown and interfering with children at a party that featured the blowing of soap bubbles (hence the nickname) – word spread fast. Four people were arrested. Fluit's first call after the charges were laid wasn't to his superiors but to the tabloid media. When the story hit the front pages, parents who'd been interviewed only days before and said their children were behaving perfectly normally suddenly had a complete reversal of their views. The only problem with the case was there was not one skerrick of competent evidence to support the allegations and most were logistically impossible. But it lit a fuse.

In working on their defence, rumours came back to our team that people in the Grusovin orbit had allegedly posited we might have been paedophiles as well. While there was nothing to support the notion, there was plenty of whispering and sideways glances by those who reckoned we were doing the work of the devil in representing these people. Fortunately, the magistrate threw out all the cases, but the brutality of the rumour is still a clear memory. The 'Mr Bubbles' case was in the media at precisely the same time as McNamara's Kings Cross work.

The utter failure of the Mr Bubbles case coincided with Grusovin and Arena agitating for a major inquiry into police protecting an allegedly high-level paedophile ring. Evidence was in short supply, but the pair were operating on the 'where there's smoke there's fire' theory, which is something experienced investigators know can be incredibly dangerous.

In this climate, Grusovin and Arena found strong support, ironically, from the church, and from a slew of lobby groups including victims of crime, politics, child protection workers and so on. Joining them in an odd mix of politics was NSW Liberal right-winger Charlie Lynn, Labor's Paul Gibson, the inevitable Fred Nile and NSW Liberal right-wing senator Bill Heffernan.

Grusovin and Arena talked relentlessly under the privilege of Parliament about lists they'd compiled of high-profile people they believed might have been involved, and a constant theme to these lists was the men were gay and powerful – there was the whiff of a witch hunt in the air.

On 1 June 2003, Alex Mitchell in the *Sun-Herald* wrote of the enduring yarn: 'Psst! Want to hear about the senior politicians, judges, QCs, solicitors, captains of industry, police top brass and church leaders who belong to a secret society that engages in wild sexual orgies with teenage boys? So would I. But the story has been around for as long as I've been in Sydney journalism – and older hands can trace it back to the 1950s – and no proof has ever been forthcoming. Yet it remains one of our most enduring urban myths.' Mitchell wrote the 'Brotherhood' as it had become known 'defies all attempts to expose its activities'.

While writing this book, a source contacted me and talked of allegations about highly placed men, mainly former politicians and lawyers now either dead from old age or long retired. I groaned. The story being peddled could have legitimately celebrated its twenty-first birthday party a few years ago. Now, as back then, the intentions were good but the evidence wasn't.

With all this as a backdrop, McNamara's anger and frustration against the NSW Police simmered. He pushed the allegations about drugs to one side and sought out Grusovin and Arena to champion his anti-paedophile stance.

He'd also waited until the prosecutions against Churchill and his coterie were finalised, and the risk of prosecution against him was negligible.

Like Rogerson, McNamara had a deft touch with public relations and used the paedophile issue to propel him from the career backwater in which he'd landed and back into the spotlight. But the process wasn't as quick as he'd hoped for.

Glen's work began with hunting for a lawyer who'd help him persuade a settlement from the government as compensation for his ruined career. Again like Rogerson, he'd convinced himself that any notion of his complicity with Churchill and the crew was false and that he truly was a white knight. He approached the Police Association of NSW for support and they turned him down, which, for a man with pariah status and surrounded by rumours of his own complicity, came only as a surprise to McNamara.

It took him another 12 months to find lawyers to represent him and in 1994, they wrote to the state government seeking an ex gratia payment, which was rejected.

At the same time he was dealing with lawyers, he'd done other research and thought that Grusovin and Arena might be the right people to whom he could take his allegations about paedophiles and cover-ups. 'I couldn't let the paedophiles get off scot free,' he said. Glen said he was attracted to Grusovin because she was well respected, experienced, connected to the powerful and regularly brutal NSW right faction of the Labor Party, and that her success was due to 'her sharp intelligence and thorough methods'. That latter comment a skilled and experienced criminal investigator may doubt, along with the men who made it on to one of the lists. He wrote she'd been an observer of the Churchill saga and 'her intellect told her there was more to it, a lot more'.

According to McNamara, he became a prime source to Grusovin with the two meeting in her office in Parliament House – she'd moved from being a member of the Legislative Council to the Legislative Assembly in 1990 when she was elected as member for Heffron, the eastern Sydney seat vacated by her brother Laurie Brereton when he moved into federal politics.

When the Wood Royal Commission started, Grusovin, Arena and McNamara had high expectations of their allegations getting a starring role. They were out of luck.

10

IN DEFEAT, MALICE

The Wood Royal Commission was established in May 1994 and showed its colours early on by preferring to assess incoming information independently and do its own investigations. To give them a prod and make a public point about her concerns and information-gathering, Grusovin rose to her feet in Parliament – the chamber known as 'the bear pit' for good reason – on 1 December 1994 and spoke in a debate on ICAC and its 'investigations into allegations of corruption concerning police and paedophile activity', and primarily clear up who was going to take the lead, ICAC or the Royal Commission.

In the middle of the usual argy-bargy of state politics over who was to blame for any confusion of roles – if there was confusion – Grusovin launched her own bombing mission. She said she was prompted in her course of action because, 'I did hold the belief that the royal commission would finally be able to attend to these matters, but because that course of action is in jeopardy, I should like to place on record the contents of a statutory declaration I have received'. She then read a statutory declaration made by Colin Fisk in which he said, 'that five weeks after I was arrested on March 31, 1989 I made a series of records of interviews with the NSW Police Internal Security Unit (IPSU) in which I named a number of prominent people I knew to be pederasts, including the solicitor John Marsden, MP Frank Arkell and other leading members of the community. I told the IPSU that Marsden had helped me establish a disco for young people in the Campbelltown area.'

After the general hubbub and points of order subsided, she continued the declaration, saying: 'As far as I was aware, while some other matters were later investigated through Operation Speedo [the paedophile investigation], the police never investigated allegations into these prominent members of the community. My copies of the records of interviews and the statements I made were subsequently destroyed and I asked Detective Chief Inspector Ken Watson of the then IPSU for a copy of all my statements and records of interviews, as well as photographs I supplied them in relation to police officers involved in a pederast protection racket, including former Detective Sergeant Ron Fluit. In fact, I made four or five verbal requests to Chief Inspector Watson of the IPSU for copies, as well as at least three written requests for copies of this material, but to no avail. In one phone conversation with Chief Inspector Watson following the creation of the Royal Commission into Police Corruption, he indicated that certain material had been "misplaced".'

Frank Arkell had been the Lord Mayor of Wollongong from 1974 to 1991 and the independent member for Wollongong in the New South Wales Legislative Assembly from 1984 to 1991.

Arkell was a closeted gay man – not uncommon for men of his age who had a private life kept separate from their public one – and was murdered in 1998 by Mark Valera who was later convicted of the killing and sentenced to life.

Marsden was anything but closeted. The prominent Sydney solicitor was loud, proud and publicly gay, and had a high profile in the state. One of Marsden's former law practice partners was John Fahey who became the Premier of New South Wales after Greiner resigned in 1992 in the wake of an ICAC inquiry in which Commissioner Ian Temby QC said his conduct could be found 'by a notional jury as conducting himself contrary to known and recognised standards of honesty and integrity'. The Court of Appeal later found ICAC had 'exceeded its jurisdiction'.

Fahey was Premier at the time of the Grusovin reading. Marsden had also been a member of the Police Board of New South Wales, President of the Law Society of NSW and a Councillor of the NSW Council for Civil Liberties. He also had one of the best contact books in state politics and enjoyed using it. Marsden could be magnificently indiscreet and when trying to make light of the allegations levelled against him in Parliament, described himself as a 'promiscuous homosexual', which for those who knew him was a fair and accurate description, but Marsden wasn't a paedophile. The allegations prompted a media storm with Marsden as the focus of programmes by the Seven Network's *Witness* and *Today Tonight*. The result was a long-running and lurid defamation case by Marsden against the network, described by *Justinian* editor and journalist Richard Ackland as 'without doubt the largest, longest and most comprehensive defamation case in the history of Australia. And probably one of the biggest in the history of the common law world.' Marsden won.

Grusovin wasn't a winner either, with Opposition Leader Bob Carr quickly distancing himself from her comments. She was moved from her position as housing spokesperson to the backbench where her career ended after losing a battle for preselection for her seat to Kristina Keneally. Arena took up the public stirring under privilege on 31 October 1996 in the New South Wales Legislative Council after the topic of paedophilia was introduced in a motion by Fred Nile. The motion related to preliminary reporting of the royal commission on its specific child abuse investigation that had begun in March 1996 and Wood was seeking an extension of time.

She asked, 'Have informal discussions or preliminary investigative sessions been held with prominent people outside the commission's formal hearing sessions? If so, who are these prominent people? What about former Supreme Court Judge David Albert Yeldham? Was he or was he not interviewed? I am not insinuating anything about the character of the former judge by naming him; I am saying only that this is but one example of a person who appears to have received preferential treatment when, for instance, Anglican and Catholic bishops were not.' While she might not have been insinuating about Yeldham's character, she certainly added his name to the list.

She added, 'Too many children have suffered. The "Mr Bubbles" case in 1989 and the Wahroonga preschool case in 1988 are examples of that. We all know that some people were never charged because the children were too young to testify and/or the police botched the entire investigation, or worse.' All charges were dismissed. Journalist Ben Hills wrote in the *Sydney Morning Herald* of 26 October 1992 that Reg Blanch QC, the

Director of Public Prosecutions at the time of the prosecution, had said, 'There was simply no case from the beginning.'

Yeldham publicly outed himself that day in response to Arena's speech. He said, 'I'm bisexual, let's face it. I've got a wife and three children and four grandchildren and I love young children and I'm involved in children's charities. But I've never ever, nor would I ever, have any sexual conduct with anyone who is under 18. I mean, I abhor paedophilia.' The media went digging and found Yeldham had been an *habitué* of public lavatories – beats, in gay parlance – and had paid men for sex in these places. He'd also been caught by the coppers who'd called in the Special Branch who dealt with sensitive matters where politics was in play and the case went away, again not an unusual occurrence with high-profile and connected people literally caught with their trousers down. Yeldham was subsequently interviewed by the royal commission and said he felt ashamed by what he'd done, asserted he was sure none of his partners was under 18, and that he believed what he'd done was 'relatively minor'. On 6 November 1996 just hours after the interview, he committed suicide in his car at the family home in Hunter's Hill.

McNamara said of Grusovin that she was 'very brave' and pointed the finger at Premier Fahey and Opposition Leader Carr for her failure to get traction on the issue. They were 'standing solid and condemning Deirdre Grusovin for her bravery. If there were a war today, you would have Grusovin next to you; this is the power of this woman.'

McNamara, according to McNamara, had some plans to make the paedophile allegations a core investigation. When he put the word on the street to find Dunn, he was allegedly approached by a 'couple of my criminal friends' who suggested Dolly Dunn, then out of prison, be murdered, but he kiboshed that idea because aside from the legal ramifications he 'wanted to find the people responsible and make them pay'. Allegedly Dunn eventually contacted him and they met in a café in Redfern, close to Dolly's old haunts, on 2 April 1994. McNamara demanded to know who'd put the contract on his life, with Dunn replying, 'we panicked, we thought you were going to expose us, we're sorry'.

Dunn, and it's impossible to verify as Dunn is now dead, handed over an envelope containing $20 000 in cash to make amends for the trouble he'd caused McNamara. Glen said he refused the money and then told him, 'I spoke to some people high up in the Police' and 'there were a few' police involved, but names weren't named. McNamara said he'd not mentioned his subsequent meetings with Dunn to the royal commission in his submissions but had been pivotal in the *60 Minutes* story in 1997 where Liz Hayes and producer Steve Barrett had tracked Dunn to Honduras.

Despite their best efforts, Arena, Grusovin and McNamara didn't get much in the way of justification. The royal commission found Arena's claims of high-level paedophile networks to be 'false in all respects', and McNamara, much to his chagrin, was never interviewed by them in spite of his offers and submissions.

However, Glen was multitasking, putting together his evidence for a claim against the NSW Government. Glen wasn't going away. The primary target of his grievances was Lola Scott, and curiously not her superior, Ken Watson. It appears that one of the motivators was Scott's rapid progress in the police since their 1989 encounter. In 1993 she became the first female patrol tactician in police history to be posted to Redfern, a hot spot at the best of times, and more so at that point as the controversial

ABC documentary *Cop It Sweet* on policing in Redfern had only just been aired. Tactics needed an urgent rethink to deal better with the community. In November the following year she became the first female Detective Chief Superintendent, and was appointed as Commander of Internal Affairs. She'd also successfully completed a law degree, and two masters – one in public policy and administration and one in crime prevention. Lola was everything McNamara aspired to be.

Internal Affairs can't boast a glorious history of achievement, and I speak as someone who spent around three years there in the early 1980s. You had to do something blatantly obvious or exceptionally stupid to have them recommend you be prosecuted. In a period where 'get tough on crime' committed by the public was part of the political mantra, getting tough on crimes by police was in its infancy. Scott inherited an outfit with a reputation that had been publicly savaged in the lead-up to her appointment. There had been cover-ups of drug thefts at Frenchs Forest Police Station, harassment of whistleblowers, the attempted suicide of a young man in police cells that left him brain damaged, with the truth of the circumstances still elusive after three investigations by Internal Affairs.

Scott walked into her new job with the task of dealing with the longstanding task of proving that police can investigate police. It's an issue that gets a regular outing, but in criminal investigation who can do the task better? Lola had to sell an agenda of ability, objectivity and results, made more difficult as she was a woman. As she noted on her appointment, 'in 1972, there were only 100 women in the organisation and they weren't allowed into the detective training course. But I had good mentors.'

The *Sydney Morning Herald* of 13 November 1993 reported she 'is not the hard-bitten type you would expect at the anti-corruption frontline. Her gentle demeanour seems a million miles from the classic macho cop chaser who knows all about the temptations of police power.' Scott, then 42, and only a few years older than McNamara, was described, as a 'calm, warm, sympathetic individual who clearly sees her main fights as managerial'. She told the paper that incidents like the shooting of Michael Drury weighed heavily on her and that 'I know the difficulty that police officers have in coming forward to report corruption – anyone who comes forward in my time to complain about police behaviour knows they will be treated fairly. It's like dealing with victims of crime, a caring attitude is important.' Lola also told the paper, 'I am not aware of any corruption. I don't believe there is entrenched corruption in NSW and the public can be proud of that.' It was a statement that toed the corporate line and one that would bite her years later.

Geoff Schuberg, then head of Professional Responsibility, and a great copper McNamara admired, said of Scott's appointment, 'Lola is a person who understands she will be under the microscope by the royal commission. It's going to be an intense and trying period but I'm sure at the end of the day, the public will be confident in the way we do the job.' The *Herald* correctly pointed out 'Scott is in a particularly hot seat'.

What neither Scott nor Schuberg knew was the greatest problem for her was Glen McNamara and he'd bide his time. In 1998 McNamara's lawyers filed their case against the NSW Government and after a number of directions hearings – legal housekeeping – they reached a settlement in 1999, but the terms were not to be made public and never have. However, the result stimulated McNamara rather than stopped him. The 'undisclosed settlement' didn't include an agreement to silence, and on 19 September 1999, Candace Sutton in the *Sydney Morning Herald* published an interview with Glen with the headline: 'Police trying to buy my silence – Angry former undercover detective tells.' He'd had a decade to craft his story and told her he'd received a cheque marked 'damages' from the NSW Police.

If the police thought he'd finally go away they were wrong. He told Sutton, 'they want to buy me off, silence me. But I'm still angry that much of the evidence I collected when I was wired up never went anywhere. Isn't one of the risks of assaulting children that you are turning them into psychopaths, or at least misfits, drug addicts or paedophiles themselves?' McNamara had finally had his few moments of public fame and he wanted more.

On 17 October 2002 he wrote to Bronwyn Bishop in her role as chair of the House of Representatives Standing Committee on Legal and Constitutional Affairs looking into 'crime in the community' and offering to give evidence. Fans of politics will find that her chairing of the committee gives a glimpse of her work as Speaker. In his submission to her, he took aim at Lola Scott and Ken Watson, with Scott the focus of his allegations. Scott, as the junior partner in the team and in her own words 'the driver/typist' was being cast as the villain.

Warming to his theme he wrote, 'During a Police raid on "Dolly" Dunn's residence in relation to the drug inquiry a box of video tapes was located by Lola Scott. The video tapes displayed "Dolly" Dunn committing sexual offences on young boys. Lola Scott told me that she had viewed these tapes and that they were disgusting. They constituted evidence of felonies against "Dolly" Dunn. When preparing an advice for DPP and the Attorney

General in relation to Dunn's indemnity Lola Scott indicated on the questionnaire that there was no evidence of Dunn being involved in any other felonies.' He was half right. McNamara's undercover recording, and the finding of the videotapes had started a separate investigation. Lola Scott said the form had clear questions asking if the subject has a criminal record, which at the time he didn't, and did he have a consorting record – when the subject is observed by police to be associating with known criminals and that association is recorded – which he didn't. Scott filled out the legal form correctly and told me that when reviewing the case prosecutors Mark Tedeschi and Margaret Cunneen said McNamara's allegations she was being misleading were 'ridiculous'.

Painting himself into the role of martyr, McNamara wrote, 'I was forced to leave the New South Wales Police because of the unfounded criminal allegations against me and the destructive behaviour exhibited by Lola Scott and Ken Watson against me. My career in the Police was destroyed and my reputation was destroyed. This caused incredible physical and emotional difficulty directly for my wife and me and indirectly for my parents and extended family. I have attempted to put this behind me but from a career perspective my opportunities exist only as a sub-contract investigator for various insurance companies – a mind numbing and soulless pursuit. I have previously applied on several occasions for investigators positions with the former NCA and with ICAC. Despite my considerable investigative expertise and experience and the fact that I worked at the NCA on secondment as an investigator from the New South Wales Police, I have never even been offered the opportunity of an interview for any of these positions.'

In Bronwyn Bishop, McNamara found a sympathetic ear – or at least an ear attuned to the political opportunities evidence like his could offer, and particularly if it went unchallenged. One rule of political spin is get in first and keep repeating the message – do it often enough and it will become the 'facts'.

McNamara's Christmas came early in 2002. On 6 December, the committee was sitting at Parliament House in Macquarie Street when the four Labor members of Bishop's committee, and Daryl Melham in particular, tried to stop evidence, including submissions, becoming public at that point. On the following Monday, Lola Scott, then one of the few women to reach the rank of Assistant Commissioner, was called into Commissioner Ken Moroney's office around 9 a.m. on her first day of duty after being on leave for two weeks. She recalled that Deputy Commissioner Dave Madden and a legal officer were also in the office when she walked in. Moroney read a one-paragraph statement to her, telling her coldly he was empowered under the legislation governing her employment that he could remove her from office 'for any or no reason without warning'.

Scott recalled she protested, saying 'there is nothing I've done that is corrupt that warranted me being sacked,' and asked 'could I have somebody here, so they can listen to it as well?' However, it was all over in three minutes and the response of the three men was to walk out of the office, leaving her alone and 'looking for a phone to ring someone, to get somebody to come'. Police chaplain Barry Dwyer was waiting outside as she exited the office but she declined his ministrations. The *Sydney Morning Herald* two days later wrote that she'd said, 'if a truck ran over me I couldn't feel worse than I feel now,' and described it as a 'witch hunt'. At that point in her day she didn't know that one of the prime motivators might have been Glen McNamara.

Moroney later issued a press release announcing the sacking and noting Scott had been warned on 8 November that year she was under review and a spokesperson offered, 'it was not a pleasant thing for him to do, but he did it for the good of the police force'. Premier Bob Carr told the media he supported Moroney's position, who he'd appointed to make the 'hard decisions about policing'.

Ian Ball, the President of the Police Association of NSW which represented the rank-and-file police officers told the ABC's *The World Today* that Scott was distraught and added some context saying, 'Commander Scott's had 30 years in the cops. Bit over 30, actually. She's the most senior ranking female officer in NSW. And quite frankly she's come into the cops 30-odd years ago when it was no bed of roses. She's survived that. And there's no question there's been some difficulties. There's no question about that. That's not an argument. But no one, no one deserves to be treated in this fashion.'

Rumours that her sacking was caused by her management style followed swiftly, along with the story her time leading Internal Affairs had been reviewed by Operation Retz that had recently reported to Moroney. With similar speed, rumours she'd fallen victim to a boys' club or that Moroney was cleaning house did the rounds. Moroney had been appointed commissioner earlier in the year following the early resignation of the controversial British import Peter Ryan who'd been a Scott supporter over his six years as commissioner.

That night, Bishop publicly tabled McNamara's submission with its inflammatory comments about Scott.

Bishop appeared on Alan Jones's 2GB programme the next morning. She talked of McNamara's submission and said of her overall inquiry, 'It is so shocking that there are so many people who want to come forward.' Jones took the opportunity to read some of McNamara's allegations to his listeners.

Jones and Scott had a past. Over the last year he'd talked about 'a very senior female police officer' and it was obvious he was talking about Scott, and she later sued for defamation.

Scott responded by talking to Mike Carlton, Jones's arch-rival and said of McNamara's list of allegations they were 'totally untrue'.

With battle lines drawn, someone in the police did as they usually do in circumstances like these, and leaked. The *Daily Telegraph* on 11 December, claiming an exclusive, reported in detail the reasoning for Moroney's decision. Scott, the paper reported, had been the subject of a report prepared by two of the department's psychologists in which she was described as having 'displayed fits of crying and anger', an 'inconsistent, threatening and intimidating management style' – which sounds precisely like the style of some senior police I've encountered over a long career – and recommended 'appropriate disciplinary processes, education, counselling and mentoring and an independent psychiatric assessment'. Scott was fortunate things had changed since the days of Philip Arantz. She commented, to the paper, 'I don't like to say this but it's a reality as a woman if I do something it's the worst thing in the world but when one of the blokes do it it's acceptable practice.'

The next day the *Sydney Morning Herald* returned fire, observing that when Scott was the only serving police officer at the July 2002 launch of former police commissioner Peter

Ryan's biography, she said, 'they'll make me pay for this,' which gives a glimpse of the tribal nature of the force. Scott told Ryan biographer Sue Williams, 'I'd been praised for my work getting crime down in my region which had been among the worst before I took over. I'd only just been told my contract was going to be renewed on March 1. So why has this happened? I don't know, I do know however that my association with Commissioner Ryan played a role. If he wanted something done, I got on and did it. I didn't play politics.'

McNamara and his allegations were almost completely forgotten in the brawl that followed Lola's sacking and it wasn't until Wednesday, 19 February 2003 that he returned to the limelight.

Bishop set the tone for the hearing when Duncan Kerr (Labor) opened by challenging her right to release submissions prior to the hearing, and argued 'those adversely named have a right to procedural fairness'. After a bit more discussion, Daryl Melham (Labor) entered the debate saying 'It is pretty obvious to everyone present that you have a predetermined course of action in relation to the calling of witnesses and in relation to stymieing proper inquiries' and 'Madam Chair, this is a farce, this is not a parliamentary inquiry, this is a circus.'

McNamara was calm and composed – he knew his script and their interjections didn't faze him. He recounted his version of the events of 1989, and took aim at Scott, making her the de facto leader of the investigations and the one who 'through the leak, was able to allow Dunn flee justice'. He alleged that Dunn, when he was caught and pleaded guilty, had a 'letter of comfort' given to the sentencing Judge Roger Court by Lola Scott to support 'an ample discount' on his sentence. Burying the knife deeper into his target he said, 'so you can supply high-grade amphetamine in New South Wales, you can even make it, and do not even worry about being charged with that. But you can supply it to undercover police, you can have it on tape, you can go and see Lola Scott, you can cut a deal that ascends her career into the stars, she will send you a letter, she will pervert the course of justice and you get 2 [and-a-half] years for a $1 million supply.' Ms Scott vehemently denied any wrongdoing.

After the committee had asked him a few questions he moved to contemporary matters, talking about the investigations into Scott around 2000, including conversations with then Deputy Commissioner Moroney and senior police, which, at best would have been a rumour, and mentioned a psychological report on her that had come into his hands. McNamara had found a soapbox on which to air every piece of alleged dirty linen he could find, and read it straight into the public record without much in the way of interference. Liberal MP Alan Cadman, either out of genuine interest, or a Dorothy Dixer, gave McNamara the opportunity to sink one last nail into the coffin of Scott's career, and asked, 'regarding your relationship with Inspector Watson, who was one above your direct superior in the period you have taken us through: why did you not refer to him?'

McNamara took the opportunity to kick one further goal by responding, 'I did but, although Watson was senior, it was apparent to me that Scott was running the operation. Watson was approaching retirement and it appeared he was taking a back seat in this inquiry. It appeared later, in the police royal commission, when the whole issue of the indemnities arose in a limited form, that Watson took the heat. There was never any mention of Scott being examined as to her complete involvement in the whole process. But the answer is: Scott was in charge of the operation.'

The subsequent examination of McNamara wasn't probative or challenging, it was an opportunity to let him take the role of teacher and they as students, in the art of policing in general and that of an undercover operative in particular. In questions about the sentences of the various players he told the committee that 'everyone got a deal except me,' an intriguing comment given his assertions of innocence, but one that wasn't explored.

After questions by Labor's Duncan Kerr, Bishop asked, 'Mr McNamara, I think it is fair to say to you that your career and you personally were destroyed behind closed doors, were you not?' To which he replied, 'Absolutely correct,' and she followed with, 'You never got an opportunity to speak. You tried to before the Wood commission and they denied to call you there, and you have come forward to this hearing.'

Recalling his days as a legal aid lawyer cross-examining police, Melham went on the attack, pointing to McNamara's submission and noting he made a 'self-serving' statement when he claimed to be 'an experienced criminal investigator and a professional witness'.

McNamara bridled, telling Melham it was fact, not an opinion and that he 'often attended criminal trials and gave evidence' and it was 'at least once or twice each week, sometimes more', which, if you were a detective around the same time as McNamara, was nonsense. If you were in court that often, backed up with the mountain of paperwork needed to get you into the courtroom, you'd not get the chance to arrest anyone unless they walked in and gave themselves up.

Melham let that issue pass, and asked McNamara if he had a 'trained memory' to which he replied that he relied on contemporaneous reports and notes – an essential in policing of the time. Having lured McNamara into bragging of his expertise, he asked if he'd kept contemporaneous notes of his dealings with 'superior officers and fellow officers', referring directly to his alleged conversations with Scott. After blustering that 'you do not take notes when dealing with other police,' he said he hadn't and offered, 'What I am telling you on oath is that the discussions I had with Lola Scott are not only in my memory but are burned in my memory.'

Most coppers make notes of potentially important conversations and these can be used to support their testimony. McNamara didn't and tried bluster instead. He might have thought he was a professional witness, but he'd been caught out easily by a slightly rusty criminal lawyer.

As Melham pushed him over his lack of any supporting notes, Bishop told Melham 'perhaps you should move on', and to the witness, 'just take it slowly Mr McNamara. You've been here for nearly three hours. Anyone is entitled to feel a bit sad.' Melham responded, 'It is interesting that I only just got to ask questions and I am now being interfered with by other members of the committee.' Bishop made one of the few jokes of a heavy day's proceedings, saying, 'I would not dare interfere with you, Daryl; it would turn me off!'

Bishop wound up McNamara's testimony and moved to another witness. Melham took his last shots before Bishop closed him down completely, asking if McNamara viewed the committee as his 'last hope', and McNamara agreed, saying, 'I had been denied, effectively, by Lola Scott, through her fraudulent and misleading behaviour, any chance of being able to go to court, give evidence and be cross-examined vigorously by people.'

When asked if he was embittered towards Lola Scott, McNamara said, 'It is a good question but it is a difficult question to answer, because at some stage there has to be a component of forgiveness. You have to say, "I have to forgive this to move on." Certainly, it was a phenomenon with me that you have to let it go; you have to free yourself of it. Am I embittered towards her? No, I feel sorry that such a clever person has finished up in the way she has. I feel great sorrow for people who have been her victims. I am not embittered towards her. I think that she should look at herself and realise that the only way that she can proceed is by accepting what she has done. I feel sorry for her for those reasons.'

Bishop and Melham repeatedly clashed over his questions and her handling of them and interjections from other Liberal committee members. The circus stopped at 1.48 p.m. and resumed, with McNamara still in the witness box, at 2.15 p.m., with some odd exchanges including McNamara suggesting some senior police should be charged for 'obtaining a financial advantage by deception' for accepting their fortnightly pay cheque. The committee ended for the day at 2.36 p.m. McNamara's evidence, given under privilege, was published.

McNamara's performance didn't amount to more than headlines the next day, and he went back to the drudgery of investigating insurance claims.

Lola Scott fared better. In April 2003 her defamation action against Alan Jones was in court. The substance of the case was that in July and August 2001 Jones had been talking about police corruption on air and referred to a 'very senior female police officer' which in the boys' club of the NSW Police reduced the probabilities dramatically. Jones commented she'd had 'a curious rise during the Ryan [Commissioner Peter Ryan] years,' and was 'commanding little more than her desk'. Scott gave evidence and said Jones's comments were 'very embarrassing' and were 'general talk' in the gossipy world of police headquarters. On the morning of the 23 July broadcast, police media had contacted her and asked if she wanted a tape, telling her that, 'Jones was having a go at you this morning.' She told the court, 'he described me to a tee. My rank, my position, my role and my function.'

The jury later found Jones's untrue and defamatory comments 'would have conveyed to a reasonable and ordinary listener that Lola Scott was corrupt and that cronyism was behind her promotion'. Moroney also changed his tune after being sued by Scott. As part of a confidential settlement, Scott was reinstated at the rank of chief inspector then retired on medical grounds.

In 2007, Simon Cohen, the NSW Assistant Ombudsman, found Moroney's decision to sack Scott was 'disproportionate' and referring to the report of Operation Retz which started with her time as boss of Internal Affairs, said, 'It is apparent that none of the findings indicate that Ms Scott was untruthful, misleading or deceptive.' The Ombudsman found that Internal Affairs lacked resources which added further stress to all officers. To put it into police speak, Lola had been handed a shit sandwich for lunch and dutifully dined on it.

11

THE TASTE OF FREEDOM

Rogerson, barely out of prison, was hauled into the Central Local Court in March 1996, but this time as a witness against his former mate Neddy Smith who was facing murder charges. It was these charges that precluded the TV series *Blue Murder* being shown in New South Wales. However, it didn't preclude the state being flooded with copies on tape smuggled across the border and watched discreetly – or something along those lines. I watched it with my father who was a retired copper and we both sat quietly with jaws hanging loose. Some of it may have been fiction, but it all had a chilling sense of reality. Rogerson, the talented publicist, would use the show during his campaign to build a new and respected public persona, casually brushing off the allegations he was a cold-blooded killer, drug dealer and manipulator of our justice system.

The feisty Winston Terracini QC appeared for Smith, and the Crown Prosecutor was Chris Maxwell QC. Rogerson and

Terracini clashed over two days, with Roger asserting he wasn't corrupt and that his problems were caused by a 'vendetta' by senior police, prompting Terracini to ask 'you hold yourself out as someone who has been dreadfully wronged?' to which Rogerson said, 'yes'. He'd used the notion before and to some success so why not give it another airing? He also denied he was corrupt and when Terracini accused him of 'extensive criminal activities' he replied, 'that's absolute rubbish,' which would be a catchphrase of his during his evidence in the 2016 trial. When Terracini had tapes of conversations between Rogerson, Smith and two other detectives played to the court, Roger was muttering under his breath, stimulating Terracini to shout, 'Don't be impertinent. Behave yourself!' After a brief exchange, ended by Terracini saying 'behave yourself and listen to the tape', Roger glowered at the barrister and said, 'if you'd shut up, I could hear it'.

Under Terracini's persistent and vigorous questioning Rogerson lost it and as one detective who'd been in court and knew Rogerson said, 'You could watch the facade drop. The smile, the charm and the twinkling eyes disappeared, and at that moment you caught a glimpse of the lethal man. Winston was lucky Roger didn't have a gun!' The cross-examination ended with Terracini getting in the last word – 'Look, you're a convict not a lawyer. You've got a hide like Jessie the Elephant!' Roger would next see Chris Maxwell in a courtroom in 2014, with Maxwell again the prosecutor and Roger back in the more familiar role of defendant.

At the beginning of his evidence, Rogerson had given his occupation as 'factory worker'. His front businesses were Scafco Scaffolding Pty Ltd and Re-Con Holdings Pty Ltd, set up in July 1997, both primarily to rent scaffolding to the building trade. On the other side of the line, he and Loveday went back to work in the protection and enforcement business.

The Bandidos, under the command of Michael 'Kaos' Kulakowski, their new national president, were changing quickly from bit players to slick operators to take advantage of their national presence, international links and opportunities to manufacture, import and sell drugs to the most prolific per capita drug market in the world. Amphetamines were the mainstay and cocaine was becoming a popular item on their product list. Michael Hurley's gang that included former footballer Les Mara and surfer Shayne Hatfield were bringing in shipments of all sizes from small up to around 200 kilograms at a time via Hurley's waterfront connections and bent baggage handlers at Sydney's international airport. The Bandidos were their main clients, pushing the drug through their well-developed and longstanding national distribution chain, though in the cocaine business the greedy nostrils in Sydney's eastern suburbs were the biggest consumers.

Roger's re-entry into this market was well timed. Greg Bearup in the *Sydney Morning Herald* of 22 April 1999 wrote, 'In 1997, police intelligence suggested that Roger Rogerson was heavily involved in brokering a deal with crime figures in Kings Cross for an orderly carve up of the drugs trade following the removal of dominant player Bill Bayeh'. The Bayeh brothers had hit major hurdles at the Wood Royal Commission and were either in, or about to go to, prison. Their days at the top of the pile in the Cross were gone, and in their place the outlaw bikers had taken over, running the doors of the nightclubs – ideal to keep the clubs supplied with product and make sure other entrepreneurs didn't get a foothold. Working with Hurley and with the Bandidos courtesy of Loveday was ideal.

To add to the biker connections, Loveday married Catherine Vella, the cousin of Alex Vella who ran Australia's biggest biker gang, the Rebels. Roger was a guest at the nuptials, and at one of the long and drunken celebrations that followed in the clubhouse he took the opportunity to settle a score with a criminal who was a guest. The criminal, by that time in poor condition from long-term heroin use, was having a quiet drink when, at Rogerson's request, two Bandidos took him outside the clubhouse and gave him a beating. When the man was on the ground, Roger put down his beer, strolled out and gave him a kicking. The poor sod was then hauled off the ground, put headfirst into a wheelie bin, and pushed down the street and left, much to Rogerson's amusement. He had a cold beer waiting for the two men when their job was done. It entertained a few of the onlookers, but one told me, 'Roger's a gutless bastard. The poor bastard who got the hiding wouldn't say boo to a fly.' A byproduct of the marriage was it gave Rogerson a link into the Rebels.

His Bandido connections brought him close to Felix Lyle, who would bob up in events later in Roger's career. The New Zealand–born Lyle, known as 'Big F', looked like the biker from central casting – an imposing physique, moustache, and long, dark, greasy hair pulled into a ponytail all of which highlighted the scourge of middle age, a receding hairline. Lyle was business first and brotherhood second. He ran the club's 'downtown' chapter based in Harris Street, Pyrmont. Lyle had brought his club's affluence into the limelight when he'd tried to buy the Blackmarket nightclub for $3.5 million, where his boss Michael Kulakowski had been gunned down in 1997. The NSW Crime

Commission were intrigued about where the money was coming from, and after an investigation found they also owned an apartment in Kellett Street, Kings Cross, just around the corner from 'the golden mile' of *Underbelly* fame or more accurately 'the grubby half mile', and a block of five home units in chic Double Bay. One of the top cops at the Crime Commission was Mark Standen, who like Rogerson, would end up with the adjectives 'disgraced', 'notorious' and 'imprisoned' before his name, and Rogerson on the list of people he consulted when in strife.

In August the same year, Rogerson and his partner Anne Melocco bought their first house together, in Churchill Road, Padstow Heights for $346 000 with a modest mortgage. It was a big step up from his old Condell Park home. The '60/70s brick veneer property sits on beautifully manicured grounds in a dead-end street with bushland on the other side of the road. It's built on a sloping block and underneath Roger created his own man cave where he and his mates could sit around and enjoy a beer and a chat. One visitor described the house as 'meticulously kept inside, but looks like a '70s time capsule'. A used white Daimler was parked in the driveway – Roger was always a 'car perv' and a slice of British luxury motoring was one of the few signs of affluence in his career.

For a former factory worker in the first years of his new small business, Roger seemed to be doing quite well. He'd also kept the Long Jetty weekender that was one of the few things he'd wanted in his divorce from Joy. A hint that Roger might have a few assets he wasn't talking about came when he was drinking with a few ex-coppers at the Bangor Tavern, a short drive from his home in Padstow Heights. An affable Bankstown real-estate agent – now dead from natural causes – was introduced to the group and when shaking hands with Roger commented, 'Good to meet you, I look after a few of your mother's rental properties.' One source in the group told me, 'Roger went off the deep end. He called the bloke everything he could lay his hands on, and told him never, ever, mention properties again. It was the first time I'd got a glimpse of the other Roger I'd heard about.' A search of property titles for Mrs Rogerson didn't yield hits aside from their old family home.

Unfortunately for Roger and Anne, both their Padstow Heights home and the Long Jetty weekender were infiltrated by stealth by the technical staff from the Police Integrity Commission (PIC), and it was prompted by Roger's actions. He'd never left their radar. Welcome to Operation Oslo and electronic surveillance that would, yet again, be Rogerson's downfall.

The operation was prompted by intelligence gathered by the NCA some years before, and from the Wood Royal Commission to which Roger, then in Berrima Gaol, had been invited to come along and roll over and give evidence. He'd declined and kept quiet – in contrast to Glen McNamara who'd volunteered to tell all, but had his offer declined. The operation targeting Rogerson placed listening devices in both their homes, and included physical surveillance. Roger didn't tumble to either.

Oslo gave a snapshot into Rogerson's busy life and Roger wasn't happy about their intrusion, beginning his stint in the witness box by telling the commission he'd 'been forced to leave my lawful form of livelihood' to be at a 'Star Chamber, a Kangaroo Court' and that his children had been embarrassed by his treatment over the years, and now it was the turn of his grandchildren. Roger the victim was in full flight, but the commission wasn't interested in his 'lawful employment', they were focusing on the 'unlawful'. The commission found Roger had been collecting $500 per week in protection money from Allan Chrara acting for his mate Kostas 'Con' Kontorinakis who was in prison. Like Rogerson, Con had been a Lennie McPherson crony. From June 1996 until December 1998, the commissioner investigators alleged Roger had collected around $40000.

Rogerson's evidence was he knew Con was involved in seedy strip clubs but didn't know of any involvement in prostitution, even though he visited the business – the Eros Cinema in Goulburn Street in the CBD – which featured 'exotic' dancing by scantily clad youngish women, offers of private dancing in the cubicles off stage, and alcohol for sale even though the place didn't have a liquor licence. The once church-going Rogerson who spent years working the vice dens of the Cross, and post police was an *habitué* of establishments like Lady Jane where lingerie lunchers included lawyers, business leaders and Bandidos should have noticed the sort of business Con was running.

Chrara later admitted in evidence that he and Con 'had a falling out' and that 'alcohol and drugs were sold on the premises [the Eros], prostitution occurred and some of the girls were belted and had money deducted for not working'. He also added that some of the money he'd given Roger was for repairs to a horse float, but Roger the welder had been more costly than he'd thought, with the bill coming to $8700.

Roger passed off the $40000 as a loan to Chrara – unusual for a man with a reputation of being tight-fisted – with the cash supplied by him and his mate Trevor Saul. Surveillance police caught many of his meetings with Chrara and Kontorinakis on video, and Roger hadn't noticed he was under observation.

When Roger stepped into the witness box at the PIC in April 1999 for the beginning of what would be frequent visits, his evidence on the so-called loan was described by the commission as 'evasive and obstructive' and he frequently resorted to a 'defective memory', which was in stark contrast to the confident and concise evidence he was famous for as a detective. However, the commission was unable to nail the reasons for the payments, noting 'in absence to evidence to the contrary, it is not possible to say the payments were for police protection or any other corrupt purpose'.

Following his examination on the Eros Cinema, the commission switched to evidence they'd found on Roger and his dealings with Sam Masri of Liverpool Council. Roger, they found, had let his criminal life overlap with his business life. As was becoming a habit, the evidence was substantially from electronic surveillance. The investigation was done jointly with ICAC, as allegations about Masri were in their bailiwick and not the PIC's. Questioning of Rogerson began on 25 May 1999 with Roger telling the commission he wasn't aware of Liverpool Council employees getting 'some sort of kickback or secret commission from certain tenderers or tenderer'.

Roger, who was tendering to supply scaffolding through businesses Re-Con and Aramco Building Services (an earth-moving and plant hire company in which Roger was allegedly an investor), was asked if he was 'well aware' Masri was an employee of Liverpool Council. He denied Masri had ever asked for a kickback. The commission heard that Aramco went into liquidation in November 1998, and on 30 November that year, Masri had written a letter confirming Aramco was a 'preferred supplier' and had work in progress for $75 000, and 'further work in excess of $1,000,000 was required and that Aramco was expected to be successful in tendering for a substantial part of that budget'. A nice littler earner for all, including Masri whom Roger had nicknamed 'Mr Ten Percent'.

Roger should have smelled a rat when he was again asked about kickbacks, and he stated under oath, 'No, I never paid anyone anything.' He compounded his problem by denying he'd been tipped off that the ICAC 'had taken an interest in the tendering process at the Council, and the tip had come from a former police officer who'd been told of the investigation by a police officer seconded to the ICAC'. To his list of denials, he added he hadn't told Anne Melocco to delete information from the computer. Roger is a Luddite who as one former mate said, 'wouldn't know how to turn on a computer, let alone use it, and look at his mobile phone – the Powerhouse Museum want to put it on display!' As the questioning progressed Roger resorted to 'I don't recall' or similar as his answer, and finished the segment of questioning with 'I wasn't doing anything wrong. I wasn't doing anything illegal or improper.' Then came the 'gotcha' moment.

A tape of conversations between ex-detective Ray Johnson and Roger was played, with Johnson giving Roger the tip-off he'd just denied, and Johnson saying 'he did say the whole thing's going to blow wide open'. It was followed with Roger instructing Anne to destroy computer records and to 'make sure the computers are clean. Remove all that shit out of that computer.' Anne did as she was told and unfortunately for her, also corroborated Roger's evidence. The following day, Roger switched tack, denying he'd given Masri money but recalling he'd given Masri $3000 which was repayment of a loan to his [Roger's] business partner, Kenneth Weldon.

The commission then moved on to what was drily called 'the Austral Matter', which again was based on evidence gained through electronic surveillance and 'related to an apparent conspiracy between Roger Rogerson, Raymond Johnson and Kenneth Weldon to carry out the offence of break, enter and steal on a property at Austral in western Sydney'. The conversations were recorded in Roger's car. Roger started his evidence by saying he didn't know where Austral was and didn't think he'd been there.

When he returned to the witness box a few days later he said he'd found out where it was and recalled Johnson had been speaking to him about 'some stolen property, and it seemed a little fanciful. He thought it could be some stolen gold bars.' The stolen gold bars were rumoured to be the haul of 25 gold bars weighing 285 kilograms stolen from the safe in Kerry Packer's Park Street office over the weekend of 28–30 April 1995. Roger told the commission he recalled Johnson had said to him something like 'if we're going to recover these stolen gold bars, we might need your expertise because you know a bit about safes and locks et cetera', but he didn't agree to be involved.

The story told to me by a source close to the action was different. The gold bars were allegedly under a concrete slab in an outdoor toilet on the property at Austral, which was owned by the man who'd done the robbery. When Roger heard the story 'his eyes lit up and he rubbed his hands together'. According to the source, Roger contacted Packer's security team to discuss a reward, then tasked Johnson and Weldon to carry out surveillance on the property to see when it would be an appropriate time to strike. Rogerson is a consummate networker and bragged of connections to the Packer empire, when, still as a detective, he'd sorted the problem of a person stalking a prominent female staffer.

The gold-recovery team needed a few uninterrupted hours on the rural site as there would be a bit of noise as they hacked their way through the concrete slab, but what the two didn't know is they were also under surveillance themselves. They didn't notice the car watching them watch the property. Roger, when briefing his team, told them if they were successful, there would be a reward, and 'we'll keep a bar for ourselves,' a bonus worth close to $200 000 these days. The source told me Roger had his team doing a few surveillance jobs, but didn't brief them on why or pay them: 'Roger was big on promises of money, but didn't deliver,' he said.

The commission concluded its hearing by asking Rogerson about his plans with former Sheriff's Officer Boris Link – who had been jailed in 1994 for his role in a cannabis growing scheme – to develop a marijuana plantation at Peats Ridge on the New South Wales Central Coast. Roger told them he was keen to grow vegetables on the site, but wasn't sure what sort of vegetables he had in mind, though his friend had mentioned cabbages. He conceded 'well, I mean marijuana might have got a mention. I think it might have been wishful thinking.' Roger later acknowledged, after listening to a tape of him and Kenneth Weldon discussing the market for marijuana and its distribution, that they may have been discussing growing 'cabbages and marijuana together'.

Justice was slow in catching up with both Rogerson and Anne Melocco, and it wasn't until July 2002 that both received summonses for perjury over their evidence to the PIC back in 1999. Their day in court would take a little bit longer. In the interim Roger's business empire fell apart, his businesses were deregistered, and an attempt to buy a quarry at Riverstone failed.

Rogerson's embarrassment in court continued in January 2000, when he was called to the inquests into the death of law clerk Brian Alexander, and Lyn Woodward. Alexander disappeared just before Christmas 1981 shortly before he was due to give evidence to the royal commission into drug trafficking. Alexander had been the go-between for bent coppers and criminals keen to get out of trouble and the NSW Police treated his disappearance as a routine missing person case. *Blue Murder* had a far more interesting take on the disappearance, with the most memorable scene from the series that of Alexander taking a harbour cruise with Neddy Smith, Rogerson and a few other detectives, and being attached to an Early Kooka stove and heaved overboard. As the Kooka and crook slipped beneath the waves, Neddy uttered 'Drown, cunt.' Rogerson joked about the scene in his pub shows – Roger started his stage career in 2003, touring with footballers Mark Jackson and Warwick Capper in a show called *The Good, The Bad and The Ugly*, and later with Jackson and Mark 'Chopper' Read in *Wild Colonial Psychos* – and once quipped he 'kept a supply of Early Kookas' just in case the need arose. The inquests followed Neddy Smith's acquittal the year before for the murder of Sallie-Anne Huckstepp and the two men allegedly with him still haven't been charged.

The allegations the inquest heard were that Roger had lured Woodward to Alexandria Park and after an argument over incriminating tapes she had relating to the Lanfranchi case, an angry Rogerson had shot her in the head, then asked Neddy to bury her. Rogerson told Coroner John Abernethy – the same man who'd taken Drury's deposition at a time when he believed he might die – 'that's the allegation and I deny it. It is a vicious attack on me by Ned Smith.' The allegations and denials weren't new. Smith had told a similar story to the NCA in 1993, and the NSW Police had followed up in 1995. Abernethy found Woodward was deceased and had died after 5 November 1981.

By 2000, Roger had given up the idea of being a legitimate business operator and was back to consulting work and working on the redemption of his image, using his deft media touch to do so. In September 2001 he appeared on *Hypotheticals* compered by expat barrister Geoffrey Robertson, and offered his acting talents, honed in the witness box, for a short film *Dealt a Bad Hand* in which he played a Supreme Court judge. He told the *Sunday Telegraph* on 15 December 2002, 'I'm taking the whole thing as a bit of a joke because the law is a bit of a joke and you shouldn't take it too seriously.'

In the first days of 2003, Rogerson did something that would have saddened his staunchest supporters at his luncheon club that met in Chinese restaurants at Roselands and the Grandviews Bowling Club. And he did it for money.

Dennis Ferguson was one of the most loathsome and saddest men in Australian criminal history. He was born in Sydney in 1948 and was legally blind from birth, with just a slight amount of sight in one eye. His parents separated and Ferguson later alleged his mother's new partner had sexually abused him for years and when the man died, he bragged he'd 'pissed on his grave'.

By 1987, he'd amassed a lengthy criminal history for sexual offences against women and children, and fraud offences and was in a relationship with 23-year-old man, Alexandria George Brookes. Shortly after his release from Long Bay Gaol in 1987, he and Brookes kidnapped three children – a six-year-old girl and her brothers aged seven and eight – of an inmate he'd befriended, drove them to a motel in Kedron, in Brisbane's northern suburbs and sexually abused them over three days. The pair were arrested and in 1988 Ferguson was convicted of kidnapping, gross indecency and carnal knowledge. Ferguson claimed he was set up and the charges were part of a conspiracy against him, a defence that failed. In sentencing Ferguson to 15 years without parole, Justice Derrington said he was a 'cunning and scheming man, not without some intelligence' and 'a danger to children and foolish parents'. The judge also observed Ferguson had no chance of rehabilitation.

Ferguson served his full term and was released on 9 January 2003. He gave an interview to ABC Radio's *PM*, in which he denied being a 'predatory paedophile' and maintained his innocence. He asserted, 'the community has nothing to fear,' but Dennis did. His face was on the front pages of newspapers around Australia, and communities were revolted that such a man was again on the loose. Enter Roger Rogerson. Through his criminal network who valued money above all, Rogerson was asked to find a minder to make sure Ferguson wasn't attacked, and 'grab him by the scruff of the neck' as one source told me, if Ferguson looked like he might re-offend. Someone who had a large amount of cash was prepared to invest in Ferguson and who that was remains a mystery.

Rogerson, with the promise of a large dollar fee, approached his Bandidos contacts. He wanted someone who looked sufficiently fearsome who could deter would-be assailants, or deal with them fast and hard. One Bandido told me 'believe it or not there are some things we won't do for money, and minding that prick was one of them'. Another former colleague of Rogerson was then approached – he's a hard man with a fearsome reputation, and a few years in prison to hone his fighting skills. He reckoned Roger was offering 'big money' for the job, but the man declined. He said, 'Roger was on the nose with me by then anyway – for him it was always about the money. I've done some things in my time, but not something like this. It was contemptible.' When he refused point blank he recalled, 'Roger got quite shitty and told me Ferguson's money "is as good as the next bloke's", but I didn't agree. There'd been a few incidents with Roger, and I didn't want anything more to do with him.'

According to another source, Rogerson found a man with a long history of violent crimes including armed robbery and with connections to an outlaw motorcycle gang, to take on the job, but it didn't last long. Ferguson was ousted from communities in New South Wales and Queensland before settling in a Housing Commission apartment in Sydney's Surry Hills. In 2010, a portrait of him was entered in the Archibald Prize, but like one of Rogerson a few years later, it didn't make the shortlist. Ferguson died of natural causes in December 2012. After his death, a young man who'd been his victim in 1987 told *Nine News*: 'He made me have sex with him and his friends. They used me as a sex toy. He got 15 years and I've got a life sentence for it.' Roger took the cash to protect a vile man – just business.

In 2004, with criminal charges looming over them both, Rogerson married Anne at a registry office service. The reception was held at the Rag & Famish Hotel in North Sydney, then part owned by his mate Steve Farley. Rogerson wore a suit with a striped tie and crisp white shirt and Anne looked elegant in a black dress. Both looked delighted when snapped by a photographer from News Ltd who had been invited along to catch a few moments. On the guest list was a smattering of outlaw bikers.

Roger the consultant had a growing reputation as the 'go to' man if you'd been charged with crimes and planned on defending them. His years as a detective, cunning mind, and contacts meant Roger could give the insights needed to create reasonable doubt, and given his dodgy reputation it was intriguing that Sydney lawyers still referred clients to him. Referrals came from underworld sources too. *Daily Telegraph* crime reporter Mark Morri recalled meeting Rogerson for a beer at the well-worn Chinatown Cultural Club in Sydney's Haymarket. Morri said it was Roger's 'de facto' office for the day and while they were there 'a disbarred lawyer joined us, and over the next seven hours or so a stream of men visited the pair as we drank. One young guy on an assault charge came in, bought Roger a schooner of Reschs (always Reschs) and handed him his brief. He had a bail hearing the next week and wanted to stall going to jail to get married. Roger moved to the corner, spoke quietly to him and came back saying "we'll sort something out for him".'

Roger's consulting also dabbled in civil litigation, and he brought Morri along to the negotiation of a defamation case. The pair met at the East Village Hotel in East Sydney, once the Tradesman's Arms Roger had frequented as a detective. Roger had found himself in strife over the place when a young plainclothes copper called John Williams had been investigating drug sales allegedly happening in the pub, and arresting a few patrons. Roger had taken the young man aside and allegedly threatened to 'load him up' if he persisted. Williams wasn't intimidated and told Rogerson he'd go straight to the media, a smart move in the wake of the investigations into Lanfranchi and Drury. However,

Williams was out-manoeuvred and transferred from duty on the streets to security duty at the Darlinghurst court complex.

Roger was helping a Melbourne contact resolve a defamation action brought against him by a Sydney identity. According to Morri 'there were drunken crooks everywhere, both from Sydney and Melbourne. Negotiations were getting more complicated as the booze flowed.' One of those present was former detective Bill Duff who'd got to know Rogerson after both had left the police. Morri said, 'the old pair left with a cheque for $50 000 in Duff's top pocket. It was renegotiated upward later.' Duff agrees he was there but denies leaving with a cheque in his top pocket, telling me the negotiation was all Roger's doing.

Morri commented, 'You could tell Roger loved it. He was in his element with all the villains and being the negotiator.'

12

THE DODGER DOGS

Zoe Zou died on 19 November 2003 in a car on a lonely stretch of the Bells Line of Road in the Blue Mountains from two shots fired at point blank range to the back of her head. In the back of the car was her 13-month-old daughter Yasmine. The killer then dragged Zoe's body from the car and buried it in a shallow grave in low scrub not far from the roadside. It was a place where only bad luck for the killer would see someone stumbling over the grave.

His ghastly business done, the killer then turned the car around and drove to North Head – a remote spot where suicides weren't uncommon and tossed Zoe's wallet and car key on a path not far from the cliff face where they were found a few days later. He left the baby outside the nearby Manly Hospital. His clever plan was to make Zoe's disappearance look like a planned suicide after making sure her child was safe. With rough surf and tides, police knew that recovering a body was not guaranteed.

Zoe could join the ranks of the missing and presumed dead. It was a smart plan conceived by a man who knew his way around police operations.

Zoe's killer was Michael Wallace, once an officer in the Corrective Services NSW who'd later joined the AFP and become a detective in their Sydney drug unit based in Redfern's TNT twin towers.

The drug unit had a reputation for, according to one source, being 'gangsters with police badges'. Wayne Sievers who'd spent time there commented it was like 'living inside a grubby episode of *Miami Vice*'. One of Wallace's fellow detectives was Mark Standen, who'd later come to prominence as the Assistant Director of the NSW Crime Commission and then arrested, charged and convicted of drug trafficking crimes. (Standen's appeal from his conviction and sentence was dismissed by the Court of Criminal Appeal in NSW in August 2015 and in July 2016 he lodged an appeal to the High Court.) Standen, as his drug deals hit hurdles, turned to Rogerson for counsel.

In 1990, Wallace was convicted for stealing $20 million worth of heroin the unit had seized in raids. Given his prior and current employment, he was a prisoner with a high risk of being beaten or murdered and so he joined the likes of Colin Fisk and Larry Churchill at Berrima Gaol. He was there in 1993, when Roger Rogerson arrived to serve his sentence and the two became friendly. It was a friendship that continued after both were released, and Wallace joined Rogerson and his cronies for their regular lunches in Chinatown or clubs around the Bankstown area.

Wallace bragged that in his post-prison career he was thinking of becoming a professional killer and 'the next Roger Rogerson'.

His fellow lunchers laughed heartily. However, the murder of Zoe Zou wasn't a professional hit – it was an old-fashioned crime of passion.

Zoe Zou's day job was on the IT help desk of the Boston Consulting Group, and at night she was a part-time escort working at the Ultimo brothel An Evening Affair. For Wallace, then 54, portly, and with grey hair finished in a bouffant at the front, a commercial transaction became infatuation – at least for him. For Zoe, the bragging ex-policeman presented her with an opportunity to sort out her complex private life – to her advantage.

In 1998, Zoe met a wealthy businessman who commuted between his rural holdings and his businesses in Sydney, where he stayed at his apartment in the CBD. Living with him in the country was his partner and their children. Both women were aware of each other's existence. Around May 2002, Michael Wallace met Zoe, who by then was in the early stages of pregnancy with the businessman the impending child's father. At this point what had been a reasonably well-managed relationship between Zoe, the businessman and his partner started to become tricky with Zoe suffering the most. It didn't work, and when the businessman married his partner shortly before Zoe gave birth in October that year, she became distraught. Her relationship with the businessman was coming to an end. He'd made sure financial arrangements were in place for mother and child, but Zoe wanted the businessman too, and turned to her besotted client Michael Wallace to help.

In July 2003, Wallace got his first offer of work as a contract killer, when Zoe paid him $20 000 to murder the businessman's partner. Unfortunately with the contract came the realisation that

Zoe was in love with the businessman and not him, and so he decided to 'rip her off' as he told a police informant. Wallace told the court at his trial he believed Zoe 'was obsessed with killing this woman' and that she'd thought of blowing her up using gas cylinders or buying a gun and shooting her before deciding to head down the professional route. When asked by her if he knew anyone in that line of business, Wallace reckoned he said no and laughed at the suggestion, and when asked if he'd do it he said, 'I don't do shit like that,' which was in contrast to his bragging with Rogerson and the lunch club. Her plan, according to evidence at Wallace's trial, prompted a cunning plan of his own and one that mirrored some police antics of the time. With the $20 000 secured, he thought he could approach the businessman and extract $45 000 to kill Zoe.

However, when Zoe and Wallace were driving up to the Blue Mountains he alleged the two were discussing their relationship and she told him she didn't love him. Wallace told the jury, 'It was like a knife to my heart,' and that 'I just completely, I just blew up. I just lost control of myself . . . She's screaming and she got hold of me and I got hold of her and I don't know . . . I just, I don't remember taking the gun. I reached into the bag, I obviously produced a weapon and she was in the front seat and I fired the weapon. I don't remember shooting her. The gun went off.' One problem with that entire scenario – and an attempt by Wallace to get a manslaughter verdict rather than murder – was why a convicted felon not that long out of prison after a long stretch felt the need to carry a loaded handgun while on a nice day's drive to the mountains.

The killing had another problem that needed resolving – Zoe's car. It's unlikely that someone contemplating suicide would use public transport to head across the city with her baby, when she could simply drive, and if you've left car keys where they can be found, chances are there should be a car nearby – and there wasn't. Wallace's response was to persuade a young man, later known under the pseudonym of Alex – who he'd met in Berrima and was a young man who also knew Rogerson – to take Zoe's car and burn it out. At least that could imply the car had been stolen from North Head after she'd killed herself.

Alex was out of prison, working in the motor trade and was a talented car thief. Wallace contacted him, spinning a yarn that 'the Triads had knocked her [Zoe]' and that he was frightened 'the Asians' were after him. Alex decided to help his mate. A few days after dealing with the car, he read media reports that detailed Zoe's disappearance, the discovery of Yasmine at Manly Hospital, and the finding of Zoe's belongings and realised his supposed mate had made him complicit in murder and one probably not committed by the Triads.

Alex had two choices: either stay quiet and hope the police failed in their investigation, or do the right thing and contact them – an act that, given his background, put him in treacherous waters. He chose the latter and for the investigating police, it was a breakthrough in a perplexing case. Alex told ABC's *Lateline* in 2006 the police 'told me that I was the only lead that they had and that it would be vitally important for me to wire up on him' and that 'I would receive $100 000 reward from the NSW Government. I'd also receive the $100 000 reward that was offered in the paper from the family of Zoe Zou. Also, I would receive a new identity, relocation to wherever I wanted to go to, and, if any problems in the future, I would be relocated again.'

The police were telling the truth about the significance of Alex's role. A few days after Zoe's disappearance, police released CCTV footage of her in the foyer of her apartment with a mystery man. On 28 November, with Zoe's car burned out, and Wallace believing all the loose ends were tied, he walked into Manly Police Station and identified himself as the man on the film. In the subsequent interview he said he'd come forward after seeing the footage on television and that Zoe 'was a very much-loved person and certainly I would not want to see her come to any sort of harm'. He added his reason for coming in was 'I've not always had a happy relationship with the police, and I thought, phhhh . . . I don't need this, you know, I'm just trying to get on with my life.' He told them he'd last seen Zoe on 17 November, and had used her car, returning it the next day and parking it on the street near her apartment in Chinatown. He left the key in the exhaust pipe for her to collect.

The detectives weren't impressed with Wallace's public-spirited admissions and though their instincts were telling them they had a murder on their hands with Wallace as the prime suspect they had no useable evidence. Wallace had done a good job of covering his tracks.

Australian police have a dismal track record in managing informants like Alex – something with his background and contacts he knew – but with the incentives along with a promise not to prosecute him for his work on Zoe's car, Alex accepted the offer. Alex reckoned Wallace was 'extremely paranoid' and worried that the reward from the businessman would cause people to try and set him up for the murder even though he hadn't admitted his complicity. To add to the danger for Alex he knew Wallace was an illegal gun dealer to Sydney's underworld.

Over the following four months, Alex (who was wired for sound) and Wallace met in parks and pubs around Sydney, with Alex prodded into the meetings by his police handlers and the promise of a substantial chunk of cash. Alex added 'confidant' to his relationship with Wallace.

As the months wore on and Wallace hadn't disclosed the location of the body, the police decided to ratchet up Wallace's paranoia. On 25 March 2004 they faked the arrest of Alex for the theft and torching of Zoe's car.

By late March 2004, Wallace was convinced the police were close to arresting him but the only impediment to them acting was the lack of a body. He decided to ensure Zoe would never be found by recovering her body, taking it back to Sydney, and then dumping it at sea.

On 29 March, Wallace acted. The two men headed towards the Bells Line of Road in Alex's utility that was wired for sound, as was Alex. Plus they were being tracked by GPS with the police helicopter maintaining discreet surveillance. Wallace was on edge, terrified they were being followed, but unaware of modern techniques that didn't require two coppers in an unmarked car lurking behind their target. In his state, he didn't see the surveillance vehicles that were keeping a watch from a distance as back-up for Alex if something went wrong.

About 35 kilometres east of Lithgow, Wallace ordered Alex to park the ute on the side of the road. Alex recalled Wallace 'put on a tracksuit, put on gloves, wiped himself down with ammonia and started getting his tools ready: a hacksaw, a small rake. He took a doona cover out of the back of the ute. He then scurried down the edge of the cliff where the body was.' A short time later, Alex was terrified that Wallace was alerted to the surveillance when he emerged from the cliff line and said, 'I can hear that bloody helicopter. I can hear that helicopter,' and Alex said, 'Stay there. Stay there 'til it goes away.' Being wired up and listened to in real time has other uses; the police got the message and the helicopter moved away, with Wallace's justified paranoia slipping back a notch.

Wallace then approached the ute, carrying the doona with its grisly contents. He put the doona into the back of the ute, closed the tarp and said to Alex, 'The animals have done a good job. You're not going to believe it. There's only a bloody skull left.' The two and their cargo then motored back towards Sydney and just near Kurrajong Alex told Wallace he needed to stop at the pub to buy some beers to 'steady my nerves'. That was when police swooped and both men were ordered out of the ute at gunpoint. Police got their man, and Alex got only $40 000 – $15 000 from the police and the balance from the $100 000 reward promised by the businessman. The police running the case had recommended payment in full, but the committee that manages rewards had opted for the smaller amount. Alex lost his job and ended up in witness protection.

Wallace's first gambit was to try and plead guilty to manslaughter, citing his well-rehearsed story of a moment of blinding anger brought on by rejection, but the Crown declined his offer and pressed on with the murder charge – they knew they were on a winner.

The murder trial ended in April 2006. Wallace gave evidence with the judge commenting on his 'general lack of credibility' and the 'implausibility' of his version of events, but it was Alex's evidence that nailed the case. It only took the jury one hour of deliberation – just enough time for a cup of tea and a Scotch

Finger, which is the usual police quip when a jury is this quick – to find Wallace guilty of murder. Even though, as the Court of Criminal Appeal later observed, 'the Crown had eliminated any reasonable possibility of provocative conduct on the part of the victim such as would justify reducing the criminal culpability of the respondent from the level appropriate to the crime of murder to the level appropriate to the crime of manslaughter,' Justice James sentenced Wallace to 20 years with a non-parole of 14 years – a sentence the Crown reckoned to be 'manifestly inadequate' as they'd expected a non-parole of 20. They appealed, but the Court of Criminal Appeal dismissed it.

The evidence presented to the Wallace trial and the story later told on *Lateline* by Alex didn't disclose one important ingredient – the master manipulator who'd orchestrated a great result for the police and the prosecutors, but more importantly a great result for himself. Roger Rogerson.

In those frustrating early days of the investigation when they had their suspect, but no useful evidence, the Homicide team headed by Detective Sergeant Steve Leach had done a thorough background check on Wallace. In combing through his past they decided it might be useful to talk to some of the detectives who'd been in Berrima Gaol when Wallace was serving his sentence there. They approached one detective who was out of prison and getting his life back in order. He decided to meet Leach on neutral ground and crossed Sydney for the meeting at Manly Wharf. A few moments into the discussion, he knew Leach had the wrong man. He later told me the following: 'I said to him, "Mate, I wasn't in Berrima when he was there. You need to talk to Roger Rogerson – I know they were there at the same time."' When the meeting ended, the former detective rang Rogerson, not out of friendship as the two weren't close, but as he told me, 'to give the cunt a heads-up. I'd rather have him onside than offside.'

When Leach arrived unannounced at Rogerson's home in Padstow Heights, the most notorious detective in Australian history was waiting for him, and he had his act polished and ready for the stage. He later told my source, 'I was shocked, I was surprised they'd reckon I'd turn on a mate and be a dog!'

Rogerson had long experience with informants – or dogs as he derisively referred to them, but also declared that he was an expert in handling these tricky people. He'd used his Bankstown links from childhood to gather the intelligence to help him secure the calibre of arrests that ultimately smoothed his way into criminal investigation. Ray Kelly and his successor Don Fergusson (who died in 1970) had handed over one of their prize criminal sources, Lennie McPherson, to him, and later he'd landed Neddy Smith in a relationship that hadn't ended well, particularly after Roger outed him as an informant while defending himself on Channel 9's *Willesee* program on 1 April 1986. Neddy was run over by a disgruntled criminal the following day outside the Iron Duke Hotel in Alexandria.

Roger played his part beautifully with Wallace, and with police desperate to crack the case, he got the deal he wanted. At the time Roger was awaiting sentence for perjury arising from his evidence to the PIC back in 1989. Sharing his wait for sentence was his wife Anne. With her past free of blemishes and her role in the lies motivated by obedience to her husband, she had a good case for a lesser sentence than her husband. Roger, however, with his track record was odds on to go back to prison, so the assistance he could garner from a deal with the police was a reduction in the time he'd spend in prison. The ever-thrifty Rogerson was looking for the best discount he could get.

His role was as a consultant. Both Alex and Wallace were under the Rogerson spell. With no luck in finding the body, the wily Rogerson later bragged to a contact of mine that he'd 'wound him [Wallace] up. I told him the police were getting close to finding her body and that he'd better move it! He was shitting himself. So I told him the best thing to do was to recover the body and take it out to sea and dump it.'

Rogerson's hand in the Wallace case would have gone unnoticed except that he felt the need to brag about how he'd 'played them all off a break' and received a 'letter of comfort' that had given him the discount he'd been after. His brag was to drinking mates at the pub and to his lunch club that now had an empty chair thanks to Wallace's departure. The NSW coppers who were the core of the lunchers didn't flinch at Roger's candour or his actions – Wallace was only a 'plastic' anyway. Not even the B team.

While the details of Roger's assistance were never made public aside from his own pub talk, Clive Steirn, his barrister in his 2005 sentencing hearing, told the court, 'Mr Rogerson's actions in coming forward and informing Police of the identity of a man wanted for murder in itself amounts to very particular circumstances.' He went on, saying, 'In the present case Mr Rogerson came forward to identify the person responsible for the murder when police investigations had come to a dead end. But for Mr Rogerson's public-spirited action more than likely the offender may not have been caught. Given the circumstances under which Mr Rogerson volunteered this information it should not be equated with an offender who comes forward to assist the authorities merely to assist himself on sentence. Accordingly he is entitled to an even further discount in relation to sentence.'

Wallace's case added another page to the Rogerson story. His own case had multiple delays and when it was close to finalisation, Roger suffered a stroke, though the doctors weren't quite sure. One source in court at the time noted that when the word 'stroke' was mentioned, Roger turned to him and winked, fuelling speculation that it was a ruse to delay his inevitable sentencing.

When he was called to give evidence in an attempt to mitigate the looming penalty, he spoke of his mindset at the time of the PIC hearings, and what he intended to do with the rest of his life. For Roger it was another opportunity to shine in the witness box. It was a vintage Rogerson performance, looking the judge directly in the eye then moving to engage the audience, and particularly the media, who'd filled the courtroom. While he'd publicly railed against the injustice of the PIC's bugging of his houses and their hearings, it was a reflective and contrite Rogerson who said to the judge, 'I was in a high state of anxiety. I had been really annoyed about being there, about how we'd been treated and I didn't really have any respect for what was happening there.' When asked about his belligerent attitude when giving the evidence that landed him in hot water, he said, 'Maybe I was too smart and too smug. That may be one of the problems I have today. Had I no experience [as a witness] maybe I wouldn't have done what I did, but as I said, it's spilt milk now, but that might have been the problem, I was just too smart for my own good and too smug and that's why I'm in so much trouble today.' Roger was so moved by his own testimony, he shed a tear.

The judge took into account the conflicting views of two forensic psychiatrists – Dr Thomas Clark who'd examined both Roger and Anne on behalf of their lawyers and Dr Greenberg for the Crown. In his report, Greenberg observed, 'I am therefore of the opinion that I could not agree with the statement made in Dr Clark's report that Mr Rogerson is most unlikely to re-offend again.' The judge said, 'There is much in Mr Rogerson's life about which he is entitled to be proud. There are many aspects of the offender's character which are admirable and he is able to call a great deal of evidence which has demonstrated the offender's kindness towards others. He has helped friends, family and strangers. He has assisted in raising money for various charities, including the Oncology Unit at Westmead Children's Hospital and a young girl with cerebral palsy. He has donated a considerable amount of money himself.' He also said, 'not without some hesitation I also accept the offender is remorseful'.

His good deed, combined with a guilty plea, age, disability and the likelihood he wouldn't re-offend, and Roger got his discount with a sentence of two-and-a-half years with a non-parole of 12 months. Michael Wallace will be eligible for parole in 2018.

A sad postscript to a very sad tale was the fate of Steve Leach. He'd been a police officer for 35 years, and included in his work was the investigation and arrest of serial killer Ivan Milat in May 1994 and for the European War Crimes Tribunal from 2000 to 2003 investigating murder, rape and ethnic cleansing, and the massacres in Montenegro – a task that required him to be at scenes when they were being excavated and forensically examined, and then interviewing survivors and the families of the victims. On 2 August 2004, the 51-year-old went to police headquarters in Parramatta where he was based, walked into the armoury and shot himself with his service pistol. A fellow officer found his body around noon.

The only one to emerge in front in the Zoe Zou murder case was Roger Rogerson; he continued dining out on it after his release from prison. Michael Wallace's place at the table was filled a few years later by another Rogerson acolyte – Glen McNamara.

13

ANOTHER OPENING, ANOTHER SHOW

Roger served the bulk of his sentence in Kirkconnell Correctional Centre near Lithgow, and was released at 8.30 a.m. on 17 February 2006. Waiting outside for him, along with media who'd been alerted to the event, were three knockabout blokes leaning against a limousine. When questioned by a reporter from the *Sydney Morning Herald*, one responded, 'We are here to get our uncle, don't take his photograph.' The chances of them being doting nephews was slight – one of the men was Tony Butler, the best man at Roger's wedding two years earlier. Rogerson limped towards the limo and motored off. When the entourage stopped at Blackheath for Roger's first decent coffee in a year, he was unusually subdued and declined an interview.

Roger's wife, Anne Melocco, was still doing weekend detention. One source told me Anne was depressed when she started periodic detention prior to Roger going to prison, but the depression deepened when he was released and she was still serving her weekly time behind bars – 'It put a real strain on the relationship, but Roger didn't seem to care. Water off a duck's back for him.'

Within weeks, he'd given up his media hiatus and was back on the public relations trail, kicking off on 12 March 2006. His choice was an intriguing one – instead of a feature piece with one of the coterie of journalists he'd mesmerised for decades with his stories, he opted for the high end – an interview on ABC's *Sunday Profile* with Julia Baird. A small but influential audience.

Baird opened by asking him if he was worried that people 'are out to get you?' Rogerson responded not by talking about underworld figures who might want to settle up with him, but instead painted himself as a victim of the Police Integrity Commission, 'a group of police that were out to get me' and the Australian Crime Commission, which at the time was an organisation that wasn't particularly interested in an ex-detective turned felon only weeks out of prison. With major organised crime, and particularly drugs as the main targets, Roger seemed to be quite innocuous, or was it a Freudian slip on his part?

He excised a large slice of his post-police career and hoped his audience had a short memory by saying, 'Basically, I cut my criminal ties you might say when I left the cops. Now all right, when I left the Police I set up an engineering business and I would get the odd phone call from Neddy Smith for a couple of years, but don't forget Neddy Smith has been in jail since 1988.'

When Baird asked him about using his gun, a fair question as Roger is rare in NSW Police history in having shot two people while on duty and fired at a few others, he said, 'Well look, I did everything in the line of duty,' which in the case of the late Warren Lanfranchi wasn't a sentiment with which the jury agreed. Rogerson, asked if the shootings had 'shaken' him, replied, 'Not really, I don't think I had any bad dreams about it or anything like that. I mean you were given a gun to protect yourself and use it to effect the arrest of a fleeing felon, that's what it's for, maybe they should use it more often.'

Roger then took the opportunity to begin rewriting history. This interview set the tone for the numerous appearances that followed – Roger wasn't a crook, Roger wasn't a corrupt police officer, he was a victim. He denied his relationship with Neddy Smith ever moved beyond professional – 'I've never done the social thing with Ned Smith' – neatly omitting while on a family day in the city, he slipped past the Lord Nelson Hotel at The Rocks where he introduced Ned to his family.

He then expanded on his handling of informants saying 'I'd mainly have a drink with them. They might have a problem themselves. There were problems I know over their children, I'd go and see the headmaster or something and say, look, "You can't blame the kid, you know, it's the father." Little things like that, they appreciate it because when you've been in custody as I have been myself, locked up, everything becomes monstrous, the slightest little problem with your wife or with your family becomes a monstrous problem inside.' Handling a criminal informant is a tricky task, and police generally take a hard line with them. Not so Rogerson.

Moving on to his family, he said of the collapse of his marriage to Joy – 'Well maybe she got just fed up, you know maybe it was my fault. I'll take all the blame, I'd never blame my first wife. I mean she, we had two beautiful daughters, I've got seven beautiful grandchildren. My daughters are very close to me.'

Joy hadn't spoken to him since the divorce, and according to sources close to him, one daughter was in contact and the other preferred not to be.

As for current wife, Anne, she was 'unbelievably strong and she's an absolutely fantastic woman but she's being punished because she's married to me' – or perhaps because she'd lied under oath to protect her husband in a prosecution which he reckoned was 'a trap'.

Of his stage show with Chopper Read and Mark Jackson he said: 'I crack a few funny lines which I think are funny, and say, "Look, ladies and gentlemen, when I was in the police, it was well known the New South Wales Police Force was the best Police Force money could buy." And then they laugh, and I say, "but the Police Force we've got today, no one wants to buy it," which usually gets a better laugh, a bigger laugh!' Earlier he'd taken a swing at contemporary policing and the long-running debate on bail, when he told Baird, 'I get rather annoyed at the way the police carry on now. They blame magistrates for allowing people out on bail and then when you read into the story you find there's not much evidence there anyhow. You need evidence to keep people in custody.'

Winding up the interview, Baird asked him, 'You were a hero of the force, now you've served two jail sentences, you said to me then you've been a bit naughty, you haven't always been a white knight' – a reference to the story that in the 1980s there had been a battle for supremacy in the NSW Police between black and white knights, though serving coppers thought it was a confection and that much of their leadership was grey. Roger agreed with Baird and confirmed he didn't wish he'd done things differently, and as for regret, 'No I would never, well. Look, the regret is I should never have been a detective, I should have looked at some of those people who went on to be Deputy Commissioners and Assistant Commissioners. I should have got a job at headquarters and bummed my way through there and got a nice easy job and that's the way to do it. That's the way to get to the top.'

Rogerson's knack for public relations had picked up on the ongoing law and order debate which called for tough men and tough penalties – and a return to the good old days of policing, a popular theme with the nation's shock jocks as they peddled their ill-informed views on morning radio. Roger the ex-felon was rebuilding his image as the grand old man of crime fighting – and as a man persecuted because he was too good at keeping the public safe. One of Rogerson's favourite songs is Sinatra's version of 'My Way', a song he plays often on the piano at home – Baird didn't cue it to conclude the interview.

Instead she posed the question, 'Do you think you can put the past behind you now?' It wasn't a happy ending for the interview and Roger replied, 'Well, what do you mean put it behind me, the only people who bring the past forward are people like you again, I don't, I never talk about it.' It was an intriguing answer, as aside from his regular media outings the past was something he talked about at length in his stage show, but Roger preferred his journalists to be unquestioning rather than capable with a mind of their own. Baird reminded him of the show, to which he said, 'Yes, on stage, what I did, that's right, but how can I when people ring up and say, "Roger, come on here, would you have an interview with us?" And it all comes out again and then you'll say to me, "Can you put it behind you?" How do I put the past behind me when everyone wants to bring it out all the time?'

•

One constant in Roger's life is his energy – something many of us, me included, hadn't factored in when thinking that after his release from prison he'd shuffle into a twilight of grandkids, fishing from his boat, and sipping a beer and lunching with his old mates. When Roger got out of prison in 2006, we all should have known that he'd go back to what he did well – crime. Ego, power and greed – along with a strong work ethic – were still driving him hard in his mid sixties.

One matter he attended to was putting the author of an unauthorised biography of him in his place and he did so by phone. Roger had bought my book, *The Dodger*, and wasn't happy, which didn't come as a surprise. The call came mid-afternoon from an undisclosed number. Late in the one-sided conversation, after the usual set-piece menace like 'I know where you live', the real Roger emerged – bringing up one of the saddest moments I can recall, just to give me something to remember him by. In the very early 1980s a colleague and good friend had run over a child on a pedestrian crossing. He was on the way home from a police training course, and it's a fair bet he'd had a few drinks and wasn't alone in the car. Rather than stopping, he drove on. The child died.

At the office the next morning, we'd been concerned to hear he hadn't attended his course, couldn't be contacted, and the overnight crime reports noted a car similar to his was wanted in connection to the accident – we did the sums. Around lunch-time he came to the office, red-eyed and haggard, his usual good humour gone, and went straight to see our boss. A brief conversation behind the closed door followed. Shortly after, with the barest of acknowledgement to the gaggle of detectives trying to look the other way while eating their lunches, he went to an office at the back of the building to wait for Internal Affairs.

As our boss was giving us a thumbnail of what had happened, we heard a shot. In the dingy small office, our friend and colleague had taken his own life – a bullet wound to his head and a warm Smith & Wesson .38 service revolver in his hand. I had the task of telling his parents. The whole sad incident is etched in my mind and will be forever. Nearly 25 years later it was an appalling event Roger thought appropriate to bring up, and did so with relish – it was designed to wound but didn't. Events like these are never forgotten and come to you all too frequently – but it was a reminder of the real Roger.

His source was obvious – a corrupt detective caught in Operation Florida that began in 2000. The man was among the coterie of corrupt detectives who'd been caught and joined Roger for drinks, and complaining. In his early career he had been a police cadet at Manly and memorable for his ability to adjust his testicles with one hand while picking his nose with the other.

Roger took another swing in 2013, telling journalist Erin Free of *FilmInk* that *Blue Murder* was a 'masterpiece' but his view on me, and *The Dodger*, was less flattering. After a few snarled comments, he said, 'I gave him all these opportunities to talk to me, but he didn't wish to. He doesn't have much going for him as far as being a cop is concerned. He's a bloody big sook. He wrote a book which was completely slanted. I've had people come up to me and say, "Mate, you wrote that book, *The Dodger*? What a terrific story!" I didn't write it! I think it's shithouse, but a lot of people think that it's fuckin' fantastic!' Roger never let the facts get in the way of the story he wanted to tell, so he missed the part where he cancelled an interview then wrote to me saying he'd be 'too busy' to be interviewed – all recounted in *The Dodger*.

As a detective, Roger considered himself the head of the A Team, with everyone else a varying degree of lightweight – a point he reiterated during our chat. Then he told me he was writing a book and in it, 'I'll make sure you get sorted out.' When Roger had obviously run through his script, I said, 'Well thanks, Roger, you've confirmed everything I thought about you,' and put the phone down. While feeling confident that his threats had been purely that, I did spend the next few days looking over my shoulder just in case, which is the art of delivering a competent threat.

Nearly a decade later I recounted Roger's call to a former detective who'd left the force, become an outlaw biker and done some time, but was now back in the 'straight' world – he told me he enjoyed being dull. He also told me that he'd known and worked with Roger in the 1990s when Roger was 'running hot'. When I mentioned the call to him, he said, 'Typical bloody Roger. He knows how to deliver a threat by phone, and he's a force to be reckoned with if he's got a few of his bruisers with him. Ha,' he smiled, 'I was one of them! But what nobody knows is he's gutless one on one. Don't let him bluff you. I got the shits with him when he tried to shaft me back in the old days when I was less charming. The prick burst into tears. Bloody sook.'

However, as one other former detective who'd been careful in what he said during an interview in late 2005, told me in 2016 post-Rogerson conviction, 'I didn't have a choice back then. I've got a few kids and Roger was still a powerful, devious bastard until the time he got locked up for Gao. He's a psychopath; charming one moment, and capable of killing in the next. But what also worried me were the young punks who revered him and wouldn't think twice about putting a few rounds through the window of my car or house, just to get a pat on the head from the man.' It was the view of so many men who'd known him for years. Another said, 'I'd deliberately kept away from him. He's capable of acts of generosity and compassion, and I bumped into him at a funeral of a mutual mate from years back. There he was sitting in the pews bawling his eyes out. Then you contrast that with everything he's got up to over the years. There are definitely two Roger Rogersons.'

Roger, like many others leaving prison, was facing a void. Adding to his problems was his prime connections with the underworld were all either retired, or looking towards retirement.

In the absence of any compelling opportunities, Roger made his own, deciding to put some oxygen back into his public image by returning to the stage and for cash. One of his first public outings was in early July 2006 at the Taren Point Bowling Club for the annual fundraiser for the Cronulla Police Rugby League Club. Over 200 local police and small business operators paid to hear Rogerson followed by Chris Anderson, the former Kangaroos football team coach. Rogerson kept his routine light and entertaining, and ran his usual theme of 'things aren't what they used to be' and poking fun at recent and current police leaders. The audience lapped it up.

When the speeches were done, the event's MC stepped up to the podium for a fundraising auction of memorabilia including a framed copy of the NSW Police P79A 'Report of Death to the Coroner' form for the late Warren Lanfranchi. Along with the form was a photo of Rogerson standing over Lanfranchi's body. The tasteful pair went to an unknown bidder for $1000, and a smile, handshake and hearty congratulations from the man who'd pulled the trigger.

Roger resumed his professional stage career, resurrecting the touring show *Wild Colonial Psychos* with Mark 'Chopper' Read and Mark 'Jacko' Jackson. He also returned to the airwaves, repeating a favourite theme that he'd never done anything corrupt or violent.

By 2007, Rogerson's media career was back on track and about to swing into top gear and along with it another business he'd pooh-poohed years earlier – the sleuthing game.

14

ELEMENTARY

If you're a copper putting together a brief of evidence against a criminal, one of the tricks of a seasoned detective is to swap roles and play defence counsel, poking around the brief for its strengths, weaknesses, vulnerabilities and credible alternative scenarios. You not only know how the investigation and evidence has been conducted, but also the cast.

With his forensic skills, history of excellence, expertise in the dark arts of criminal investigation and old-fashioned rat cunning, Roger was well qualified for defence work. The problem was with his criminal record he'd never get a licence to be a private investigator and he believed he needed to at least have the vestige of legitimacy. This is a cultural curiosity possibly belonging to his generation.

Roger comes from the 'job for life' generation where you started work in the public service or police and you were there until you retired. You moved up the ladder by seniority – in the police the seniority list was nicknamed the 'stud book' and station officers who maintained it would neatly draw a line through those who died, resigned or were caught doing something illegal and kicked out or sent to prison. Careers progressed by the numbers. It was this sense of order and place that drove Roger to seek legitimacy in having a licensed private investigator to provide a front for his work, and quid pro quo, having someone like Roger working on your criminal cases was good for business. He might have been a crook, but he knew his stuff, and he also knew plenty of criminals with sufficient funds to pay for an insightful defence or a cunning negotiation. No more hanging around dingy clubs with lawyers who had professional issues.

To get his first private eye was easy. Roger the mesmeriser turned the charm on a young former police officer he'd known since the man's childhood, but it didn't end well.

With Roger given the green light into the sleuthing business one of his first actions was to consolidate the arrangement by admitting the young man to his exclusive lunch club. The investigator told me that Roger 'was on the scrounge for a quid' when he left prison, and what he learned in their relationship was Roger was greedy and at the same time, 'as mean as cat shit'. He knew Roger had an extensive network of criminal contacts, particularly in the outlaw biker world that was particularly prominent in south-west Sydney, but he'd made it clear to Roger his business was strictly legit. Roger told him he was 'on the straight and narrow, mate. I just want to make a quid every now and then.' During their relationship he not only introduced the man to his luncheon mates but also to his longstanding Melbourne friend and colourful identity Mick Gatto. Like Roger,

Gatto was charming, made you feel like an insider when he met you, enjoyed his notoriety and loved being in the limelight.

The unofficial partnership went well initially with Roger living up to his promise as rainmaker and offering advice as required. It wasn't a full-time pursuit, but the investigator noted 'it kept him from getting bored and pestering his missus, and made a bit of money along the way'. However, the young man twigged to a problem after taking on a client for a debt recovery. It was the normal sort of task a licensed commercial and private inquiry agent takes on – X owes me a debt on a commercial transaction, can you see if he's got the assets or cash flow to make good the debt or sort an arrangement for paying, rather than spending a chunk of cash on lawyers. The usual routine for an agent is to do their homework, then approach the debtor and talk. It can be faster and cheaper than litigation.

The debt was six figures and arose from work the client had done and billed, and the debtor was in a remote part of the state. The investigator got an advance of $10 000 to cover travel and costs, which is common practice in the business, and a sensible move to preclude you having to chase your own client. Roger volunteered to keep the investigator company on the long drive but didn't ask for any fees – just pay for his drinks, food and accommodation. The investigator said, 'It was all sweet until we got there, and the first thing the bloke shows me is a Supreme Court document. My bloody client didn't tell me he was already suing the bloke. It's before the court so I can't go near it.' The pair returned to Sydney and the investigator admonished his client for not telling the whole truth, and telling him he'd also wasted his money and the investigator's time.

A few months later, the client called for a progress report, which surprised the investigator who reiterated it was all done months ago – and that's when the problem appeared. Roger had visited in the intervening months, telling the man they'd re-thought the issue and he'd need a bit more cash to continue their work. The former client, believing Roger to be both credible and representing the investigator, handed over a further $22 000, usually in $5000 lots, but hadn't heard from Roger since. He'd also paid in cash and didn't get a receipt. The investigator straightened out the client, telling him he had nothing to do with Roger's visits and as far as he was concerned the matter was finished. He told me, 'Roger's pulled about 20 grand more out of this bloke and done precisely nothing aside nearly landing me in the shit. Looks like he's snipped the quids [taken money] from the bloke then driven to Melbourne for a weekend on the piss with Gatto.'

The end came very shortly after. The investigator, with his licence and reputation put on the line by Roger, decided to end their professional relationship. Their personal relationship hit a hurdle around the same time, when Rogerson offered him a great deal on his old fibreglass runabout, complete with trailer and outboard. The boat had done sterling service taking the kids out for a joyride during his Australia Day barbecues at Picnic Point, and was the same boat he'd taken Christopher Flannery's children out on to take their minds off their father's recent disappearance. Roger wanted $7000 for the boat and represented it as a 'great deal, mate's rates'. The investigator, who knew very little about boats but lived near the water and thought having one might be a good idea, was interested.

As Roger increased the pressure to do a quick deal, the investigator, now more objective in his views of Roger, decided to get a rough valuation done, and found the market price for the SS *Jolly Roger* was half what he was asking. Roger called him a 'weak cunt' and shared that view with their mutual acquaintances.

Another sleuth in awe of Rogerson would fill the investigator's seat at the lunch table, and it was another affair that would end badly. The replacement was Glen McNamara.

15

GOING THE BIFF

The contemporary outlaw biker from major clubs like the Bandidos, Hells Angels, Rebels and Comancheros is more likely to be found hanging around a gym than a seedy pub. Times have changed with grunge, poor diet and obesity consigned to history.

Roger's last major contact with the outlaw biker world was in 2004 when some of its luminaries had been at his wedding. Since then ill health, his court appearances and then prison had kept him busy, and for the bikers, being seen in the presence of someone so publicly on the nose wasn't good for business. His desire to return to their company was well timed. Sam Ibrahim, John's brother, was head of the Nomads and was in prison in 2006 for an internal fracas a few years before in Newcastle when Sam decided discipline could be instilled by shooting a few of the members of the local chapter. His club was fracturing and in late 2006, would become the parent of an outlaw gang called Notorious who, with Ibrahim's guidance, took over the Cross and with their gym-buffed bodies, good hygiene and sharp clothing would be known sneeringly by other gangs as the Nike Bikies.

One ray of sunshine for Roger in the outlaw biker world was Felix Lyle, who'd done something rare and usually fatal, and swapped clubs. After internal battles in the Bandidos over money, Lyle was kicked out, and joined the Hells Angels, then working to be a dominant gang on the Sydney scene. Under his command, the club opened chapters in Chinatown and Bondi Beach and had their sights set on becoming the bikers in charge at Kings Cross, then the nation's nightclub and party drug capital. Lyle and his fellow Angels were also targeting Surfers Paradise, then controlled by the Bandidos.

However, Lyle's well-crafted plans hit a hurdle in 2010, when he and an associate, Terrence 'The Black Prince' Reddy, found themselves embroiled in a civil fraud case in the Supreme Court over dodgy mortgages. The case prompted investigations that led to both men being arrested on a number of criminal charges.

The indefatigable Rogerson was working other angles to make a quid. Mark Standen was the Assistant Director of the NSW Crime Commission, and the man who'd led the operation to catch Michael Hurley and his gang. Around crime circles is the story that for a large part of his New South Wales career, Standen, a man with allegedly a major gambling problem, had also been a source of information to Hurley in return for cash. For a man who'd risen to the lofty heights of criminal investigation, his career had not been without blemish. Standen had started his professional life as a customs officer and after some strife with the Stewart Royal Commission into drugs in 1979, joined the Australian Federal Police (AFP).

One senior and unnamed AFP officer told *The Australian* in June 2008 that Standen was 'viewed as the new breed of Commonwealth copper on the rise. They were smart, forensic in their methods and played the part.' A source of mine who'd worked with Standen when he was a detective at Sydney International Airport had a different view: 'He was a crook pure and simple, but he was a charmer and knew how to play the game. When I tried to sort him out after a few hair-raising incidents, the bosses looked after him and I ended up back in uniform.' Standen was also unscathed by the arrest of his friend and one-time colleague in customs, Allan McLean. Like Rogerson, Standen was destined for greatness but in 2006 the wheels fell off. That year, he sanctioned an informant to sell the Hurley gang seven kilograms of cocaine, of which six kilograms got into the market.

The plot to import the chemicals had a few problems. A tip-off about the deal led to the co-ordination of an international investigation in which electronic surveillance featured. Standen and his business partners were double-crossed by their supplier and the chemicals never arrived and, even worse, around one million dollars lent to the would-be drug barons to fund the Australian end of the venture was lost in what appeared to be a slick con job on Standen and his colleagues by a team of fraudsters based in the Bahamas. They'd decided to make some quick cash in a deal that, had they been more commercially savyy, would have looked too good to be true, and it was. With the drug deal looming, the men had to get the money back, so the call went out to Sydney's underworld Mr Fix It.

In May 2007, with Standen and his colleagues being recorded on the phone, Roger Rogerson entered the game. One of Standen's cohorts, Bill Jalalaty, was taped ringing him to tell him, 'Roger Rogerson is on the case.' Roger alleged he'd been called in by Frank Wheeler, who was an old friend, to see what could be done, but had only made $200. According to the *Daily Telegraph* of 4 June 2008, Wheeler was a 'former employee of the late standover men Tim Bristow and Michael "No Thumbs" Pestano'. Bristow had died of natural causes, but Pestano had died from gunshot wounds after unsuccessfully trying to evict a family from a rural property near Wellington in the NSW Central West in 2004. Wheeler told the paper Standen had approached him in December 2006 because he had a friend who'd lost one million dollars, and Standen couldn't help him.

On 2 June 2008, Standen was arrested for his involvement in a deal to import 300 kilograms of precursor chemicals needed to make ice with an estimated street value of $120 million. The chemicals were to be hidden in a shipment of basmati rice.

Rogerson was offering his wisdom within hours, not to Standen this time but to his media colleagues at News Ltd. Rogerson, adding features writer to his list of talents, was in print in News Ltd papers on 4 June as well, and he put the boot straight into Standen. He wrote, 'They're smart cookies and they know it. They're cocky and arrogant. They're greedy. Very greedy. And they know they can get away with it. A lot of them are bad gamblers and that's the worst situation for a cop with potential to turn.' He went on to say the commission was 'a law unto themselves, accountable to nobody,' and about their methodology he wrote, without a trace of irony, 'I honestly don't think you could say corruption exists because cops are poorly paid. It's because of greed, simple as that.' He added, referring to Standen, 'They live two totally different lives . . . It's the thrill of the chase for a lot of them ... For some people it all comes tumbling down, others get away with it.' Roger may have been sketching out his autobiography.

The article was followed by regular contributions to News Ltd and appearances in true crime shows on television. Roger used his media outings to rewrite Sydney's recent criminal history, casting himself in the most favourable of lights. Writing in the *Daily Telegraph* of 13 December 2008, he described Neddy Smith as 'nothing but a rapist and a drug-dealing murderer who also loved to do armed hold-ups'. Michael Hurley was 'charming to the point of charismatic', and Roger fingered him as responsible for 'the great Chinese takeaway', a snappy line for the January 1988 robbery of the National Australia Bank branch in Sydney's Haymarket in which thieves broke into the bank from an adjoining building and looted 80 safety deposit boxes. Only 42 boxholders came forward to tell police about their losses. A police guesstimate of the amount plundered was between $10 and $100 million, and the crooks were never caught. Roger wrote 'his gang got away with millions'. Of Christopher Flannery, he wrote 'there has never been any evidence as to who did it or where he is buried, if he was buried,' and Lennie McPherson told him years after, 'Roger, you can control a bad man but you can't control a madman.' He said of the comment that it was 'Lennie's way of letting me know he killed him'. In the 2011 television series *Tough Nuts* Roger asserted Stan 'The Man' Smith killed him, although Stan was probably in Texas at the time, but why let another good story get in the way of the facts?

What the bosses at what was once unkindly referred to as 'The Harlot of Holt Street' didn't know was that the genial old bloke was up to a few nefarious activities at the same time. On

17 June 2016, the *Daily Telegraph* reported 'UK Gang hired Aussie Enforcer', and reported that at the time Roger was offering his wisdom to their readers, his 'infamy extended as far as the UK with a Manchester drug gang allegedly hiring the ex-cop to threaten their own crew with having their hands cut off if they stole drugs or money from their crimes'. Apparently the UK gang had set up a local operation in beachside Coogee and had been importing 'tons of amphetamines into Australia when a large sum of money and drugs disappeared'. Nothing stimulates action faster in a major crime gang than loss of profit and product. The gang had come under notice in the global investigations that snared Standen; again it was a reference to Rogerson, captured on surveillance tapes, that prompted an investigation. One of the Coogee crooks called Nick was caught on tape recounting a conversation with one of the principals of the drug gang. Nick said, 'He also told me he knew "the Dodger" who I know from a movie he showed me was a former corrupt police officer in Australia. I took these comments as warnings that I better be careful and give him a wide berth from now on.' Roger told the paper he 'knew the men but wanted nothing to do with them'.

The story wasn't an isolated tale. Roger, if the price was right, was available for a 'whack job' (contract killing). One story was about a medical practitioner who was on the brink of a long, messy and expensive divorce. It's not an unusual occurrence and homicide investigators, when assembling their list of suspects, put spouses and family members at the top. Between 2008 and 2010, 66 per cent of domestic murders in Australia were classified as 'intimate partner homicides'. The doctor did some networking and his network overlapped with Rogerson's, and the two men met at a club in Sydney's west, a place in which neither man was known. The doctor outlined his problem and Roger offered a solution that included murder of his wife in circumstances that would distract investigating police from putting him on top of the suspect list, and advice on a bullet-proof alibi. Payment for services rendered was $50000 up front and a further $50000 on successful completion. Roger, obviously not in a sprightly state, assured the doctor he had associates to assist. Where Roger ran into trouble was when subsequently trying to recruit helpers. As a contract killer Roger had presented a couple of problems. While he was still capable of planning and being the wheelman, he was only good with a handgun and his physical condition meant he'd need to be very close to the target to do the deed, which increased the probability of being spotted by witnesses. The other problem was Roger loved to brag, with his exploits as the topic, and as he got older he became more indiscreet. Murder Incorporated meets Dad's Army never got to fire a shot.

16

AUTHOR AUTHOR

When Roger and I had our one-sided conversation in 2006 he threatened 'I'll sort you out' in the book he was planning on writing. I responded by asking if it would be something for the fiction section or was he planning on 'doing a Neddy' – a reference to Smith's 'tell almost all' books of the early '90s which featured The Dodger and torpedoed his reputation more than any police investigation. Roger didn't rise to the bait. His literary path began in earnest in 2008, the year that his rehabilitation in the eyes of the public and his transition from criminal to commentator began.

In creating his new persona as the grand old man of crime and policing, Roger got a leg up from the combination of Channel 9 and News Ltd. In 2008 he became their star rogue, taking advantage of the *Underbelly* series on Channel 9 by blogging for News and offering his insights, or rewriting history to suit his purposes. He began in February with a review of the first episode on the Melbourne gang wars, giving it a four-star rating. He reckoned, 'I never liked Melbourne or their crooks. And watching *Underbelly* last night reminded me why.' No one reminded him of various longtime 'mates' or the memories of debacles involving Alan Williams, Dennis Allen and Christopher Flannery two decades before. He said, 'We had more control over the crooks and I reckon most of the crooks would agree.' He thought it stacked up well against *Blue Murder*, noting 'the guys that wrote that didn't like it [*Underbelly*] but it was good drama'.

The blogs were a great hit, and to further capitalise he was the guide for bus-tour groups around Kings Cross, weaving tales of the place's seedy and criminal past. It gave him an audience and he made a few dollars.

Just before Christmas that year, Neddy Smith, with nearly two decades of two life sentences served for murder, and his Parkinson's disease advancing ruthlessly, applied for early release and was refused. It was timely for his old mate Rogerson, who was the go-to man for the media. First up was Alan Jones. Rogerson told Jones that politicians would be too scared to release someone with a high profile like Smith's.

The interview prompted a flurry. Roger told the ABC that from his experience some were kept in prison 'because of the political correctness of the time', a theme he would apply to his own problems of the '80s and '90s. Roger wrote in the *Daily Telegraph* of 11 December 2008: 'I think these days Ned is a political prisoner and it will take a very strong politician to allow him to be released. I occasionally listen to Hadley and Jones and they have got the politicians terrified . . . Having been on both sides and spent time in the slammer, I can tell you there are hundreds and hundreds of prisoners that could be released back into society without posing a danger to anyone. I have become very cynical of the NSW justice system.' Compassion out of the way, he nailed his former mate, writing 'so should he be released? Of course not. Ned was always an unbelievably conniving bastard. Always been well known as a shocking liar and a shocking give up.' His article two days later, on 13 December, canvassed his view of Sydney crime figures over the recent decades, but avoided his connections to men like Michael Hurley and Lennie McPherson – both of whom were dead by that time – and one notable omission was Stan 'The Man' Smith, who wasn't dead, and of whom Roger was terrified. Roger would wait until Stan was dead to offer his view.

There was more in the same vein for the next few months, with Roger expanding to include the ongoing travails of the Ibrahim family, then with rolling problems involving Sam, Michael and Fadi.

In early October 2009, Roger made good part of his threat to me and became an author with the publication of *The Dark Side*, a book that accentuated his positives, eliminated his negatives, and consolidated his new image in the mind of the public. I didn't get a mention. The launch was on 14 October and the venue was one made famous by Roger and Neddy during their bromance – the Iron Duke Hotel in Alexandria, once owned, allegedly by Smith.

The launch was magnificent media fodder, bringing together stalwart crime reporters, retired or disgraced coppers who were still on friendly terms with Roger, a few underworld figures and some loyal fans he'd built up during his shows, assorted sticky beaks keen to see who was chatting to who, and lawyers from both sides of the criminal justice game.

The ambience of the Iron Duke got a boost from screens showing *Blue Murder* and, poised behind the table where Roger would be signing the books, a painting by Adam Cullen of Roger standing over the late Warren Lanfranchi in Dangar Place and with the added touch of a bullet stuck on the canvas with the note 'he had a real bad day'. Cullen had been best man at Chopper Read's second wedding and Chopper had introduced him to Rogerson. The painting was done as part of a number of works by prominent artists to be auctioned in aid of The Alphabet Foundation, a charity supporting orphaned children. Each work had a reference to the alphabet, with Cullen using X to mark the spot where Lanfranchi died after being shot twice in the chest by Rogerson.

Doing the launch honours was Alan Jones AO, introduced as 'Number one in the nation' and 'you don't dial 000 if you want to get anything done, you dial Alan Jones's studio number!' Jones had been asked to do the launch (by either Paul Kenny or the publisher) and agreed after being sent a copy. The *Sydney Morning Herald* reported on the day of the launch, 'Alan wrote back to say he'd never met Roger but had interviewed him several times. He said he found him a fascinating and interesting person.'

Jones, his sombre banker's grey suit offset with a perfectly knotted blood-red silk tie and with a matching pocket handker-chief flourishing on the breast of his jacket, stepped up to the podium amid the shouts of adulation and in his introduction evaded unpleasant memories of Roger's numerous major problems – and also giving himself some wriggle room if questions about their association ever arose – saying, 'I'm not suggesting Roger Rogerson is Mother Teresa. I don't know Roger Rogerson. I don't know his past.'

Jones spoke about the need for 'old style' cops and 'fear is a necessary corollary of discipline' and lamented the current police force, saying, 'what we have now is not a police force but a police service that consults and conciliates. We have a permissive society and the loss of standards' and bizarrely his example in his crime diatribe was 'just look at spelling and punctuation'. Jones must have been unfamiliar with the spelling and punctuation of many 'old school' coppers.

It was a speech in tune with Roger's theme of being a brilliant copper fallen victim to the less able. Jones's finish was timed perfectly to coincide with the shooting of Lanfranchi in *Blue Murder* on the screen behind the podium – Roger's years in musical theatre production had paid off. Time for your entrance, Mr Rogerson.

With the screen depicting Richard Roxburgh as Roger, Alex Dimitriades lying on the road as the late Warren Lanfranchi and the smoking Smith & Wesson .38 revolver as itself, Roger stepped up to the sound of whoops, wolf whistles and applause. His face split in a wide and warm grin, eyes twinkling and like any great performer he connected with everyone in the room, making them feel as though he was there just for them. He was back precisely where he wanted to be.

He opened with a joke, telling the crowd that if Jones hadn't been available he'd have asked Jeffrey Archer because 'he and I have a lot in common. We're both writers and, like him, my memory got a little here and there in court and I ended up doing time just like Jeffrey.' With the audience lapping up every word, just like the juries he'd spun stories to decades before, he confessed to a fear of public spaces, and said, 'all the things that have happened to me make me quite agoraphobic,' and then was on to his regular theme – the decline in the once great police force and how he became a victim of lesser men. He packaged the story into a recollection of his last day in the police, saying, 'I remember quite clearly throwing my gun and handcuffs straight in the bin at Police headquarters. And the Superintendent at ICAC thought my gun was going to explode – I don't think he'd ever seen a gun, really, being at headquarters.' The audience loved it, even though it was utter nonsense – ICAC was a few years into the future, and at Internal Affairs many of the staff were detectives from the CIB, like Roger's old mate Angus McDonald.

After the speech he set to the thirsty work of autographing books, with a cold schooner of Reschs at hand and news photographs and film crews recording the moment.

Aside from the chuckling of journalists and crime insiders who have long memories and bad experiences with Roger and collectively dismissed his book and the event as 'bullshit', the other dissenting voice was Debra Smith, Neddy's ex-wife, who'd seen the Smith/Rogerson bromance at its most passionate, and at its bitter end.

Jones had followed up by interviewing Rogerson on his radio show, introducing the segment with: 'I'm not one of those politically correct people and it mightn't be politically correct to say it but if we had – you talk to people at the grassroots – if we had a few more of the man I'm about to speak [to], then we'd have fewer problems in society, confronting society at the moment. A bit of old-style policing wouldn't do any harm.' Debra rang the show and was put to air. She said 'all Roger did was make a mockery of the police force' and of Jones's speech, she said, 'if you are going to say things about people that are negative, you've got to be able to prove them'. As for Rogerson, the book stimulated speaking engagements and book signings.

In mid-November, a piece by journalist William Verity was published in Fairfax papers. Commenting on the recent fascination with Roger and his rehabilitation in the eyes of the public, Verity made the point that Rogerson was like the disgraced cop in a thriller who 'prevails and he walks away from the final battle in the derelict factory scarred and exhausted into the arms of an adoring and beautiful woman who's forgiven him for his many faults. The story is so deeply imbedded in our psyche that it may go some way to explain the continuing fascination with Roger Rogerson, the nation's most famous detective, more than 20 years after the commissioner told him he was off the case.' Verity tried to get a comment from Jones – and Margaret Cunneen who attended the launch, and Clive Steirn SC, who'd represented Rogerson in his 2005 court case. All were elusive. He had more luck with fellow scribe Graham Henry, who wrote his autobiography *Abo: A Treacherous Life* in 2005 and was a man never shy of offering a comment. Henry said he'd offered Rogerson $10000 at Christmas when he was still a copper 'to get him on my side, but he told me to stick it up my arse. Roger was always good company and a man's man but he was one of the most feared on the streets of Sydney.'

Henry also joked that contrary to Roger's claim that after publication of the book there were no secrets, 'that's probably why his book is so skinny – because there is still so much he can't say'. Henry didn't comment on whether Roger's rejection of the cash was what coppers of the time described as the unforgiveable crime of 'offer insufficient bribe'. In recent years, his view of Roger has changed for the worse. Graham told me in a recent interview he hadn't heard much from Roger until he got a call asking for his address so he could send a few signed copies of *The Dark Side*. The books didn't arrive but two heavy criminals did. He said, 'I don't believe in coincidences. The mongrel tipped them,' and he didn't elaborate on the reasons for the visit or the outcome other than the matter was sorted. He'd also known McNamara during his brief tenure at the NCA, and said, 'I don't know why Roger was involved with that fool.'

One regular luncher with Rogerson, one of a crew of local identities from business, law and football around the St George area, made the comment to Verity that Rogerson was a 'pillar of society' and a 'leading Freemason' which touched on the police era of the '60s and '70s in which there was a popular notion that Catholic groups and Freemasons vied for prominence in the force. There was credit to the proposition – but ultimately it was the trinity of 'cash, bash and gash' that ruled. You were either a player or your career prospects were hampered. He said, 'he was a very courageous person, if you were going to an armed robbery, he'd be the first through the door,' but there was a downside to Roger and he added, 'I wish I knew what motivated him to go to the wrong side, but I don't know why.'

Rogerson didn't offer any insights either, but took the opportunity to hammer out his key messages to Verity of how effective police were when he'd been the golden boy, his brilliant handling of criminals and then slipped in mention of Chester Porter QC's comment of him that 'had he fought in a war, he would have been a VC'.

Chopper Read offered some balance, telling Verity, 'I think Roger was as bent as a dog's hind leg myself. He swears black and blue that he wasn't – he looks you straight in the face and tells you he wasn't corrupt.' Chopper was wise enough to avoid going boating with Roger, commenting 'because I would end up getting thrown overboard with a gas cooker around my neck'. While the comment was made as a joke, Read was serious when he talked of their failed relationship and like others in Roger's life, it was over money. Read said, 'on a couple of occasions Roger started moaning and groaning under his breath when I couldn't pay him the full amount [from their touring shows]. I could only pay him $500 not $700, because we only had 60 people on the night. I thought it was a bit churlish.'

At the end of 2009, Roger had taken up an interest in boxing and mixed martial arts, though for him it was more networking with audience members than enjoying the art of the biff. Big bouts were ideal places to mingle with members of the outlaw motorcycle gangs and others without questions being asked – it wasn't consorting, it was blokes with a mutual interest enjoying a night out. Roger, however, couldn't resist tipping off the media he was about to make a public appearance with some colourful characters. His ego needed the massage, and it sent a message to the underworld that Roger still had the juice.

On 2 December, Roger was in the audience at Sydney's ACER Arena to watch Danny Green defend his cruiserweight title against American Roy Jones Jr. In the front row of the audience was Rebels head honcho Alex Vella, Mick Gatto, Rogerson and Rodney Adler. Rogerson had met Adler while both were in Kirkconnell Correctional Centre and had kept occasional contact. Sharing the best seats in the house with them was the new President of the Comancheros, who'd taken over after the incumbent 'Mick' Hawi had been charged and was on remand after the fatal brawl between his gang and the Hells Angels at

Sydney's domestic airport in March that year. Rogerson was in top form, chatting with both gang leaders. The synergy between Rogerson and the two gangs would recur in the aftermath of Jamie Gao's murder.

17

A FINE BROMANCE

Glen McNamara was one person who shared Roger's views of Roger and the decline in policing and it was these views, and their books, that finally brought them together. In spite of the perception of Rogerson and McNamara being polar opposites – one the most corrupt copper in the nation's history, the other the self-promoting brave crime fighter with a hatred of drugs, paedophiles and corruption – both had cast aside reality and believed themselves to be victims, and they both loved the limelight. It's a sign of Glen's entrenched bitterness that when he registered a new company on 12 February 2013, to run his private inquiry work through, that he called it FUIPSU Pty Ltd – less politely known as 'Fuck You IPSU [Internal Police Security Unit]'. The registered address was his mother's house.

The two men met through former detective Brian Harding. Harding told me in an email, 'In about 2007 Glen McNamara contacted me and indicated that he was writing a book. At this point Roger Rogerson, Glen McNamara and Tim Priest were all writing books. Each interviewed me as part of their research for their books and it was obvious to me that the three potential books overlapped each other. I put the three authors in touch with each other and that is how McNamara and Rogerson met. I was not aware that following the initial meeting McNamara and Rogerson formed a close friendship. I last saw Glen McNamara at a book signing in Camden in 2010.'

McNamara was a man Roger should have loathed for being a 'dog' (in this instance an informer, rather than a surveillance officer); however, he saw an opportunity. His relationship with the other private investigator was headed towards the rocks – the man was an astute operator and not in sufficient awe – and it was obvious that McNamara was suitably starstruck and Roger has always needed an acolyte. McNamara was like many of his predecessors – he craved a strong and decisive male in his life, would do as he was told, was easily manipulated and didn't ask too many questions.

The result of their first meetings was McNamara writing himself into the Warren Lanfranchi story, and putting Roger on the high moral ground when he'd 'blasted Warren out of this life, express style'. *Dirty Work*, McNamara's maiden outing as an author, was published in March 2010 and launched at the Woolloomooloo Bay Hotel by Tim Priest. In the audience was Alan Jones. Rogerson didn't appear, but he was there for the launch of *Savage Obsessions*, McNamara's second book, at the Potts Point Bookshop two years later. Like Rogerson's, the book attracted some solid press coverage with Nick Galvin in the *Sun-Herald* of 11 April 2010 headlining his piece 'Good Cop, Bad Cop' and writing, 'Glen McNamara still looks like a cop. Solid. Dependable. He could play himself in an episode of *Underbelly*.' And like Roger, Glen hit the road, touring libraries and bookstores to promote his book and enjoying a brief moment in the limelight. After appearances in his home territory in the Sutherland Shire, McNamara told the local *St George & Sutherland Shire Leader* 'people should not be naive about the nature of violent crime. It's real. It's part of our world.'

As a curiosity, in the 'About the Author' blurb at the back of McNamara's *Savage Obsessions* he's said to be a guest lecturer at the University of New South Wales. The university hadn't heard of him as a guest lecturer.

It's unlikely McNamara knew what sort of world he was walking into when he arrived in Rogerson's inner circle, and while he was tolerated by the mix of lawyers, businessmen, hardworking blokes and ex-coppers, not everyone was happy. At one of their regular lunches, Roger introduced Glen to the table as a mate, and instead of the usual nods, handshakes and offer of a beer, one former detective stood up and said, 'I'm not staying if that cunt is joining us,' then left the table. For some older detectives, McNamara's work in Kings Cross was neither forgotten nor forgiven.

Rogerson's pragmatic approach to life in general and McNamara in particular was evidenced by his performance at the funeral of Graham 'Chook' Fowler in May 2013. Around 500 people, including a few journalists, were at the service. Roger stood by the coffin at the Hillside Chapel of the Palmdale Crematorium on the New South Wales Central Coast and told the crowd that Fowler's nemesis Trevor Haken was 'a Judas, a drunk, a blackmailer, a thief, a wife beater,' and reminded them he'd turned on his mates. With the crowd warming to his speech, Roger pressed on, telling them he had visited the desperately ill Chook at his home in Bateau Bay two months before he died. They'd talked of the 'good old days' and Fowler told him he wanted to live long enough to attend Haken's funeral. Chook didn't get his wish, but his mate Roger assured the crowd, 'I speak for many here when I say that I am going to make sure I'm around to attend the funeral of that lowest form of life.' The crowd gave Roger a rousing round of applause, though after recent events, the chance of Roger making it to Haken's funeral is remote.

In the early days of their relationship, McNamara was unaware of the depth of Rogerson's involvement in Sydney crime, but he soon got a crash course. Roger, with the promise of bringing some more business into McNamara's unspectacular investigation business, initially kept his word. His reach into Sydney's legal and criminal community was long.

Not all the new business was illegal. Private investigator Ken Gamble, the nemesis of fraudster Peter Foster, is now based overseas but referred legitimate debt recovery and investigation business to them. Roger, he said, was an excellent negotiator and with Glen as a licensed investigator and commercial agent the work was done properly. However, he wasn't dazzled by McNamara's detective work. He said, 'He reckoned he knew his way around a fraud brief, but as the job progressed it was obvious he didn't. It turned out to be a bit of a mess, which I had to fix up, so I didn't use them again.'

In addition to their legitimate work, the two were allegedly doing more aggressive debt collection work and commercial negotiations. One alleged story was they'd approach their target, with Roger smiling and charm on full, and Glen standing by his side, and with the target lulled by the nice old man, the situation changed. Rogerson's smile dropped at the same time as he produced a pistol, and with McNamara in the role of thug, would put the hapless person in the boot of the Falcon and take him for a ride – which involved plenty of speed humps and sharp high-speed turns. It was a technique both had learned in the police to soften up their quarry. After a suitable time, assessed by the pre-boot attitude of the target, they'd stop, open the boot, and Roger made his demands and gave his timeline, with his points reinforced by the pistol in his hand, and the consequences of failure to comply. It was old-fashioned extortion – simple, brutal and effective. Though in his declining years, Roger was always chuffed his name could still manipulate and intimidate.

His reputation was bolstered by stories of these events, and along with his networking and successes in criminal briefs with his dogsbody McNamara, Roger found himself in demand with a new generation of criminals.

One Padstow local who was a regular at a chic cafe in Padstow Heights, not far from Rogerson's home, said she'd recognised Rogerson as a fellow regular who'd sit at the rear of the cafe, and have one coffee while reading the *Daily Telegraph*. Where it got interesting was Rogerson attracted other non-local patrons – all male, twenties to forties, tattooed, tough looking but all well-dressed – a mix of Caucasians, Southeast Asians and men of Middle Eastern appearance. High-end four-wheel drives were their favourite transportation and would be parked outside in the quiet backstreet. The men would arrive separately, take seats at separate tables, have one coffee each and wait, looking uncomfortable amid the other patrons who were retirees and young mothers. Roger would beckon, in strict order of arrival, each of the blokes to his table, have a quiet conversation and when done, the next would be called. The ageing King of Crime was holding court. My source said the conspicuous mob didn't help business, and 'the stingy old bugger only had the one coffee'.

The firm of Rogerson and McNamara had a big win in 2013, in a case that started back in 2009 when Roger was recommended as the man to negotiate a settlement in a divorce case where money and emotions were running high. Roger's client was Virginia Nemeth, then locked in battle with her husband, millionaire property developer Ferdinand. The jewel in his crown was the then run-down Hampton Court Hotel in Bayswater Road in Kings Cross, a once-grand old pile that had seen the Cross at its best and worst. At one point in its career it had been the dormitory for sex workers taking a break from their shifts at nearby brothels.

According to a 2014 Supreme Court finding, the relationship between the couple had soured when Mrs Nemeth 'was unhappy about what she considered to be a degree of control over Ferdinand exercised by Anthony, particularly in relation to the companies' financial matters'. The problems deepened when she claimed Anthony was not his son, and had DNA evidence to prove it. The judgement noted, she used 'the DNA analysis in an attempt to persuade Ferdinand to disinherit Anthony, who she saw as a competitor'. In 2008, a settlement was offered to her in which she would get eight million dollars in cash by instalments, plus their large pile in Mona Road, Darling Point.

Into this messy case came Roger Rogerson. The judgement noted, 'It seems that Mr Gordon Scurr, who worked with Mr Hall, recommended to the appellant in early 2009 that she consider mediating the dispute privately using someone like Mr Roger Rogerson who he said was a very successful mediator despite his reputation.' In December 2009, Roger and Jim Byrnes met with Nemeth, who was then unrepresented and had no funds to get new representation, which is where Byrnes, then involved in litigation funding through his company Australian Litigation Funders Pty Ltd (ALF), came in. Byrnes was accompanied by Felix Lyle, introduced as his driver. The tattooed, long-haired hulking ex-Hells Angel and Bandido, was a conspicuous sight in Nemeth's Darling Point salon. The judgement said she was seeking an 'unorthodox solution' and 'believed that by retaining Mr Rogerson and Mr Byrnes (through her agreement with ALF) – whose reputations she was aware of – it might be possible to persuade, cajole, or pressure Ferdinand to provide her with a more generous outcome'. She signed up with Byrnes, whose deal was a commission of 25 per cent on the settlement, which Nemeth later realised included the house. The outcome of their deal wasn't quite what she had in mind.

One of Rogerson's tasks was to see if he could find a 'brief' (in this instance, a possible criminal offence) on Anthony, but he failed. In August 2010, Nemeth terminated her funding agreement with Byrnes' company and instructed new solicitors. Ferdinand died in November 2010 with Anthony as the executor of his estate. The Family Law proceedings, reported in a subsequent Supreme Court case, were settled in November 2011 with Nemeth getting the house and nine million dollars. Then the saga got messier with Byrnes claiming his 25 per cent, and Nemeth taking ALF, Byrnes and another company, Australian Corporate Restructuring Services Pty Ltd, to the Supreme Court to get out of the funding agreement.

In February 2013, a very Sydney story came to the Supreme Court in Phillip Street, when Roger took a seat in the witness box, put a Bible in his hand and swore to tell the truth, and confirmed he'd done some work for Mrs Nemeth and had offered to use his links into the NSW Police to protect her if needed. Nemeth's barrister asked him if it was common for people to ask him to commit criminal acts on their behalf. Roger replied, 'it's not unusual at all,' but added with a straight face, 'I deny I did anything in the past. It's what people think I did in the past,' and 'I'm getting a bit old now. If I was interested in doing it, I probably couldn't. I'd probably get caught.'

Rogerson told the court he'd known Nemeth's husband when he'd run a strip club at the Cross and Roger had been a detective. He reckoned she'd hired him 'because of who I was and everything else. I might be able to get through the barricades and get something that would suit her.'

The questioning then moved on to his former client who he described as 'very greedy' and was happy to involve Byrnes in the deal as 'I'd seen the situation with him and Alan Bond. I knew he'd been very successful in business in Sydney. I knew he had a company that did this sort of conciliatory work, debt collecting on a grand scale you might say, using lawyers and so on. I thought this bloke might just be the one for this.' When the barrister observed the deal with Byrnes would get him somewhere between two million and $15 million, Roger, with eyes at full twinkle and suppressing a grin, said, 'That's a great deal for him.' Roger commented that Byrnes' reputation as a 'standover thug' was undeserved.

The Supreme Court found against Mrs Nemeth, and her subsequent appeal was dismissed by the Court of Appeal. She had to pay the respondents' (Byrnes and the companies associated with him) costs. Byrnes was thought to have pocketed somewhere

Top: Roger Rogerson outside the Darlinghurst court complex in 1982 (Fairfax/SMH/Peter Morris)

Right: Sallie-Anne Huckstepp, Sydney, 19 February 1982 (Fairfax/SMH/Paul Mathews)

Below: The bullet pen owned by Roger, engraved with the name of Warren Lanfranchi, one of the three people he shot while a police officer (Jonathan Ng/Newspix)

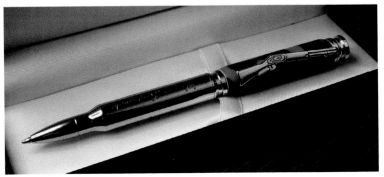

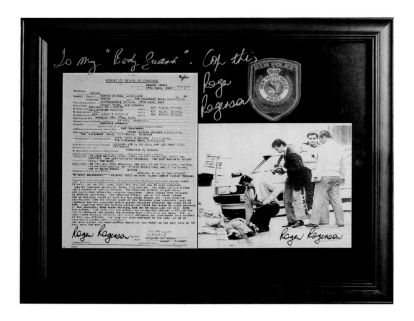

Above: 27 May 2014, gift from Roger Rogerson to Mark 'Hammer' Dixon at his gym in Redcliffe, Queensland. In the frame is a signed photocopy of the P79A report to the coroner on the shooting death of Warren Lanfranchi, and a print from the scene of the shooting
(Mark Calleja/Newspix)

Left: Former NSW police detective Roger Rogerson prepares to leave Long Bay Gaol, 11 December 1990
(Fairfax/SMH/Craig Golding)

Above: Glen McNamara giving evidence to the House of Representatives Standing Committee on Legal and Constitutional Affairs chaired by Bronwyn Bishop in Sydney, 19 February 2003 (Fairfax/ Edwina Pickles)

Right: 1 February 2016. Glen McNamara leaves the Supreme Court of New South Wales during the trial (Adam Taylor/Newspix)

23 April 2004. Roger with Anne Melocco and Graham 'Abo' Henry following Roger and Anne's registry wedding ceremony (Erica Harrison/Newspix)

23 February 2006. Out of prison. Roger relaxing at his home
(Michael Perini/Newspix)

22 February 2006. Mark 'Chopper' Read and Roger prior to their performance as the Wild Colonial Psychos at Bronte RSL (Sam Ruttyn/Newspix)

27 May 2014. Roger is arrested at his home in Padstow, with the media in attendance (John Grainger/Newspix)

CCTV captured crucial images used in evidence. *Top left*: Rent A Space, Padstow, 20 May 2014, 2.09 p.m. Glen with the silver surfboard cover *Top right*: 4.20 p.m. Roger and Glen inside Kennards Hire at Taren Point, hiring a block and tackle

Bottom left: A hard day's work. Roger and Glen enter the lift of the Cote d'Azur Apartments with a six-pack of beer, 6.40 p.m. *Bottom right*: Glen's blue Falcon towing his boat exits the Cote d'Azur carpark, 21 May 2014, 7.28 a.m.

(Supreme Court of NSW)

Roger Rogerson's barrister, George Thomas, at Sydney Central Local Court on 25 August 2014 (Fairfax/Ben Rushton)

Crown Prosecutor Chris Maxwell QC leaves court, Wednesday 15 June 2016
(Fairfax/Peter Rae)

Roger Rogerson is led from the Supreme Court after giving evidence, 6 May 2016
(Fairfax/SMH/Walter Peeters)

between two and three million dollars from the deal. Roger, always one to brag about his exploits, never bragged about money and kept very quiet on how much he'd picked up from this deal.

While this case was running, Glen McNamara made an offer to Byrnes. McNamara had been one of the police who'd arrested Byrnes for possession of heroin. Byrnes told me 'I'm no Pablo Escobar [a reference to the late head of Colombia's huge Medellín cartel]' and after a few unkind remarks about McNamara when he was a copper, said McNamara told him he might be able to help get the old conviction set aside. The case was one that had rankled Byrnes for decades and he said, 'Why not, what have I got to lose apart from some cash?' He alleged McNamara's fee, paid to him by bank transfers ended up as somewhere between $30 000 and $40 000.

With the team of McNamara and Rogerson on the case, McNamara suggested Byrnes engage and brief barrister Charles Moschoudis. Byrnes said McNamara was erratic and often missed meetings, and after a while on the investigation he prepared a statement for his client that 'contained some things which were utterly wrong'. The statement was the death knell of the investigation, and Byrnes said, 'I'm not a bloody idiot and wouldn't sign the thing.'

18

THE NEW FACE OF CRIME

The criminals that Rogerson and McNamara had faced in their police careers were mainly of the old school. With a few exceptions, they were male, from poor or working-class backgrounds, had a basic education but not the opportunity for university or even six years of high school. Many came from families who'd been involved in crime for generations. They were shoplifters, housebreakers, car thieves, armed robbers and safebreakers, who learned their trade through mentoring. Their jobs were risky, the money was sometimes dismal, and the chance of being caught was high. Prison was a paid holiday and a chance to network and get some professional development. The irony of getting it from someone who'd been convicted escaped them.

The contemporary breed of criminals is very different. They're enticed into a business dominated by drugs like ice and cocaine, where the profits are staggering and the risk low. Most finish high school and many have gone on to university – an MBA, finance or law degree are great sales tools if you're looking at entering a life of crime rather than the 'straight' world. Unlike the older crims, they don't factor in getting caught, and many don't quite understand the dangers and brutality of the world they're entering. Jamie Gao was one of these young men. As he'd find out in 2014, a life of crime wasn't like the one he'd seen so often in the Hong Kong action films he and his mates loved.

Jamie's family was well-to-do middle class, originally from Hong Kong. He'd grown up with his mother and grandmother in their large family home in a quiet street in Hurstville. It wasn't a flash home, but it was obvious the Gaos weren't short of a quid. Jamie went to Caringbah High School, one of the state's selective schools that, according to the NSW Department of Education, 'cater for gifted and talented students who have superior to very superior academic ability which is matched by exceptionally high classroom performance'. Jamie was a tall, handsome lithe young man with long black hair that swept over his face. He was charismatic, funny and had an edge that made him stand out from his studious mates. As Sydney crime writer and former detective P.M. (Pam) Newton wrote of Jamie in *The Drum* on 28 May 2014, 'It's the face that stays with you. The photo of the bright, beautiful boy, with the funky haircut, the shiny smile.' And as Newton observed, 'Sydney's underworld isn't glamorous – it's cruel.'

Jamie didn't have Newton's insight, nor does it seem he did any research on the two older men he'd encounter just after his twentieth birthday. At school Jamie had a close group of mates, and following the HSC they went on to university and stayed close. For Jamie, his higher education was a business degree at UTS, located near Sydney's Chinatown.

One of Jamie's friends, Bing-Jie (known as BJ) Wang, was Jamie's ticket into the underworld. Around late 2011, Wang was working as a drug dealer, pulling in big money and living the life that Jamie wanted. BJ and his cohorts, the Lam brothers, ran a drug ring that was likely to be affiliated with one of the Hong Kong Triads, but they were clumsy. They talked openly of their business on mobile phones and handled the packages of drugs without the sense to use gloves, thus leaving fingerprints and DNA evidence. Their stupidity resulted in them being arrested in May 2012 for drug trafficking, but the arrest of his friends didn't deter Jamie Gao. Instead of learning that crime was a dangerous business – by being arrested and also risking offending brutal gangs such as the Triad – he went the other way, believing that he was smarter and could build a similar business with greater profit potential and less risk of being caught.

It's likely Gao's relationship with Wang also put him on police radar. The *Daily Telegraph* of 31 May 2014 reported the AFP had been interested in him from around late 2011 because of his connection to drug importations. One legal source told me Jamie had also come to police attention because of a few deals he'd done with large numbers of cheap mobile phones used for pay-as-you-go customers – popular in the drug trafficking business for single use then discarded, thus making electronic surveillance difficult. Police also confirmed they were looking at links between Jamie and casino high roller Peter Hoang who was shot dead at Croydon Park on 7 September 2014, and the former Bakers Delight franchise holder Paul Nguyen, who went missing on 1 May 2014. Police were suspicious the three were involved in drug trafficking and money laundering.

In early 2014, Jamie met Misaki Takebayashi who was from Japan and studying at UTS. Misaki had rudimentary English and even less Cantonese and Mandarin, but the two fell fast for each other. However, while she knew her boyfriend had interests other than study and her, she had no idea of his growing involvement with drug trafficking.

Jamie had his first direct brush with police when he was arrested for unlawfully detaining 19-year-old student Jaiwei Yu, and assaulting him causing actual bodily harm. Gao and two other young men went to Yu's home unit in Sydney's Carlton, allegedly to sort out one of Yu's flatmates, Alex Li, over his bust-up with a girlfriend. Yu said the girl had wanted revenge and Jamie had taken on the job as standover man and punisher. Unfortunately for Yu, Alex wasn't home at the time, so Gao decided Yu would do. The three men took the slightly built man out to their car, manhandled him into the boot, took him for a brisk drive around, and finally stopped at a park where he was unloaded, and taken into the park where Jamie punched him in the mouth. The three left him. Unfortunately for Jamie and his crew, Yu and Li weren't intimidated and went to the police. Gao was arrested on 22 March and faced his first time in court on a criminal charge at Kogarah court on 15 April 2014. The case was later adjourned to 10 July and then withdrawn, because by then Jamie was dead.

Another lawyer source told me the incident with Yu wasn't Jamie's only standover venture, telling me he'd kidnapped and assaulted a Sydney businessman over a debt. The police had also visited Jamie's home in early 2014 with a search warrant looking for drugs, but the visit hadn't resulted in charges. His mother Katherine said in a statement, 'Since the drug search with the police I would talk to Jamie about drugs and he told me that he wouldn't do that. He was cranky that he was involved in this and kept saying that the police always have eyes on him and that he hasn't done anything wrong.'

In late February Jamie flew to Hong Kong where he caught up with a mix of Sydney and Hong Kong friends and relatives, and allegedly with Triad connections made probably through BJ and the Lams. It was on this trip Jamie was likely to have started work on the deal that would eventually lead to his murder. The original deal he put to the alleged Triad heavies was 10 kilograms of ice on credit, with payment in full as soon as it was sold. Jamie, by that stage well entrenched with the Rogerson/McNamara team, had a tantalising opportunity for the Triads – access to the outlaw bikers and their distribution networks. The bikers didn't mind where the product came from so long as it was of good quality, and for the Hong Kong criminals, traditionally insular in who they dealt with, it was an opportunity to plug into Australia's most successful distributors. It was a win for everyone – in theory.

However, the Triad heavies had generations of experience behind them and decided that while they'd risk a shipment to a new network, the risk would only be three kilograms. If that deal worked to their satisfaction, then the amount would increase. Jamie didn't have a choice and readily agreed. The Hong Kong connection would arrange for the drugs to be couriered to Sydney from their sources in mainland China and delivered to Jamie. Two trusted Triad henchmen would be sent to Australia to keep an eye on Jamie and the deal.

Gao's likely involvement in organised crime was why the NSW Police Robbery and Serious Crime Squad became involved when his disappearance was finally reported.

19

TOPPING UP THE SUPER

January is the dead time for many Australian businesses, with normal life on hold until after Australia Day, then it's kids back to school and us back to long days. For criminal lawyers, there is a bit of work about in the lower courts getting adjournments and bail for those unfortunate enough to have been arrested on charges at the more serious end of the scale. The higher courts are all on vacation until the end of the month when they head to church to kick off the new Law Term. Anglicans usually go to St James Church, and Catholics to St Mary's for the Red Mass that also offers pre-Mass robing in the crypt. Jewish and Muslim services are held later. Atheists don't bother and quip over coffee at the faithful then heading off to preside over a tribunal of fact.

At the beginning of the 2014 legal year, Glen McNamara was contemplating his future and his dwindling finances. Making a quid as a private investigator without soul-destroying insurance work was tough, and more so if your practice was in crime. Legal aid funding, the lifeblood of the criminal defence world, doesn't run to investigators too often, and fully funded criminal work is scarce because most crooks who get caught have been in crime to make a quid at the time they're caught. Affluent clients with money to spend on investigations are rare. What Glen had found was Roger's promises about bringing in mountains of business hadn't quite come to fruition. Roger had talked a grand game, but it was slowly dawning on Glen that Roger was using him and his licence to take the cream and leave him with the dog work.

He was also wondering just how much Roger and Jim Byrnes had made in the Nemeth case, because he'd done okay but nowhere near the rumours he was hearing of $2.8 million total settlement. If it was that much it certainly wasn't split three ways. In the minds of most detectives who had been around in the mid '80s was the story that Roger had taken $50 000 from drug dealer Alan Williams to offer to Michael Drury, after which Roger had 'trousered' half and then offered the leftovers to Drury. The only person to come out of the incident relatively unscathed was Rogerson.

Adding to his problems, he and Cheryl were divorcing, which resulted in selling the family home and renting for the first time in decades. McNamara was spending more money than he earned and the bottom line was there was little chance his business was going to dramatically improve. Cheryl was living overseas, but the positive was their daughters were living with him. They were loyal and looked after their father. The other positive was he was back at work rather than spending a long January doing very little, and it was this return which brought him into contact with Jamie Gao.

Charles Moschoudis is a Sydney barrister specialising in criminal law, taking on anything from traffic crimes such as driving while under the influence to major drug cases, and in an earlier life was a member of the NSW Police force, working undercover in drug investigations and as a member of the Special Operations Group and later as a prosecutor. He has a reputation for honesty and integrity.

In January 2014 he was running his practice from chambers at 185 Elizabeth Street, Sydney above the Bambini Trust Restaurant & Wine Room, one of the favoured lunch and drinking spots for the city's well-heeled legal types. On cases that needed some shoe leather, he frequently used Glen McNamara. Glen wasn't an inspiring detective but was capable and experienced to do the grunt work Moschoudis needed. Two of his clients were Hong Kong nationals, brothers Lok Lam and Kit Lam who were friends with Jamie Gao and living in Sydney when they were arrested for serious drug crimes. As their English was limited they needed a translator for all legal conferences and Jamie, with his fluency in Cantonese and English, was ideal for the role. Both were allegedly Triad members with Hong Kong connections, and Jamie came allegedly with the Triad's approval. With his aspirations to be a criminal mastermind, they also knew they could rely on him to keep quiet if the conversations headed into murky waters.

McNamara and Gao met at one of the conferences in January and the two started talking afterwards and not about the case both were working on. Moschoudis wasn't aware of their developing relationship. According to McNamara's version of events, he was working on a book on the ice epidemic that was finally on the national agenda. It's a compelling tale, but McNamara hasn't explained why he didn't ask Roger for an introduction to his outlaw biker connections that are the main distributors and retailers of the drug in city and regional Australia.

In Gao, he saw a young man he believed had connections to both the recreational users around his age, and to the men from Southeast Asia who supplied the drug. He was aware that Jamie was on bail for assault occasioning actual bodily harm and unlawful detention. Any experienced detective could pick Jamie Gao as a wannabe bad boy, and best handled to their advantage by giving the kid an audience, an ego massage, and a vicarious thrill by offering a glimpse of a career as a detective. McNamara came on hard as a tough old detective, and Gao was rapt. The two met occasionally over the next few months and, according to Jamie's friends, he'd bragged about McNamara being a hard man, a former detective and private investigator who was connected in the city's underworld and knew influential people. McNamara, he reckoned, had talked of being an ice user, and importantly for Jamie and his image, could 'hook me up for guns' and was connected to the biker gangs.

There's no evidence to suggest McNamara was an ice user and dropping it into a conversation with a callow youth like Gao may have been a clumsy, yet ultimately effective, tool in gaining Gao's confidence. The problem with McNamara's story of building a relationship with Gao for research purposes is the speed with which the anti-drug campaigner and would-be author of a book on the evils of ice could pivot so quickly to become a drug dealer.

Rogerson is quiet on the subject, but the likelihood is his acolyte and he were having a beer or lunch – they were as thick as thieves at the time – and Glen mentioned his meeting with an eager young man translating for the Triads. The word 'Triad' is magic to someone like Rogerson who saw opportunity and all he had to do was persuade McNamara that an easy dollar was at hand. Given his knowledge of McNamara's financial situation and his still serious case of hero worship, getting him over the line wouldn't be that hard.

What he was also considering was a chance of a longer term and profitable association. With the right networking it was the opportunity to bring the Triads, who could supply, together with the outlaw motorcycle gangs who could distribute into areas in which the Triads were weak. A prime example was the lucrative inner-city market dominated by the bikers. A constant supply of quality, well-priced product is something they'd never turn down, and much safer than sourcing their own raw materials and operating meth labs. It was the sort of deal Roger loved – high profit, minimal risk and the chance to shine. Gao was the first step back to the big time or failing that, a decent, quick quid.

McNamara went from alleged book research to joint criminal enterprise without much hesitation. Roger then set about a task he did well – planning the operation to make sure he got most of the profit with the least of the risk. He'd learned the hard way that fronting the operation was good for the reputation but bad for the career, and so better to let someone else do the grunt work.

Roger tasked McNamara to deal with Gao while Roger attended to the details and worked his contacts in the gangs. He met with members and associates of both the Rebels and the Comancheros at mixed martial arts events around south-west Sydney and at the Hordern Pavilion – places where you could network and where any casual observer would assume a mutual interest in the contest rather than plotting criminal enterprises.

His contacts bit hard and fast at what Roger had to offer, and prices were haggled over. What they all needed was a sample to test the quality before the cash was handed over. Roger was trusted and respected, but his supplier was an unknown, and a man of Roger's age – though they wouldn't say it to his face – was just a bit too old to know the difference between the good stuff and the second rate. The outlaw bikers take pride in the reputation of their product and as one told me, 'We're not the fuckin' Lebs who sell you anything and shoot you if you bitch about it.' Roger told McNamara the buyers were keen, and reassured his acolyte all he'd have to do was 'follow my lead'. McNamara would be hearing that mantra repeatedly.

McNamara was instructed to chat to Gao and tell him they wanted ten kilograms to start the relationship rolling and at no time disclose that Rogerson was involved. While McNamara had a reputation – albeit self-created – for integrity, a quick look at Google for Rogerson might have soured the deal, particularly if you read the Neddy Smith allegations, and about the demise of Warren Lanfranchi.

While McNamara was wooing Gao, Roger was wooing the media – crafting a plausible yarn designed to make sure the public remembered him as the grand old man of crime now in retirement. His vehicle was News Ltd – journalist James Phelps had asked for an interview that Roger was happy to agree to. The original venue for the late February interview had been the usual cafe where he held court with his underworld connections, but he'd prudently revised that idea and invited Phelps to his home, where the likelihood of an outlaw biker popping by for counsel was remote.

Phelps was greeted at the door by the genial grandfather and his dog, Roxy, who barked fervently at the journalist, prompting Roger to quip, 'Believe it or not, she's a ferocious attack dog in disguise. A bit like me.' Phelps was getting the full Rogerson charm. Roger talked of spending the summer commuting between Padstow and his weekender at Long Jetty and of his passion for cars.

Turning to business, he said he'd been 'unhappily retired' since getting out of prison in 2006 but still did some consulting work on criminal briefs he'd 'pick apart' at the request of lawyers. He admitted the only brief he'd kept from his police career was on Warren Lanfranchi, but didn't comment on why.

On contemporary criminals, he was derisive, telling Phelps, 'Everyone has their price . . . and finally someone will crack . . . I think it is worse now with junkies. If you can offer a bit of gear to a junkie then you have them. Back in my day they were hard men, not junkies. They were just tough belligerent blokes that hated the world. They had shocking upbringings, mostly their fathers were crooks. They came from criminogenic families.' He talked about his great triumphs as a detective and that he 'wouldn't want to go back to prison'. It was a plausible interview with Rogerson comfortable, in fine form and with not a hint that he was in the middle of a plot with the new breed of criminals 50 years his junior to keep the junkies supplied with what is the most destructive illicit drug in history.

By late March the foundations of the deal were in place, and Roger was still anonymous. Gao had travelled to Hong Kong ostensibly to catch up with friends and family, and while there convinced his Hong Kong drug connections to provide the ice to him on credit – which shows the level of trust they had in him – but they'd baulked at ten kilograms and told him he'd get three. They were prepared to take a risk, particularly with the potential to link up with the outlaw gangs but not one that big on the first deal. Buying drugs on credit was also not uncommon, but the deal came with deadly consequences for those who failed to pay up when required. As trust grew through successful deals, so would the quantity.

Outlaw gangs and Asian crime gangs have a very short history of co-operation and for decades kept their enterprises separate mainly because of social and racial pressures within their gangs. The Hells Angels, for example, wouldn't permit non-white members for many years, which prompted the start-up of Latino gangs like the Mongols, and on the flip side, the Triads were similarly strict with their recruiting guidelines. The vast profits from drug sales finally broke down these walls – cash wins every time. Australian and European bikers pioneered links into Southeast Asia, and have more recently been followed by the Mexican cartels, all keen to buy precursor chemicals for amphetamine manufacture that are easily acquired in the region, or good-quality and cheap finished product.

Gao's orders from Hong Kong were to hand over the drugs and get the cash – no credit until McNamara and Rogerson had established their integrity with a successful couple of deals. What Jamie didn't know was the two older men had nowhere close to the amount he needed – somewhere in the range of $500 000 to $700 000 in cash, according to NSW Police experts. This was the moment when the future of the deal changed from developing a business relationship to a rip-off.

The former detectives' first step was to find a safe venue to do the handover. As the outcome of the deal had changed, they needed somewhere that couldn't be traced to them, didn't look threatening to Gao who'd be on tenterhooks, and offered privacy. True to form, Roger didn't want to pay for the place and so spoke to a few of his mates to see if they had a space – a shed, garage or storage unit – he could borrow for a couple of months as he had some 'old furniture' he wanted to store. One mate jokingly suggested he hire a storage unit and got an unamused glare in return.

Rogerson then visited his mate and occasional drinking partner Mick Maguire. Mick was in his late fifties and suffering from terminal cancer. Rogerson had borrowed Maguire's keys in February 2014 and Maguire had given him the access codes, ostensibly for Roger to look at some office furniture for his home and if the unit was suitable to store his box trailer. One source told me, 'Box trailer? He doesn't own a bloody box trailer!' The police alleged that when Roger returned Maguire's key ring to him, one was missing – the key to the lock on the storage unit.

On 2 April, equipped with keys to Maguire's storage unit number 803 at Rent a Space Self Storage in Davies Road, Padstow, Roger returned and the CCTV cameras at the units recorded the arrival of his silver Falcon station wagon.

The next day McNamara was recorded at the Meridian Hotel in Hurstville, an easy walk from Gao's home and a 15-minute drive from Cronulla. It was a sensible move from McNamara who was well known locally, and their meeting would be conspicuous. In Hurstville, McNamara was anonymous and he met Jamie in the bar. They were an incongruous pair – the solidly built balding mid fifties McNamara chatting intensely with the tall lithe floppy-haired boy in body-hugging jeans and a T-shirt.

On 4 April, the cameras at Rent a Space picked up the arrival of Rogerson's and McNamara's cars as they entered at 8.50 a.m. and were onsite until 9.41 a.m. The duo took the next major step towards the deal on 27 April when McNamara arrived at Outback Used Cars, a dealership on the western edge of Sydney and nearly 70 kilometres from his home at Cronulla. He bought a cheap and well-used white Ford Falcon station wagon, paying in cash and using the name 'Marvyn Turnbull' for the formal documentation the dealer was required to complete. While the origins of the car are unclear, police alleged it might have come from Rogerson's old acquaintance Karl Bonnette. McNamara kept the receipt for the purchase of the car, which he later showed to Rogerson, probably as proof of his expenses in their 'joint criminal enterprise'. Roger demands to be trusted, but doesn't trust anyone, particularly where money is involved. The preparations for the rip-off were done.

Around this time Rogerson allegedly confided in a friend he'd 'sorted a big quid' and gave a thumbnail sketch of the deal he'd had McNamara engineer with Gao. The friend, allegedly, listened but was appalled at Rogerson's greed and stupidity – ripping off a Triad associate was potentially fatal. When he asked Rogerson about what might happen in the drug rip-off, Rogerson allegedly told him he wasn't taking a risk – Gao didn't know who he was, the venue for the handover was safe and secure, and there wouldn't be a witness. McNamara was someone who'll 'do as he's fucking told or else and he's not bright enough to think for himself – tried that once and look where he ended up'. Roger allegedly said they'd isolate Gao from any friends he'd brought with him, then he'd 'put the chink off' if necessary. He added, 'Mate, it's just like the old days.' His mate didn't want to know – 'I didn't know if the prick was senile, bragging or just full of shit,' he said. McNamara had also done something rather foolhardy, developing a recent interest in firearms. On 3 May he was at the Condell Park Indoor Firearms Range honing his marksmanship with a revolver, and police later found he'd been researching .25 calibre handguns on the internet. These weapons aren't common. They're quite small and light and can fit into the palm of an average-sized man. At close range they're deadly.

At 10 a.m. on 19 May, McNamara was back on surveillance cameras as he arrived in his blue Falcon at Hunter Self Storage in Taren Point, removed his 4.5 metre Quintrex trailer boat from his storage unit and took it back to the underground car park of the Cote d'Azur apartments. Around 3 p.m. that afternoon Rogerson was also on the move, picked up on CCTV as he entered the storage unit in Davies Road, where he removed a few office chairs and put them in the back of his silver station wagon. Moving the chairs wasn't because he'd developed a need for them, but useful if you're setting up a pattern of conduct that might be later used as an alibi. Around the time Roger was moving furniture around, Jamie Gao's distinctive tricked-up white Nissan Silvia had been picked up on the CCTV at the front gate. Jamie was doing his own reconnaissance but without the security code, couldn't get in. Had he done so, he may have bumped into Australia's most notorious detective.

Gao's day on 19 May gives some insight into the young man who believed he was about to hit the big time. He'd spent the morning in lectures at UTS before meeting up with a 19-year-old female friend – who prefers to remain anonymous – for lunch at Caffe Tiamo in Pitt Street near World Square. The two had a pleasant lunch during a break between 11 a.m. and 1 p.m., with no hint from Jamie of his looming coup. She said, 'He was fine, normal. We had lunch. He didn't tell me about the meeting.' She said Jamie was naturally smart and sociable and 'he wasn't crazy about study, he wasn't the nerdy type that studies every day,' and while he talked about his family, girlfriend and some of his private life, he didn't mention or hint 'about the illegal stuff. He doesn't tell about all the stuff he does.'

However, with some of his male friends, Gao wasn't discreet, bragging that the deal he'd put together was 'going to be massive' and 'shortly I'm going to be rich!', noting it was the 'deal of a lifetime'. Jamie, even in the closing stages of such an important deal had no clue who he was really dealing with, or the brevity of his lifetime.

Just before 8 p.m., he and McNamara met briefly again at the Meridian Hotel and the two were recorded as arriving and leaving separately.

20

TIME FOR YOUR CLOSE-UP

Tuesday, 20 May 2014 was another fine and pleasant day in what was to be the warmest Sydney autumn on record. At 11.37 a.m., McNamara was at the Cronulla Mall, using one of the few payphones still in service to call Gao on his mobile. The deal was on. Shortly after, Gao texted McNamara – a popular method of communication for them both, and Gao wondered if his older mate was available for lunch. Glen responded that he had food poisoning and would be spending time close to the toilet. Gao said he'd spend the day studying and with his girlfriend. Neither were telling the truth, and shortly after midday, McNamara was recorded driving the old white Falcon station wagon out of his garage.

At 1.16 p.m. the cameras at the Rent a Space storage facility recorded Rogerson and McNamara arriving in the white station wagon and parking outside unit 803. The two men went inside the shed with McNamara carrying 'an object' that wasn't clear in the footage. The two left the door open and emerged a few minutes later, then tested the roller door on the unit by sliding it up and down a few times. They then got into the white station wagon and drove from the facility, with McNamara at the wheel.

Both men were next recorded in Arab Road, Padstow, around 900 metres north of Rent a Space in a dead-end street in a suburban backwater of light industrial operations and warehouses. Road and pedestrian traffic was minimal, making it an ideal place for a rendezvous – with one notable exception both men had missed.

Roger was now in his silver station wagon parked on the northern kerb, and McNamara parked across from it. What neither of them knew, was the building Roger had parked outside – Micks Meat, a wholesale butcher at 2C Arab Road – had a security camera on the front of the building. One small camera designed to keep an eye on a small car park would be the catalyst for the collapse of what Roger thought was a masterful plan.

The timing was ideal, as CCTV cameras on the M5 tollway had just recorded Gao's Nissan exiting and turning into Davies Road – he was only minutes away. McNamara remained in the white station wagon and as Gao's Nissan turned into Arab Road, Roger drove his car into the forecourt at Micks, and Gao pulled into the space he'd vacated and parked. The camera recorded him removing a backpack from the Nissan and heading across the road towards McNamara. The camera also recorded two other men getting out of Gao's car and watching him as he walked across the road with the backpack. So far everything was going to plan – no signs of other surveillance, no signs of aggression on either side. However, Gao had left his wallet, mobile phone and car keys in the Nissan. McNamara, with Gao lying low in the back seat, then drove up Arab Road and turned into Davies. As they departed, Rogerson drove out of the forecourt and on to Arab Road. Gao's mates didn't notice the old bloke in the bland station wagon drive by, and they didn't follow.

CCTV footage from cameras along Davies Road caught their progress, then the storage facility's cameras recorded their arrival at the front gate where McNamara, wearing a hoodie that he'd pulled up onto his head before stepping out of the car, entered the gate access code.

The station wagon pulled up outside unit 803 around 1.45 p.m. and McNamara and Gao – carrying his backpack – went into the storage unit and closed the door. Glen knew about the security cameras in the facility and thought obscuring his identity a little might be prudent. To borrow from military pundits, no criminal plan survives the first minutes in operation. The camera also recorded the fact the rear seat of the wagon was folded flat.

Two minutes later, cameras at the Bridge Street entrance record Rogerson's silver station wagon at the storage facility, which is a dead-end street on the southern side of the facility. Roger drove to the gate, entered the code, then did a lap of the site, presumably checking to see who else was about, then parked near 803 and walked to the door with, as the prosecutor later noted, 'his distinctive gait'. Roger went straight inside, closing the door behind him. Given the tightness of the timing, the likelihood is Jamie Gao died after Rogerson's arrival from two bullets to the chest. Police officers of the McNamara/Rogerson vintage were armed with .38 Smith & Wesson revolvers, usually six shot. Police were trained to use a two-handed grip, with your gun hand stabilised by the other, and to pull the trigger twice, aiming at the centre mass of their target. Shooting someone in cold blood is a hard task – McNamara had recently refreshed his pistol skills, but Rogerson is one of the few police officers in this country who has form for pulling the trigger and killing the target.

At 1.58 p.m., Rogerson was recorded stepping out of the unit and walking to his wagon. He then drove it closer to the unit door, but McNamara's station wagon obscured the number plate from the camera. McNamara then stepped through the door, wearing a pink-coloured top and removed a surfboard cover from the wagon. He didn't bother to close the door of the unit, then both men went back inside, and at 2.18 p.m. the bag obviously containing something large, was dragged through the door by them. When they neared the open tailgate, they bent down, each man taking an end of the bag, and lifted it into the wagon. The pair then re-entered the storage unit and returned with a few office chairs they piled onto the bag, then closed the tailgate, and locked the unit door. At 2.22 p.m. they left the storage facility. In the bag in the back of the wagon was Jamie Gao, victim of what is probably the most electronically recorded crime in Australian history. The well-planned crime was turning into a fiasco – without the culprits being the wiser – and had a long way to go, much of it also caught on CCTV.

McNamara, followed by Rogerson, drove back to the Cote d'Azur apartments where he parked the white station wagon in the secure underground car park around 3.03 p.m. After making sure there weren't any witnesses lurking around the lower basement car park, the two men dragged Jamie's body from the back of the wagon and put it on the ground between the wagon and McNamara's boat. What the two hadn't factored into their planning was the weight and size of the late Jamie Gao being too much for the reasonably fit McNamara and disabled Rogerson to manhandle from the ground, up and in to the boat. Plan B was formulated by the ever practical Rogerson who thought a block and tackle – or chain block – would do the trick and so at 3.51 p.m. the white wagon exited the garage, and Jamie was left on the ground, shoved as far under the boat trailer as possible. In keeping with their day thus far, they were recorded as they entered Kennards Hire in nearby Taren Point where they hired a block and tackle. McNamara paid and kept the receipt. Back in McNamara's garage, the two used their recent acquisition to hoist Jamie into the Quintrex, cover him up, and then at 6.24 p.m., the pair were recorded by the building's CCTV in the lift, heading up to Glen's apartment for a cleansing ale after a hard day's work. Thirst quenched, Roger drove home to Anne, and returned to Cronulla early the next morning to complete the disposal of what they thought was the only link to the crime – the body of Jamie Gao.

Around three kilometres out to sea, where the water is deep and with no other boats in sight, the pair manhandled Jamie Gao over the side. Fortunately for them the sea was calm because a dead body is clumsy to move, even for two able-bodied men. Smart money would suggest the murder weapon should have gone over the side as well – but whether it did or didn't would tantalise the investigation for over a year. For two experienced detectives, the pair made two fundamental errors. Jamie's body wasn't properly weighed down, and they'd failed to stab him to prevent swelling that would add to his buoyancy.

It was a full day for Rogerson and McNamara, and after cleaning the boat and returning it to the storage unit, they headed back to Rent a Space and spent an hour tidying up the crime scene. CCTV recorded their arrival and departure, and Rogerson, with his distinctive walk, hobbling from the storage unit carrying a green plastic bucket to a drain and emptying the bucket's contents.

The next job was to turn the ice into cash and Roger had his cunning plan well prepared.

21

BEST-LAID PLANS

By 2.30 p.m. on 20 May the two men who'd been with Jamie in his car knew something was horribly wrong. He'd briefed them on the location for the handover, and given its proximity there was only one likely scenario – the drug deal had become a drug rip-off. It wasn't uncommon, but with the weight and value of drugs, and the old white bloke fully aware of Jamie's Triad connections, they'd expected it to run smoothly – you'd need a death wish to screw the Triad and the man they knew as Glen didn't look suicidal. What they didn't know was Rogerson had been planning a 'winner takes all' strategy for months. He'd get the drugs plus business, cash and more respect from the bikers who wouldn't ask any questions of the product's provenance.

Gao's colleagues were now confronted with three options, none of which were particularly appealing. They could stay in Australia and hope that either police or the man Jamie had met with wouldn't come looking for them, and they had no idea just how much or how little Jamie had told the latter about his connections. Option two was to run away from the potential problems in Australia and their Triad associates in Hong Kong, but with the reach of the Triad, they'd be convicted and sentenced to a gruesome death when they were inevitably found. Option three was to flee Australia and head to Hong Kong – after all they were only bit players in the deal – and hope the Triad would be sympathetic, the notion of honesty being the best policy. It didn't take them long to decide on option three.

Their first move was to drive around the area to make sure they'd exhausted all opportunities to find Jamie and more importantly, the drugs. To that end they drove around for hours, hoping for a glimpse. After night had fallen, they dumped Jamie's car with his sports bag in the back seat, in a close-by industrial area, where they'd hoped it wouldn't be found for a few days, thus giving them plenty of time to escape. They'd also called their bosses in Hong Kong so there'd be no surprises, and booked themselves on a plane. The two men also did something compassionate. Jamie's mother and grandmother were in Hong Kong on a trip, and calling them anonymously to let them know something had happened to the lad was tricky, so instead they called the friends of Jamie who knew about his other side to let them know he was in strife.

A source told me they'd survived their return to Hong Kong but found one of the men responsible for organising Gao's deal with the Triad bosses disappeared shortly after their phone call. The men didn't return to Australia for the trials.

Jamie's friends converged on Padstow but their search for him was fruitless. They eventually found his car but decided to wait another 24 hours before calling police, just in case Jamie re-appeared.

If a 20-year-old male goes missing, experience tells police that a few scenarios come into play, and they usually involve sex and alcohol instead of foul play, so hitting the alarm buttons isn't the obvious reaction. However, they were thorough and Jamie's name was flagged in their intelligence networks as a person of interest, so rather than offering a cup of tea, a Scotch Finger and some advice on the ways of the world to his friends, they called the Robbery and Serious Crime Squad who were the designated contacts for any information on Gao. Jamie was 'hot' in police terms, with possible links to drug, firearm and fraud crimes.

Within hours, Jamie's disappearance had become part of Strike Force Album, with around 50 police part of the investigation. Police made a public appeal for information, citing 'grave concerns' for Jamie's fate and contacted his mother in Hong Kong who cut short her trip and headed home. The Nissan was found early in the investigation, along with Jamie's wallet and mobile phone. In tracing calls to and from they found McNamara's number and one from the phone box in Cronulla.

Finding Jamie's car was methodical police work, and finding his phone good fortune, and with those early snippets they started the painstaking process of interviews and gathering all the CCTV footage. Fortune came their way again when they located the camera at Micks Meat, and from that starting point they were able to piece together the logistics of the crime, tracking CCTV up Arab Road, Davies Street, Rent a Space. Contemporary technology blended with old-fashioned, detailed police work.

Murder investigations work around the clock for the first few days, with detectives putting in 48 hours without sleep, and the hunt for Gao was no different. At 2.30 a.m. on Thursday, detectives arrived at the storage facility and had a chat with the staff, telling them they were working on a missing persons case with the victim possibly being held for ransom. The detectives then did a walk around the 510-unit site.

They came back later that morning for a detailed look in daylight and left with the CCTV for the prior two weeks.

Back at Bankstown Police Station where the investigation was centred, the pile of CCTV tapes were being watched frame by frame. In most investigations of serious crime, and just like a jigsaw, one piece falls into place and the way forward becomes clear – it's a 'Eureka' moment, and in this investigation it came late on the afternoon of Thursday, 22 May. What the police didn't know was that around the same time and one kilometre away, the two men responsible for Gao's disappearance were sitting down having a beer with mates and a couple of other men – not mates or regulars at the pub – who might have called by to chat to Roger about the drugs he had for sale. What none of the men knew was Glen McNamara was already under surveillance, triggered by examination of Gao's phone records, with an officer in the pub's car park.

An older police officer was passing the younger officers examining the footage from the storage unit when something caught his eye. He doubled back and looked more closely. On the film was the man who Crown Prosecutor Chris Maxwell QC would later describe as having a 'distinctive gait'. The older officer was more direct and exclaimed, 'Oh fuck, that's Roger!' Game on and the jigsaw suddenly looked less daunting.

They had two suspects – experienced coppers, one with a lousy reputation and a track record of violence who everyone thought was retired, and one a reputation for being a fervent anti-drug campaigner with a few shadows in his past. The investigation then focused on both men – their homes, associates, businesses, cars, phone numbers, and evidence to support the granting of search warrants for electronic surveillance and to search their houses and cars. They found Rogerson had done something stupid – using his own car in a crime. They tracked the white station wagon back to the dealership and found it was likely to have been bought in a fake name but 'McNamara walked out of the description,' as one source said. Karl Bonnette was later alleged to be involved in the car deal. In court, Bonnette denied any involvement. Mick Maguire was interviewed and confirmed he'd lent keys to Rogerson for him to use the unit occasionally for storage, and forensic teams worked the scene to find any evidence that could put any or all of the men inside the unit – things like hairs, fingerprints, footprints, clothing, blood spatters or gunshot residue. With Rogerson likely to be involved and Gao missing, the chance of a firearm involved was high.

What they didn't have was any clue on the fate of Gao, but they did have sufficient evidence to get search warrants for McNamara's and Rogerson's homes, and to justify getting the expensive, time-consuming and sometimes frustrating surveillance operation underway on two men who knew exactly what a surveillance operation looked like.

Around 4 a.m. on Saturday, 24 May, when the residents and even the party animals could be expected to be in the deepest part of their evening's sleep, the Strike Force entered the underground car park of the Cote d'Azur apartments and searched McNamara's Ford XR6 – registered in his name – and the white Falcon wagon registered in the fake name 'Turnbull'.

Under the rear of its driver's seat they found the ice taken from Jamie Gao. It was later speculated to be a few grams lighter than the original weight because the pair had taken some samples to convince Roger's buyer it was a quality product. As one underworld contact told me, 'You buy your drugs in either kilos or pounds – so the deal should have been for three kilograms, not 2.78. Twenty-two grams is a very healthy taster for a bigger deal.' Dealers use a more scientific approach to testing a drug's integrity than what you see on television when a bag is cut open and the product is sniffed or tasted. Aside from being a poor method of quality control, you've got no idea of what you're about to ingest. Like police who have scientists to do the testing, the dealers had taken the sample for analysis by people in the organisation with some training.

Then the police made an interesting decision, and one that harked back to the ISU imperatives when dealing with McNamara and the speed so long ago. Do they run surveillance to see where the drugs go and try and catch the supply/distribution chain and run the risk of losing the drugs and not getting a result? Or do they seize the drugs and see how McNamara reacts? They chose the latter, and that night the wagon and its contents were taken from the car park and hauled off to be examined for evidence of young Mr Gao or anything else that might be useful. The drugs were weighed, entered into evidence logs, samples sent for testing and the rest put under lock and key.

Shortly after dawn that morning, McNamara headed down to the car park. It was business as usual and he had to drive to Cooma prison, supposedly for one of his criminal defence investigations. The criminal was Shayne Hatfield, doing time for his involvement with Michael Hurley in cocaine importation.

The CCTV cameras didn't capture the look on McNamara's face when he noticed the station wagon containing the ice was gone. Was it stolen? Had the Triad tumbled to their scheme? Were the police onto Gao's murder? These issues passed through his mind, as did the safety of his daughters. His first reaction was to ring Rogerson. He knew Roger was an early riser and would be up and preparing to head to the airport for a flight to Brisbane and a speaking engagement for a mate in the fight game.

His call was brief and careful – in the back of his mind was the possibility, correctly, that the call might be recorded. The two met at the airport prior to Roger's flight, and McNamara then headed south to Cooma. Roger had stressed the importance of making everything look normal, something he had no trouble in doing but an effort for McNamara who'd spend the next 24 hours in a state close to panic. The police put him out of his misery at 6.30 p.m. that Sunday night when he was driving his XR6 Falcon in Kyeemagh on the side of Botany Bay near the airport. He'd been under surveillance since Thursday afternoon, 22 May, and police decided it was time to act, ordering what appeared to be a routine traffic stop, but as McNamara got out of his car, detectives from the Strike Force closed in. McNamara, looking haggard and wearing a grey T-shirt, grey hoodie and jeans, was searched, cuffed to the front then taken to the St George Police Station in nearby Kogarah. Prior to his arrest, news crews had been alerted and were on hand to film the event. While police were processing him at the station, McNamara said to Detective Haithem Jouni, 'I've been a goose, look I've just been a goose. I've got a story to tell but not now, it's not all it seems.'

Rogerson showed no sign of concern when he arrived in Brisbane as the guest of Mark 'The Hammer' Dixon who was the late Mark 'Chopper' Read's bodyguard – the essential accessory for every wannabe crime figure – and ran a gym in Redcliffe on the shores of Moreton Bay. Dixon said he'd shouted Roger the trip so the two could watch some bouts at the gym on the Sunday and 'have a couple of beers and some seafood'. Dixon is a Rogerson fan and described him as a 'hero, not a disgraced copper'. He said Roger had arrived with a bag full of copies of his book *The Dark Side* which Dixon had to carry because Roger 'was hobbling. He's got a rebuilt knee. His Achilles tendon is cut. He's half cripple, and he's 73 years old. He's a grandfather.' At this point, Dixon hadn't seen the CCTV footage from Rent a Space. Dixon reckoned the weekend went beautifully with Roger meeting a 'few of the locals and he was having a great time'. Dixon didn't mention that Roger's books, along with memorabilia like his signed photocopies of the P79A report on the late Lanfranchi sold brilliantly, netting Roger around $2000 in cash.

At the Sunday boxing match, Dixon recalled, 'Mate, he looked like he didn't have a worry in the world, happiest I've seen him in ages. He was sitting here on the ring beside me at the table having a couple of beers, having a laugh.'

Roger stayed with The Hammer's uncle, Alan 'Bunger' Johnson, a former boxer now involved in harness racing, at his home in Scarborough, and after the match, they all went back to Bunger's place for a few more drinks. Tagging along for 'drinks and a few laughs' according to his statement to police, was Steve Farley. Farley was now running a hotel at Acacia Ridge near Brisbane, and Roger had rung him on the Sunday morning to invite him to the match. The Dodger was in form and planning, following his conversation with McNamara the day before. He wanted the next few days to be run on his terms, and having an unwitting and wealthy mate onside would help.

Drinking was on the agenda that night, and had they had the television on, they would have noticed that McNamara's arrest, and the police now on the hunt for their drinking mate, was leading the news. Roger also didn't mention the phone call he'd got from his solicitor Paul Kenny who'd been planning on an early Sunday night, but that idea went out the window around 7.30 p.m. when Roger's wife Anne rang him for advice. She told Kenny a squad of NSW Police officers had arrived with a search warrant. Kenny had a conversation with Detective Inspector Sheehy, though the detective didn't tell him the reason for their evening's arrival. Shortly after, Kenny's phone was ringing again, and this time it was barrister Charles Moschoudis to tell him Glen McNamara had been charged. Kenny also believed that Rogerson and Sheehy had spoken by phone while the search was in progress.

Kenny rang Roger, and the two discussed Roger's return to Sydney as soon as possible. In a subsequent conversation, Kenny assured Sheehy he'd get Rogerson back.

When Bunger got up around 6 a.m. the next morning, his house guest was gone, with neither he nor Hammer aware of the reason for the hasty departure. It's a tribute to the strength of the facade Rogerson can maintain that neither man was aware that during the evening's socialising Roger had got a call telling him they'd arrested McNamara and wanted a chat about a kidnapping. It is unlikely that a media tart like Rogerson would be oblivious to the media storm that had broken after the McNamara arrest.

I was in London – Sunday night local time – when I was bombarded with phone calls and emails from Australia telling me that McNamara had been arrested and police were hunting for Rogerson. Until that moment, I'd thought Roger was nursing a dodgy hip and bouncing his grandkids on his good knee and in the eight years since writing about him the only time I'd given a thought about the old felon was when catching up with mates still angry at the man who'd ruined their careers. I was wrong about his retirement and astounded at the allegations levelled against him and Glen McNamara – until that point I'd always viewed McNamara as an honest cop who'd blown the whistle and suffered as a result. Like many others, and in the absence of any comment from the NSW Police, I'd bought the story that Glen had crafted. In one of many interviews that night, Ellen Fanning on ABC Radio National opened our chat by capturing the moment, saying that Rogerson's career was allegedly 'spectacularly continuing'.

Back in Queensland, Farley reckoned that Roger told him early the next morning the police were keen to interview him over the Gao disappearance, and that 'Roger denied knowing anything about the man or having any involvement in his disappearance or kidnapping'. Roger told Farley he didn't want to be arrested in Queensland and would prefer to drive back to Sydney and get advice from his solicitor Paul Kenny. Farley was heading to the Gold Coast early that morning and Roger went with him, and spent the day on his own, hiding out in Farley's apartment in the Peninsula building in Clifford Street, Surfers Paradise. Farley was on a liquor licensing course. Roger was belatedly thinking of electronic surveillance and decided against using his mobile, so Farley borrowed a phone from a friend of his who lived in the building. He also left him with the keys to his silver Holden ute.

While Roger was in Surfers Paradise planning his return, the story was developing fast. Early that morning, around the time Roger and Farley were driving to the Gold Coast, a fisherman had spotted something suspicious floating around 2.5 kilometres off Cronulla's Shelly Beach, the beach closest to McNamara's apartment. He pulled his boat in closer and found a blue tarpaulin wrapped in chain, and in the tarpaulin was a silver surfboard bag out of which protruded a white running shoe. The mystery of Jamie Gao's disappearance was solved.

Early that afternoon, Detective Inspectors Mick Sheehy and Russell Oxford from Strike Force Album flew to Brisbane to hunt for Roger. The Dodger, however, was still a few steps in front, and wanted to deal with the looming storm on his own terms, so he didn't use his return ticket. In the late afternoon, shortly after Farley had returned, he slipped into the driver's seat of the ute and headed south to Sydney. In his police statement, Farley said he met Roger at the Cambridge Hotel at Fairfield and he was 'a very good friend for the past 20 years', and took the opportunity to mention he knew McNamara. Farley said, 'I am aware of who Glen McNamara is, as he was a Kings Cross Police Officer who I'd met when I leased hotels in Kings Cross many years earlier. I do not consider McNamara an associate of mine; in fact I do not like the man at all.'

Roger drove through the night – a lonely trip accompanied only by his thoughts of what lay in store in Sydney and, as ever, using his experience and cunning to work through his slender number of options. He arrived in Sydney just before dawn and left the ute with a friend of Anne's who lived nearby and who drove him home to Churchill Road, Padstow Heights. His luck was in and the house wasn't under surveillance and the news crews hadn't arrived. But that luck didn't hold.

By 8 a.m., the news pack, tantalised by the prospect of an arrest either in Brisbane or Sydney, had staked out Rogerson's home. I was still doing interviews from London, and asked one of the reporters if there was any sign of police or a possible surveillance unit. In a place like Churchill Road, a quiet dead-end street with bush on one side, surveillance would be obvious, but there was none. Rumour running through the media was Rogerson was planning on giving himself up later that morning, and that was confirmed by Kenny, who reckoned he'd been negotiating just that over the prior 24 hours.

Kenny said he'd got an agreement with police for Roger, accompanied by him, to hand himself in at a police station that morning. Just before 7 a.m. Roger rang him to let him know he was home. Kenny rang Sheehy and his colleague Russell Oxford who'd flown to Brisbane the day before to track down Roger. He told them their quarry was back in Padstow Heights and Roger would hand himself in, as arranged, later that morning after the detectives had got back to Sydney.

Kenny drove across town to Padstow and found Roger in his home office waiting for him. He said Roger tried to tell him what had happened, but Kenny stopped him. He said, 'It's the golden rule of criminal law practice – I don't want to know anything but the police version of events,' and went on, 'I learned a lot from Chris Murphy [a high-profile Sydney criminal lawyer] who told me, "You don't cut the material until you get the pattern."' He also said that talking Roger out of a recorded interview with police was one of the most challenging things he'd had to do.

The police weren't taking Kenny's word that his client would do the honourable thing (and may have been swayed by the exuberant media swarm). With exits from the property covered, the detectives hammered on the front door, and Anne let them in. They swept through the house and found Roger and Kenny sitting in the office talking. Roger, wearing a black polo shirt, jeans and carrying his trademark cream bomber jacket, was handcuffed to the front and escorted out of the house. He used the jacket to avoid the media getting a glimpse of the handcuffs – a small vanity. When the media surged towards him en route to the back seat of the police car, Rogerson gave them what would be the last grab in his media career, claiming without a hint of irony, 'We're back to Gestapo days! I'm 73 years old!'

As Roger was being driven off to Bankstown Police Station, Kenny held an impromptu press conference with a similar lack of irony. His face was flushed and he was in high dudgeon, claiming police 'had started smashing on the door,' then 'a number of them came into Mr Rogerson's office room where we were having a legal conference making arrangements to go to the city. It was completely unnecessary; everything was being done in a professional manner with the arrangements with the police. Everything was going along very smoothly and they've taken it upon themselves to burst into his home. It was very distressing, the way they spoke to Mr Rogerson was most unnecessary. He's been an experienced ex-policeman, he's an older gentleman as you know, he's 73 years old. They have betrayed our trust.' He thought the arrest was, 'an absolute disgrace; he was treated like a dog. I've been in shoot-outs, I've been bashed, I've had everything under the sun done to me. But I've never seen conduct like just occurred here, ever.'

The police response was a curt statement issued to the media later in the day, saying, 'NSW Police were not satisfied with the arrangements being proposed and took an operational decision to arrest a 73-year-old man at his Padstow home in relation to the alleged murder of a 20-year-old Sydney man.' Pitching Roger as the victim of an injustice didn't work.

While police were arresting Rogerson, in the morgue under the NSW Coroner's Court in inner-city Glebe, Dr Kendall Bailey was performing a post-mortem on Jamie Gao.

Dr Bailey's initial examination showed Jamie had been wrapped in a blue tarpaulin, which had purple, blue, yellow and white ropes around it and, she noted, metal chain. Jamie's white shoe was also poking out the end of the wrapping. Inside the blue tarpaulin was the silver-coloured Ocean & Earth surfboard bag. As she unravelled the package she observed Jamie was wearing a watch, and on his right hand was a latex glove. Gao presumably had learned from the Lam brothers' mistakes – they'd left fingerprints on the bags of ice police seized – of the need to keep DNA and fingerprints off drug packages. It also suggests that in the few minutes between his and McNamara's arrival in the storage unit, and Roger's arrival, that the two were planning to inspect then complete the handover of the drugs rather than the brawl that, according to Rogerson, led to Glen shooting Jamie before Roger walked in.

Jamie was dressed like many well-to-do students his age in a black Jay Jay's T-shirt, black jacket, blue Calvin Klein jeans, Dolce & Gabbana underpants, and a pair of white Lacoste high-top shoes. In the cold bright light of the tile and stainless-steel suite, Dr Bailey began her post-mortem, noting her subject was a 20-year-old male, and on his back were tattoos of Asian symbols, and the words, 'every saint has a past, every sinner has a future'. She found two bullet wounds, one to the upper chest around 6.5 centimetres to the right of the centre line, and the other lower. There was a downward trajectory for the bullets, and in the instance of the uppermost, it stopped 150 millimetres below the entrance point. The bullets tore through vital organs and Jamie would have died very quickly. Both bullets were recovered from the body and in good condition – great for comparison if the murder weapon was found. In policing there is no such thing as fancy shooting to wound. Point at the biggest bit and pull the trigger.

Bailey said in court later that one possible scenario was Jamie was seated in a chair when shot. With the classic two-handed grip, the infirm Rogerson could have steadied his hand and pulled the trigger with the same ease he guided a schooner to his lips.

22

LOYALTY

The Crown Hotel is at the beginning of River Road, Revesby where it meets Milperra Road, and an easy 10-minute drive from Rogerson's home at Padstow Heights. It's a friendly working man's pub with no pretensions – housed in a drab single-storey building of no merit or distinction, surrounded by a parking lot. Inside, there is an Irish bar, a sports bar with betting and big screens, and a beer garden that is heavy on beer and short on garden, but you can smoke out there.

Most Thursday afternoons from around 4 p.m. onwards, there is a drinking school of old mates who gather in the beer garden at a table immediately to the left as you exit the sports bar. On the wall above the table is a CCTV camera. The camera catches the faces of those around the table in clear and crisp film. They're all in mid to late middle age and run businesses affiliated with the building trade, the nearby Bankstown airport and several are ex-coppers. One of those was Roger Rogerson, who turned up a couple of times a month. Another ex-copper tried to avoid those visits, and said, 'Roger ruined too many careers. While I don't want to get the prick offside, I also don't want to spend much time with him.' One of the men had given character evidence for Roger back in 2005, and talked of Roger's charitable works for kids at Westmead Children's Hospital.

Another said to me the day I was there that, 'Roger said you were a bit of a cunt,' to which I replied, 'History suggests the same thing about Roger, so I'll let you make up your own mind on that topic.' They gather for a smoke, chat and a few beers – mostly schooners of draught beer, with one preferring a Corona with a slice of lime. They last at the pub until it's time to head home for dinner with their families. They all like a drink, but don't drink to excess because they know the Highway Patrol and their breathalysers are on the prowl.

On 22 May 2014, the school gathered as usual. It was an unseasonably warm night with the temperature hovering at around 20 degrees Celsius in spite of winter looming. Bill Duff, one of the ex-coppers, had been sidelined by complications from recent surgery and was at home recovering. However, Roger Rogerson was there and in fine form. The CCTV recorded him as looking well and his usual vivacious self while he held court at the table of drinkers. With him was Glen McNamara, who'd been an occasional attendee since he and Roger had become 'as thick as thieves' a few years before, according to the blokes. McNamara, introduced to the school by Roger, was tolerated rather than embraced because he could be moody and argumentative. They're a group of blokes who'd chide each other, but not take it seriously, but Glen didn't have much of a sense of humour. The Corona drinker copped more chiding than his peers. The night I went, I sipped Rosemount chardonnay, and there were a few good-natured jokes. Australian blokes in a pub enjoying mateship.

They reckoned Roger never rushed to buy his round and had, as one of the drinkers described, 'short arms and deep pockets,' but when others headed to the bar or Roger was cornered into getting his shout and gave one of the men cash to buy a round – his injured shoulder and dodgy knees made it difficult for him to negotiate his way from the bar without spilling the drinks – he insisted they present his loyalty card. The Dodger, they reckoned, was in poor physical shape to the point where he needed his left hand to steady his right (his right shoulder was the injured one) when holding a full schooner glass, but always 'had his eyes on a quid,' and with events unfolding he had his mind on a very big quid that night.

This night McNamara was notably out of sorts, and the camera caught a morose man sipping sparkling mineral water and not attempting to engage in the banter. The usual five or six drinkers swelled to around 20 but Glen remained on the periphery. To keep their strength up they tucked into the seafood platters. Among the new arrivals were three men. One was a well-known boxer, and the other two were what police like to describe as 'of Middle Eastern appearance'. One was alleged to be an affiliate of the Rebels outlaw biker gang, and the other allegedly affiliated with the Comancheros. They were involved in the boxing game, and Roger had recently taken an interest in the sport, though that interest might have been prompted by the discreet networking opportunities ringside rather than the noble art of pugilism.

As the evening ploughed on and thoughts of going home early went out the window, Roger deployed his ample charm, with McNamara casting the occasional poisonous look in their direction. One of the lads said, 'I thought they'd had a bit of a domestic.' A few months later, what had happened that night dawned on them, and tarnished their relationship with Roger.

Successfully ripping off drugs with a street value of three million dollars from a callow youth with dreams of being a criminal mastermind isn't a complex task, and particularly for two experienced former police officers. What is tricky is getting rid of it for a profit. McNamara had few criminal contacts while in the police force, and less after he'd resigned. Roger, however, had a lifetime of contacts. Thanks to his longstanding involvement and reputation within the nation's outlaw biker community, he had ample contacts to broker a drug connection with the men responsible for the bulk of the nation's amphetamine sales. For bikers, it was an imperative to have both a supply and stockpile of product, and if the price and quality were right, then a deal could be done. One compelling reason for the invitation to the two was so they could discuss the sale of the ice they'd taken from Jamie Gao. The drinking school were appalled that he may have used their social gathering as a cover for a drug deal. As I was leaving on the night I joined the school, one said to me, 'If you bump into the old cunt, can you get the loyalty card from him? It won't do him much good in jail, but it had about 90 bucks on it!'

About a week later, the publican was asked by police to provide his CCTV footage after they'd received a tip that Roger had been drinking with some interesting characters that night. Investigations move in mysterious ways and it wasn't until around late August 2015 that police began interviewing the school's regulars. They were shown still photographs taken from the CCTV and asked to identify each of the men. The regulars were at pains to point out that the men they described as 'Roger's new best friends' appeared to have been invited by Roger. They knew who they were because of an interest in the fight game, but that was the extent of the relationship.

One possible motivator for the belated investigation may have been the emergence of a story that Roger had been trying to create some smoke around his own involvement. His natural cunning and decades of experience alerted him to the potential problem of being spotted by physical surveillance on men affiliated with biker gangs. The violence of recent years meant they'd painted a target on their back and with the NSW Police and federal, state and Australian Crime Commission taskforces on their trail the risk of surveillance was high.

His other issue with the gangs was he'd been developing new networks within them recently. Roger, alert to the need to be relevant to the current players, knew that along with his reputation he needed to deliver the goods, and a three-kilogram bag of ice was a fine way to get the result he wanted – and pocket a tasty amount for his retirement fund.

In the lead-up to the first, and later aborted trial in July 2015, the story had it that Roger was pointing the finger at Bill Duff as the middleman to offload the ripped-off drugs. McNamara alleged that Roger had told him Duff would be there to do the introductions. The problem with that scenario is that not only was Duff unwell and recovering from surgery, he didn't know the two Middle Eastern visitors and didn't have the dodgy network Roger had cultivated.

Duff, in a statement to police, recalled Roger had done something out of character around the time of the murder. At 9.15 a.m. on 20 May, Bill was at home recovering from surgery when Roger rang him and, after asking about his health, said he'd call on him later in the day. Duff said, 'It's been a long time since Roger had dropped in to see me at my home, but I thought he might have wanted to see how I was going after the operation. We chatted about my health and general things before Roger left about 30 to 45 minutes later.' Duff initially believed the visit was on the day of the murder but – with his illness at the time – later acknowledged he'd got the day of the visit wrong. It was the last time Duff saw Roger in person.

When Duff didn't appear for a drink that night, Roger changed tack and told McNamara that 'one of Bill's boys' would be around in his place. An interesting story development done on the run. In most drug buys, the middleman brings the parties together, the product is checked for quality, and then the amount and the cash are discussed. When that scenario didn't fly Roger changed tack yet again, alleging that an old friend who wasn't an ex-cop would be the middleman. McNamara's misery deepened. He had a car with a bag of ice in the back, and Roger's promised connections to get rid of the stuff, and get some cash, were looking less and less likely. The Dodger, McNamara later reckoned, was 'full of shit'. Their bromance had been shaken with the cold-blooded murder of Jamie Gao, and McNamara, who'd been in a similarly dicey situation back in 1989, was seeing some trouble coming his way, either from the police who'd eventually investigate Gao's disappearance or, more worryingly, from Jamie's contacts. Drug dealers invariably react badly to being ripped off. Roger's assertions of the pair getting away with it weren't looking as certain as the old felon had made out.

The police investigated the allegations about the middleman and they stumbled at the first hurdle. Neither Duff nor Roger's 'old friend' were on the CCTV. Taking a hard look at Bill Duff, they found no evidence whatsoever to suggest any complicity or even the ability to be complicit. Duff had been at home, sick, and had co-operated at every step with the investigators. Roger was trying to verbal Duff, and it wasn't working.

The other guy wasn't a regular in the drinking school and not on the CCTV footage either, and while he talked about all his contacts in the underworld it was more talk than knowledge – he was guilty of bravado. The clincher was he was on a business trip in Brisbane the night of the drinks, and police verified his alibi. Two things were likely from that night at the pub. Firstly, the stories about Duff et al. were a ruse by Rogerson to mask the real deal. Secondly, Glen McNamara was more miserable than usual.

23

FOLLOW MY LEAD

Court cases in real life are a world apart from what is served up in TV courtroom dramas. Even criminal cases involving murder, drug trafficking and high-profile characters both in the dock and behind the bar table bring only a few moments of excitement to relieve the hours and days of grinding procedural boredom. In long-running cases you're more likely to doze off than have an adrenaline surge.

Rogerson's first appearance in a criminal court in almost a decade was on Tuesday, 27 May 2014 and it was a brief one. After being arrested at his home, he was taken to Bankstown Police Station where, after declining to be interviewed, he was formally charged.

Next stop was Bankstown Local Court – the same court in which he'd given evidence back in the first days of his police career. The court was sitting later than usual to accommodate the Rogerson bail hearing because the local police didn't want the old felon spending the night in the station's cells. He was not in the best of health, high profile, still connected to some senior police and the focus of a media swarm so the best result was getting him to prison. Rogerson, anticipating a long day ahead and plenty of media attention, had showered and shaved after his long drive through the night from the Gold Coast, and fronted the court wearing a cream windcheater – those who've known him for decades reckon he buys an identical one as the older one wears out – tailored trousers with the crease in the right place, and large '80s-style glasses. It's a fair bet he'd taken the advice he'd offered to criminals during his police career to 'pack a toothbrush, mate' because he knew he wouldn't be going home that night.

Rogerson, represented by Kenny, did not apply for bail. Kenny told Magistrate Elaine Truscott the behaviour of the police during his client's arrest was 'disgraceful'. Kenny intended to make a formal complaint. It was set-piece blustering lapped up by the media who packed the courtroom, and offered a few grabs to the journalists who hadn't been in Padstow Heights at the time of the arrest. Playing to the media has become part of the informal side of criminal law procedures and both defence and prosecution play the game. Roger was taken from the courtroom, loaded into the back of a police truck and transferred to the Metropolitan Remand Centre, a short cross-country drive away at Silverwater.

One of his first phone calls wasn't to his wife, daughters or lawyer – it was to businessman John Kizon. Rogerson, on the hunt for possible bail sureties who were cashed up, probably had Kizon on his list.

Glen McNamara beat Roger to the prison by 24 hours. He'd fronted Kogarah Court the day before after spending Sunday evening in the police station's cells. He also hadn't applied for bail and had been taken to Silverwater. Unlike the Rogerson hearing, it was a low-key affair. McNamara shifted uncomfortably in the dock and tried to look reassuring when he spotted his two daughters in the courtroom. His solicitor, Hudson Lu, didn't ask Magistrate Christine Haskett for bail but did request protective custody in Silverwater, which was a wise precaution given it was McNamara's first time as a prisoner, and as a former prison officer and whistleblowing former detective with a high public profile on law and order issues, he was a prime target for other inmates. Roger, with his numerous spells in prison, and his tentacles in the underworld was likely to have been welcomed rather than attacked. Both men were next to appear at the Central Local Court in Liverpool Street in the city on 22 July 2014.

The old sandstone edifice was where Rogerson had spent many hours either waiting to give evidence or in the witness box learning his trade, and its corridors had been the workplace of corrupt solicitor's clerk Brian Alexander.

On 4 June 2014, McNamara was taken to the NSW Crime Commission where he was interviewed at length. The details of what ensued are privileged but Glen was allegedly keen to do a deal in return for a heavily discounted sentence, but that plan faltered at the first hurdle. The police believed their case was so strong they didn't need McNamara's help. Sure, he could plead guilty and get a discount for doing so, but that was the only discount he could expect. Veteran homicide detectives reckoned the case against both men was a 'lay down misère' – slang often used by police who believe the result is a certainty. One former colleague who'd been in the Homicide Squad for nearly two decades said, 'Mate, it's the best brief I've seen. Dumb and

Dumber [the nicknames given to Rogerson and McNamara respectively in the wake of their arrests] are rooted.'

Remand prisons are less strict in their operations than prisons for those convicted, and Rogerson and McNamara communicated regularly. In the early weeks of their incarceration, Rogerson kept a close eye on his partner in crime, and after the failure of his visit to the Crime Commission assured him they could still get out of the charges, and all McNamara had to do was 'follow my lead'. McNamara, like a lamb to the slaughter, took that advice – at least for a while.

The morning of 22 July was the first time the charges against the two men came together in court, and the hearing was brief. McNamara appeared by video link from Goulburn Correctional Centre, to where he'd been shifted in order to keep the two men separate, and Rogerson didn't appear at all. The two later shared a cell for over six months.

Chris Maxwell QC appeared for the prosecution and told the court he was waiting for reports on the post-mortem on Gao – which could take up to nine months, he said – DNA and fingerprint evidence, statements from witnesses, and analysis of what the police believed was the methylamphetamine ice they'd found in McNamara's car. Neither man's legal representatives had much to add, nor did they apply for bail on behalf of their clients. The families of both men weren't in the courtroom, and the only people I could identify were Kylie and Margaret Tees, the daughter and wife of the late Aarne Tees. The case was adjourned for two months.

The first day together in court was uneventful, as these early days tend to be. The progress of the case depends on the prosecution's preparation of the brief of evidence they'll be relying on; service of that brief on the defendants; dealing with any questions arising from the brief; time for the defence representatives to work through the brief in details and plan. With both defendants in custody, the court tries to stir decisions along so people don't spend lengthy time in the cells waiting to see what their future holds. In the case of McNamara and Rogerson, the seriousness of the charges meant the case was destined to go to the Supreme Court where it carried the right of trial by jury if the pair decided to plead not guilty, or for sentencing in the event of a guilty plea. The prime decision to be made at the early stage was whether to test the prosecution case in a hearing in front of the magistrate, or to ask for both men to be committed for trial. A rule of thumb, if the evidence was not going to be tested in front of the magistrate, is around six to eight months to progress from the lower court to the Supreme Court.

However, on the steps outside the court, Paul Kenny was more talkative to the media pack of TV, radio, print and wire-service journalists. Kenny, an experienced media performer, had just the right grabs, saying his client was pleading not guilty, and 'I think Mr Rogerson will get a fair trial in due course. I think the right processes have been put in place for that to occur,' which removed the element of the impact of the high profile Roger had built for himself from defence planning. Many of us had been expecting Roger to play the card that, given his past and reputation, selecting a fair jury might have been tricky – an issue for a trial judge to consider, and a possible avenue for appeal if he was convicted. In planning a defence, always keep a few steps ahead. Kenny told the media, 'His health is not very good. Seventy-three years old, he has quite a few ailments and the conditions he's placed in are not very good. I'm concerned also about his mental health.' Playing to his audience, he told them Roger was isolated in protective custody, had spent a few chilly nights without even a blanket. His pillow was hard and uncomfortable and his watch had been taken from him. Kenny also took the chance to tell the pack that he didn't know what McNamara was planning to do. Rogerson's 'follow my lead' wasn't mentioned.

Late on the afternoon of 7 August, I got a call from a contact telling me both men would be back at Central Local Court the following morning as their solicitors had both contacted the court and indicated each man would be making a bail application. Experienced court watchers know hearings like this can yield some tasty information, and I was very keen to see any or all of the CCTV footage that was supposedly so damning. At 9.30 a.m. the next morning I was at the court and I wasn't alone – Sydney's media had got the same tip-off.

On the bench was one of New South Wales' senior magistrates, Les Mabbutt. At the bar table, the full legal cast was assembled for the first time. There was veteran Crown Prosecutor Chris Maxwell QC and his instructing solicitor, and on the other side was Ian Lloyd QC, a former Crown Prosecutor now at the private bar and instructed by Hudson Lu for McNamara. Lloyd and Lu would later be replaced as the case headed towards trial. For Rogerson, Paul Kenny had instructed George Thomas.

Maxwell is a quietly spoken, well-mannered and immaculately dressed man with over 40 years of criminal practice behind him. In a profile in the *Sydney Morning Herald* of 27 September 2009, journalist Michael Duffy wrote of Maxwell he 'is the opposite of the flamboyant prosecutor of fiction, baying for the accused's blood on behalf of the public. He is a fairly big, grey-haired man who moves slowly. In court he is firm but measured, rarely raising his voice.' Privately, he is personable and with a glint in his eye. Justice David Kirby said of him that 'When I've seen him in court, Chris is reasonable and fairly laid-back. That's a good thing in a Crown prosecutor, you don't want a zealot, you want someone who's dispassionately trying to get to the truth, not to get a conviction.'

Rogerson and Maxwell have a history. Early in his career when he was at the private bar, Maxwell defended a man charged with armed robbery by the Armed Hold Up Squad. The star witness for the prosecution was Rogerson. Maxwell recalled, 'He was the most polished witness. I'd ask him a question and he'd look me right in the eye, and then during his answer he'd turn to the jury and finish it. He was just such a charming fellow. It was very hard to make any inroads with him.' In 1989 the two met again, this time with Rogerson in the dock, charged with conspiring with Alan Williams and Christopher Flannery to murder detective Michael Drury at his Chatswood home on 6 June 1984. Maxwell didn't have better luck this time either and the jury acquitted Rogerson. Williams had pleaded guilty and given evidence for the Crown. Round three of Rogerson versus Maxwell had better odds for a Maxwell victory.

In his second career as a defendant, expensive and capable lawyers have always represented Rogerson. Thomas is a very different character to Maxwell. He sports a shaggy beard and long, wayward hair and is usually in a suit that could do with a press. On the steps outside courtrooms you can catch him taking a break with a roll-your-own cigarette. One fellow practitioner said to me, 'George looks like an unmade bed sometimes, but don't let the appearance lull you.'

In the public gallery, aside from the usual pile of journalists sporting a mix of iPads, laptops and spiral-bound notebooks were Rogerson's and McNamara's families. Jamie Gao's family and friends were absent and as one said to me later, 'We'd be the only Southeast Asian faces in the room, and none of us wanted to be set upon by the media.'

I took a seat on the right-hand side of the court on the hard old benches. To my right was a small elderly woman in slacks and a baby-blue cardigan that probably wasn't doing a great job keeping out the creeping cold of the old courtroom. Clutched in her right hand were legal-looking documents – the poor soul looked nervous and tired. Sitting close beside her was a fresh-faced young woman in her early twenties who looked equally nervous and tired. You often see people like these in the back of the lower courts, there to support their family members charged with crimes. The legal-looking documents are usually house deeds that can be used as a surety if bail is allowed, and it shows both faith and love to risk the house you've spent your life paying for to get someone out of prison. These two were people with unshakeable faith in Glen McNamara – his mother and daughter Jessica.

In the row in front was one other person in a similar predicament – Rogerson's wife Anne Melocco. Mrs Rogerson was a slender, groomed woman in her early sixties – she had the look of a professional. Beside her was a man I didn't recognise.

He was a skinny, white-haired and nondescript man in his sixties, but what twigged me to his identity was the expensive but wrinkled clothing he was wearing. The designer jeans, soft black moccasins and Loro Piana sweatshirt with label on show meant the man wasn't short of a quid. Like Mrs McNamara, he was carrying a sheaf of legal-looking documents in his hand. This was Stephen Farley, Roger's sometime mate, millionaire publican and someone who had the assets to post a substantial bail rumoured to be around $1.5 million if granted. Unlike the still fit McNamara, it was unlikely that Roger with his dodgy knees and hips, plus his badly damaged shoulder, could do a runner.

The lawyers were in place when Magistrate Mabbutt walked to the Bench at 9.30 a.m. McNamara would be appearing via video link from Goulburn, but Mabbutt and most of the lawyers were surprised when told by court staff that Rogerson was on his way in the back of a prison van that was briefly delayed by traffic. The magistrate wasn't pleased after directing that neither man was required to physically be in court for the next few hearings. By the reaction in the courtroom, the only people aware that Roger would be there in the flesh were his lawyers, his wife and possible surety, and the prison staff who'd organised the transport.

At 9.50 a.m. Rogerson made his appearance, struggling with his crab-like gait up the stairs from the labyrinth of cells and corridors that link the court building to the adjacent police station. He finally made it to his place in the bullet-proof glass–enclosed dock – a nod to contemporary security needs in the Victorian-era room that was designed to make sure you didn't miss the power and majesty of the law at work. Before sitting down, he bowed his head to Magistrate Mabbutt, then turned to his right and dipped his head and waved to his wife. He looked confident; his wife looked sad and on the edge of a breakdown. George Thomas opened by outlining that bail sureties were present in court and witnesses on hand if there was need to call evidence on alleged threats to them and hazards, if any, posed by letting his client out on bail. Then Thomas asked for a short adjournment to speak to his client. It wasn't a well-received request given the busy court calendar and that the bail application was on Rogerson's request, but given the gravity of the charges and the fact Rogerson was onsite it was granted. Rogerson shambled down the stairs again. Forty-five minutes later he was back and Thomas told the court Rogerson's bail application was withdrawn. McNamara's application, however, went ahead, which got Maxwell to his feet. It was the first time we heard and saw what the Crown would be alleging and Maxwell took us on a guided tour of the high points of the case he'd be presenting at trial, and was given consent to play highlights from the CCTV tape that captured the prelude and postlude to murder.

He began by telling the now-rapt court that to let McNamara free would be an 'unacceptable risk' given the calibre of the evidence, so much of which had been recorded by CCTV cameras. The CCTV tape was then played to the court, with Maxwell providing the voiceover. With the tape being played on screens around the court, we saw McNamara and Rogerson arriving at the storage unit at 1.16 p.m. and a short time later both men leave – Rogerson in his silver Falcon and McNamara in the white Falcon station wagon. Cameras pick up their short drive to near Micks Meat in Arab Street, Padstow where they park at 1.33 p.m., and as Gao and his mates arrive, two minutes later, Rogerson motors off. Maxwell speculated that Rogerson, who was parked directly in front of Micks Meat, was 'there to observe'.

The courtroom was silent as we witnessed one of the rare moments in criminal investigation in which most of the crime has been captured on film. As Jamie Gao got into McNamara's car and was driven towards his death, Maxwell recounted the lead-up to the crime that CCTV had also captured. The day before McNamara had taken his Quintrex boat from Hunter Self Storage at Taren Point, just a short drive from his home at the Cote d'Azur – Maxwell relished giving the only 'r' in the name a roll of the tongue – followed by meeting Gao that night at the Meridian Hotel in Hurstville. On the morning of the murder, McNamara was caught on camera in a shopping mall in Cronulla using one of the few payphones that still exist to call Gao.

Maxwell resumed the CCTV evidence from Padstow, noting that McNamara was wearing a hoodie and sunglasses as he stopped the station wagon at the entry gate to the Rent a Space self-storage units just a 900-metre drive along Davies Road from where the men met. His attempt at disguise was a disaster – traffic cameras on Davies Road had monitored his progress. As McNamara backed the car into a parking space outside storage unit 803, stopping close to the unit's door but leaving sufficient gap for easy access, Maxwell paused the film and said in his soft yet clear voice, 'It is significant the car is a station wagon – to hold the body.' We then watched as McNamara and Gao entered the unit and closed the door, with Maxwell pointing out there was no internal lighting, 'a dark place' he said.

The cameras then picked up Rogerson driving into the facility, and he does a loop of the place, and parks near the unit. Maxwell said it was the prosecution's belief he was checking to see if anyone was nearby. At 1.49 p.m. Roger entered the storage unit and closed the door behind him. Six minutes later, he emerged, and reversed his car close to the front of the station wagon, with the prosecution believing it was an attempt by Roger to ensure his number plate was obscured, which also showed his lack of grip on where the cameras were and what they were able to record. For a man who'd been able to predict the rise of drugs as the prime criminal enterprise in the nation, he was woefully ignorant of basic technology even after audio and CCTV surveillance had expedited his arrival in prison once before.

McNamara, minus the hoodie and now in a pink-coloured top, opened the back of the wagon and pulled out a silver-coloured surfboard bag, and he and Rogerson went back inside the unit. A few minutes later the CCTV recorded the two men carrying the now full surfboard bag out of the unit and stowing it in the rear of the station wagon. Both men went back into the unit and returned with office chairs they piled on the bag and then drove off.

Maxwell described the moment as 'a brazen, matter of fact crime; they just left the door open with a dead body inside; office chairs were moved and the body bag was dragged outside, both men bent down and lifted the bag into the station wagon; office chairs placed on top of the body'.

Maxwell concluded by telling the court the two men re-appeared on CCTV camera the next day, with McNamara carrying a bag of clothing containing what appeared to be the pink shirt he'd worn the day before, and the two back at the storage unit the next day, 'presumably to clean up the crime scene'. It was, Maxwell said, 'a joint criminal enterprise to supply drugs that turned into a drug rip-off' and 'we believe Mr Rogerson probably did the killing'. Of McNamara, he said, 'He is staring at convictions for two offences that carry life imprisonment. On the 24th of May, three days after the killing, 2.8 kilograms of ice was found in the back foot well of the car that the accused was driving.'

He went on, 'The evidence shows that in May 2014, Roger Rogerson, clearly an associate of McNamara, obtained keys and access to the rented storage unit at Padstow, and Mr Gao was killed in that storage unit. The crown alleges this was an execution style murder associated with the supply of very significant quantities of ice. Any sentence that would flow from these charges if convicted would be lengthy.' He paused, then said, 'It is a very powerful case,' and sat down.

Ian Lloyd then rose to do his best for a client in such obviously deep shit, telling the court the Crown case wasn't weak, but it was circumstantial and the Crown couldn't prove who'd fired the two shots that killed Jamie Gao – which in a joint criminal enterprise doesn't make a lot of difference but is handy for haggling over penalty. At this point in the investigation the results of gunshot residue tests which might prove who did the shooting weren't available – a year later they were. His client 'obviously has been involved in the disposal of the body but that does not make good the case of murder'.

Lloyd said his client taking his boat out of storage the day before the murder may have been innocuous and he may have planned a fishing trip, a comment that got a few smirks from the media contingent, followed by sniggers when he said something unexpected may have happened in the storage unit and his client may be innocent. After the CCTV, no one was giving that line any credence. One curious matter he dealt with was a suggestion by the police that McNamara's daughter Jessica was frightened of her father and feared for her safety if he was granted bail. Lloyd gestured to Jessica's presence in the courtroom and offered to call her as a witness to dispel the notion. However, after the power of the visual evidence, there was no chance of McNamara being granted bail, which was formally refused by Magistrate Mabbutt. As the magistrate departed the bench, Roger stood and nodded respectfully then turned to his wife who was looking plaintively at him. With a jaunty wave and a smile he headed back into the depths of the cell complex.

On 26 August, the action resumed at Central Local Court because Rogerson had decided to go ahead with a bail application, but this time he was on a video link from Silverwater. He was dressed in a green prison uniform and spent much of the hearing shuffling through a pile of papers in front of him. Just like any good detective, Roger had taken his brief to court, and was keeping 'au fait' as detectives of his time liked to say.

Mabbutt was again on the bench, and Maxwell opened for the Crown, this time focusing on Rogerson's alleged involvement. More about the crime unfolded in the packed courtroom. The CCTV from the storage unit was played again, with Maxwell commenting Rogerson had 'control and access to the scene of the killing'. He also told of a phone call from the prison between Rogerson and Anne that had been taped, where Rogerson said, 'Well they'd been there a fair while Anne. I thought I'd go over there and see what's happening. I thought I might be able to give a bit of a hand, a bit of old grandfatherly advice.' The conversation was Rogerson's clumsy attempt to use the technology that had caused him grief on prior occasions, to try and set up a defence, but in the courtroom it caused the crowd to shake their heads in disbelief.

George Thomas then told the court there had been 'enough time for a killing' and that a struggle had occurred prior to the arrival of his client at the storage unit. Rogerson, according to Thomas, found Gao dead on the floor from gunshot wounds when he entered the unit. The post-mortem report had arrived earlier than first anticipated and Thomas told the court Gao had been shot twice in the chest, with one '150mm down from the nipple' and the bullets had entered with a downward trajectory which exonerated his client who was shorter (Roger is around 175 centimetres, and stooped) – an interesting contention provided both men were standing up facing each other. Another minor problem with his argument was Gao was a tall and lanky boy around 185 centimetres tall, which made him also taller than McNamara who is around 181 centimetres.

In a further glimpse of how Rogerson's defence could unfold at trial, Thomas said Roger had only become involved in the drug deal because of 'McNamara's concerns Jamie Gao had associations with people said to be Triad related. McNamara wanted to be sure he wasn't being followed' and suggested that it might have been Gao who'd brought the gun.

Thomas conceded the grandfatherly former detective had helped move the body but wasn't involved in dumping it at sea, a comment that stirred the unfounded rumour of a third man. Shortly after Gao's body was found, coppers who knew Roger reckoned he'd be physically incapable of helping McNamara dump the body from the boat, and with the usual black police humour, speculated on the two ending up in the water along with Jamie. What they hadn't recalled was the clear footage of Rogerson pulling his fair share of the weight as the surfboard bag was dumped into the back of the station wagon.

On the question of ensuring Rogerson's appearance at court should bail be granted, Thomas indicated Anne Melocco had deeds to their home in Padstow Heights and the weekender at Long Jetty, which could be offered as a surety worth $1.5 million.

Steve Farley wasn't around, and according to Rogerson insiders, had decided he wanted nothing more to do with his sometime friend and on Roger's part, Farley had returned to his place on the 'shit list'. However, the surety on offer or Thomas's eloquent plea didn't sway Mabbutt, and bail was refused. In the park outside the court Thomas gave a doorstop press conference, reiterating his line of Roger being in the wrong place at the wrong time and merely offering 'grandfatherly advice'. Like the three-page script Roger had written years before as part of his play for dominance of Sydney gangland, it wasn't working.

24

THE CAST CHANGES

By Christmas 2014, after numerous video appearances in court, speculation was for a committal hearing to begin before a magistrate around Easter 2015. Justice doesn't move quickly. However, on 21 January Rogerson took the timetable into his own hands and McNamara, now reunited with his mentor in Silverwater prison, was following his lead. Sitting side by side in their prison greens, both men told Magistrate Mabbutt they waived their right to a committal hearing and wanted to get to trial at the earliest possible time. The magistrate, already alerted to this development, ordered they be arraigned together in the Supreme Court on 6 March 2015 and bail was refused. Rogerson, as usual engaged with every step of the proceedings, said, 'Yep, I understand that, thank you.' McNamara looked grim and didn't say anything.

However, the collective sigh of relief from the media, the police and most of the witnesses keen to see the matter speed to what we reckoned was its inevitable conclusion, was short-lived. At 9.30 on the morning of the arraignment I got into the lift at the Supreme Court in Phillip Street along with the clutter of bewigged barristers heading up to court. As we waited for the doors to close, in stepped Charles Waterstreet, barrister at law. Tall but not as tall as he seems on first glance, once lithe, shoulder-length hair kept under control with a headband beneath his barrister's wig, and large, dark-skinned, liver-spotted hands that draw your eyes to them.

Waterstreet looked at me through the chunky circular black frames of his very fashionable glasses, smiled and said, 'Mr McNab, I suspect I know why you're here,' and I replied, 'Oh shit Charles, please tell me you're not appearing for Roger?'

'Oh no, dear boy,' he said with his trademark broad grin, 'I have ethics you know, and I'm appearing for Mr McNamara.' In the lead-up to the Supreme Court appearances there had been rumours swirling that either or both men were looking at a change in representation with choices based on a blend of ability, profile and cost. Waterstreet's arrival in the case meant Ian Lloyd QC was gone.

Waterstreet has been a notable member of the criminal bar for over four decades and has represented alleged terrorists, murderers, robbers, outlaw bikers, and quite a few hopeless cases. Along the way he's produced two films, written two memoirs and is a columnist for Sydney's *Sun-Herald*. His friend actress Rachel Ward described him as 'sometimes charming, sometimes exasperating'. One thing you can bet on with Waterstreet – he can be painstaking to the point of irritation.

For the arraignment, both McNamara and Rogerson were brought in from Silverwater. Roger was casually dressed in beige trousers, white shirt and a bottle-green cardigan and looked like the kindly old grandfather you'd see making slow progress to the bar at your local RSL club. He was carrying his trademark sheaf of papers in a buff-coloured manila envelope just as he did back at the Armed Hold Up Squad, and was alert and engaged. For Rogerson, a courtroom was his second home, and in a perverse way, he was enjoying being on stage again and the focus of everyone's attention. McNamara was sitting to Roger's right in the dock, and was dressed in a grey pinstripe suit that had been bought when he was more slender. Nearly a year in prison had piled on the pounds, and he was pale, sweaty and melancholy. Family members of both men were absent.

On the bench was Justice Geoffrey Bellew who'd be handling the trial. Bellew was an SC appointed to the Supreme Court after a career particularly in criminal work including prosecuting major drug trafficking and terrorism cases, and representing rugby league players when they appeared before the judiciary. Tall, fit and thorough, Bellew was one of the younger justices and known to be efficient and critical of lawyers who wasted the court's time. A few days before the arraignment, he'd been appointed president of the NRL Judiciary.

The proceedings were formal and brief. The charges were read; both men stood and told the judge they were pleading not guilty. Bellew and the barristers then discussed a trial date with both Maxwell and Thomas agreeing to the first available date of 20 July 2015, and Waterstreet was uncertain if he'd be available because of other commitments. Friction was obvious at the bar table, with Thomas keen to get the trial started at the earliest possible time. Bellew made his point clearly, telling Waterstreet he'd better make sure he was ready. The trial was estimated to run for eight weeks, but that would soon change along with the trial date, which was subsequently moved to 27 July, not because of Waterstreet but to accommodate numerous housekeeping issues that could speed the trial rather than hamper it. What Bellew didn't know was the road to trial was poised to become bumpy.

In early May I got a call from a lawyer contact telling me to 'stand by for breaking news' and alleging Paul Kenny wouldn't be Roger's solicitor for much longer. The information was half right.

The venue for the trial and the preliminary housekeeping had switched from Phillip Street to Central Criminal Court at Darlinghurst. The complex of three courts facing Oxford Street on the crest of the Darlinghurst hill was also the scene of some of Rogerson's greatest victories, and the backdrop to his memorable photoshoot in 1981 where he posed in his cream-coloured safari suit for the *Sydney Morning Herald*.

The mood in the courtroom on 13 May was not much fun if you happened to be Paul Kenny or, by extension, his client. While the lawyers and judge were circumspect about the problem and Thomas was at pains to distance himself and his client from the allegation, it seemed the rumour I heard was correct and that Kenny had approached Jessica McNamara, a prosecution witness, and the content of the conversation had prompted her to contact the DPP. Ms McNamara, according to my sources, had felt threatened by Kenny's approach. Kenny has denied threatening her in any way. However, her allegation posed a few questions, one of which was why it had taken so long to report an approach that happened around nine months earlier. These were matters that would emerge in the trial. With the looming professional problem, Kenny had withdrawn and solicitor Peter Katsoolis now represented Roger.

The two also have a history. Katsoolis is the long-time solicitor of Neil Chidiac, the Sydney bookmaker who was arrested on 31 March 1989 by detectives from the Redfern-based drug unit of the AFP for conspiring to import heroin. Nicholas Cowdery QC prosecuted Chidiac, prior to Cowdery becoming the occasionally controversial NSW Director of Public Prosecutions, and Chidiac got 20 years' imprisonment. From the moment of his arrest through to the present, Chidiac has protested his innocence, which isn't unusual in serious criminal cases. At his trial, the judge commented that two of the key Crown witnesses, a customs officer called Alfred Oti, and one of his relatives, taxi driver Wilson Kwalu, were 'self-confessed perjurers and liars' as well as 'down-and-out villains' and that 'you will look carefully at what they said before you would hang a dog on their evidence,' but the jury did.

In 1994, an investigator acting for Chidiac interviewed Oti who told him he'd been threatened by the arresting police that if he didn't lie to 'get Neil Chidiac' he'd get a longer sentence and said, 'he [Neil] was not involved with me or Wilson Kwalu or any other person that I know in importing drugs'. After his release in 1997, the Channel 7 current affairs programme *Witness* interviewed Oti who repeated the comments he'd made to the investigator in 1994. In March 2015, Justice Beech-Jones of the NSW Supreme Court in reviewing submissions made by Chidiac through his lawyer Katsoolis commented 'the case against Mr Chidiac rested solely on the testimony of two confessed criminals and perjurers namely Messrs Oti and Kwalu,' and further that the material presented by Chidiac's legal team left him with a feeling of 'unease or a sense of disquiet' and 'I consider that there does appear to be a doubt about Mr Chidiac's guilt.'

At the time of writing the case has been referred to the Court of Appeal. The case has been frequently publicised by veteran journalist and now editor of the ABC National News Reporting Team, Neil Mercer. Mercer in 2011 hosted the documentary *The Life and Times of Roger Rogerson – Beyond Blue Murder*.

The two men met in Berrima Gaol in the early 1990s and like Michael Wallace, Chidiac was seduced by the Rogerson magic, and the two became friends and regularly caught up after they were released. Chidiac and his family were regulars at the annual Rogerson Australia Day barbecue at Picnic Point. When the news of a probable review of Chidiac's conviction hit the news, Roger bragged to his drinking and lunch mates that he had been instrumental in developing the 'brief' that Katsoolis was using to get a judicial review and was 'lending a hand with the publicity stuff'. Unfortunately, Roger had other commitments in March 2015 when Justice Beech-Jones announced he had sufficient doubts about the case to have it reviewed by the Court of Criminal Appeal.

The crew were back in court on 29 May, and then again on 5 June, when the cast at the bar table had changed again. Abdullah Reslan, a capable young specialist in criminal law, replaced Hudson Lu. Rogerson's earlier plan to push the 'grand-fatherly advice' notion to the court backfired and at court he was additionally charged with 'accessory after the fact to murder', which was a back-up by the Crown just in case the jury had some doubts about how joint the criminal enterprise had been. Maxwell made Roger the focus of the day when he told the court Roger had approached an old friend, Mick Maguire, who was then terminally ill with cancer, on 3 April and asked if he could use his storage unit. Maguire handed over the keys and access codes to unit 803 and it's something mates do without asking why. On 19 May, the security cameras recorded Rogerson at the unit around 3 p.m. removing a couple of office chairs. Maxwell told the court that McNamara and Gao were recorded by CCTV at the Meridian Hotel in Hurstville that night, and at 1.16 p.m. the following day, McNamara and Rogerson were recorded entering the unit with McNamara holding 'an object', but what that object might have been remained tantalisingly unknown.

McNamara, he said, aside from removing his boat from storage was also recorded putting the surfboard bag into the white station wagon used in the crime, and at 7.28 a.m. on 21 May, the bag containing the late Mr Gao was recorded in the boat, wrapped in a tarpaulin that was secured with what appeared to be rope, but more detail wasn't forthcoming. Maxwell then changed tack and talked about Jamie Gao, and not in a favourable light. Quoting from statements, he said that one friend had told police, Jamie 'always spoke to me about wanting to be a gangster'. McNamara, Gao had told his audience, was an ex-cop, a PI and a 'dangerous figure' who had 'bragged about his ability to dispose of people without a trace,' and knew influential people, he used ice and knew how to get it and 'could hook him up for guns'. In what would become a significant theme, Gao told his mates that McNamara 'was a heavy with connections to bike gangs,' which if you're bragging about your interest in the ice business is an essential connection to have for both supply and distribution.

The audience, leaning forward in their seats for more tasty snippets were slightly let down when Maxwell sat down, and Thomas took to his feet, describing much of the evidence as hearsay, and relating specifically to McNamara and not his client. The risk of a rift between the two men was increasing.

McNamara's defence team was notably quiet. Throughout the morning the difference between the two men in the dock was stark. McNamara looking formal in his grey pinstripe court suit sat hard against the right-hand side of the dock facing the judge. He stared into space, only engaging when his lawyers approached him to show him paperwork or whisper in his ear. He tried to ignore his fellow dock dweller who repeatedly leant across to comment or show him paperwork. While Roger had no success with McNamara, he dug through his ample pile of papers, beckoned his solicitor across to ask questions and show scraps of information. Roger was the most animated person in the courtroom, a bit like the overly active child craving to be the centre of attention.

On a chilly Saturday morning in the first week of July, I was enjoying my usual Saturday morning habit when in Sydney of having an early breakfast at Tropicana in Victoria Street, Darlinghurst before heading off to battle gravity at the gym. Tropicana has been around for decades and was the birthplace of the short film festival that bears its name, and haunt of Darlinghurst denizens who don't feel the urge to be hip and seen – if that's your fancy there are plenty of places across the street for display purposes. It's also a favoured place of some of Sydney's underworld insiders and their fans.

On the banquette at the far end of the restaurant I noted two other regulars, Charles Waterstreet and solicitor Chris Murphy. Polite nods, then back to the important business of breakfast and a pile of newspapers. As Waterstreet was leaving he stopped for a chat, and told me he was heading out to see his client and had a pretty serious day in front of him. Weeks away from the trial I thought every day would be pretty serious and didn't think anything more of the comment. The next morning the calls started. It had been a very serious day, with McNamara finally understanding there was no sense following Roger's lead and it dawned on him that his mate was planning on shafting him to save himself.

Roger, with his acolyte now showing some common sense, was furious. Glen, according to one source close to Rogerson, had gone from being a 'terrific bloke' to 'that mongrel' and a few anatomical expletives, in the space of 24 hours. Sources in Silverwater said Roger had nearly 'gone off the deep end' when he heard of McNamara's change. The bromance was dead, and with Roger's ructions in prison, arrangements had been swiftly made to transfer McNamara to the relative safety of Parklea Correctional Centre – a precautionary move prompted by speculation that with Roger's criminal connections both inside and outside prison, arrangement could be made 'to whack McNamara' who was Roger's greatest liability in the forthcoming trial.

In pubs, clubs and Chinese restaurants with lazy Susans on the table tops, where colourful identities, current and former coppers, and retired criminals gathered – sometimes the gathering was a mix of all three – the trial was a hot topic. Would Roger try for a separate trial so late in the day? Would McNamara take the wise path and plead guilty? Would McNamara be beaten or murdered in prison, or would his family be threatened? The one thing on which they all agreed – Roger would be giving evidence to save himself and it was a performance they 'wouldn't miss for quids!' Rogerson had turned full circle and like the time shortly after the Lanfranchi killing where Roger had gone from pin-up to pariah, he'd gone from someone with a rehabilitated public image thanks to his media performance and a loyal coterie of people in his thrall, to a man with few friends or supporters.

McNamara's pivot resulted in another visit to the NSW Crime Commission but it was as unsuccessful as the one almost a year earlier. When we bumped into each other a few weeks after our Tropicana moment, Waterstreet quipped to me they'd offered to plead guilty and tell all in return for a suspended sentence for Glen. But more seriously, they'd offered again to plead guilty and give a chapter and verse of what had happened – at least McNamara's version of the facts – in return for a hefty discount on sentence, but the Crown weren't buying. Plead guilty and take your chances with the judge was allegedly their view, which left McNamara with only one other choice – paint Roger as the mastermind and claim duress, and with Roger's track record that approach had credit. The only problem was getting the track record into evidence for the jury. This is the time wily barristers and skilled witnesses get to dazzle, and wake up those in the public gallery who may have nodded off in the long, pedantic and quietly spoken periods that are typical of the courtroom.

The barrister tries to 'open the door' by moving the witness to a point where they respond to a question that allows the barrister to then attack them on past events that would otherwise not be allowed. It could be something as innocuous as 'You're an honest man, aren't you?' and if the answer is 'Yes' then the gotcha is for the barrister to tell the court about the criminal record of the witness. On the flip side, a man like Rogerson can do the same thing, luring the barrister into asking a question that allows him to answer with what coppers call a 'bombing raid'.

Back at court on Friday, 24 July, just three days before the start of the trial, McNamara in his usual grey pinstripe was sitting in the dock and spent most of the morning cradling his head in his hands. Rogerson wasn't required to be there. He was in Silverwater working hard on his brief.

Maxwell gave an idea of the scope and complexity of the trial, telling the judge the prosecution had 141 people on the witness list, of which 45 would be called to give evidence, and with consent of the other barristers, 81 would have their statements tendered to the court without the need to appear, and 15 probably wouldn't be called. To tender the statements, the Crown gets the police officer giving evidence to mention the statement in his or her evidence and it then becomes part of the records and is read by the jury. Waterstreet, who hadn't sorted which statements he'd agree to, much to the obvious annoyance of the judge, presented the only problem.

Finally, the case spiced up as Waterstreet went on his own bombing mission and introduced the key plank of what was to be his client's defence – duress.

Waterstreet said Jessica McNamara would give evidence that when her father returned to the apartment they shared, he had Rogerson with him and was 'skittish'. Rogerson, Waterstreet alleged, looked at Jessica, then turned to her father and said, 'Glen, you have lovely daughters,' which McNamara took to be a threat rather than a compliment, and while making the comment he tapped a lump in his trouser pocket, and Jessica told police she could see a glimpse of black showing at the top of the pocket. Waterstreet said both the Crown and his client believed the object in the pocket was a gun. Moving on to events earlier in that fatal afternoon, he said that after Roger had shot Gao, he pointed the pistol at McNamara's head and said, 'I'd hate to go and see your lovely daughters.'

While he scored points with these comments, Waterstreet didn't do himself any favours when he told the judge he was acting pro bono as McNamara's cash had run out and that he might need an adjournment. In the 2008 *Australian Story* on Waterstreet titled 'Nothing But the Truth', he joked, 'I do a lot of legal aid, what is called pro bono work. My Latin wasn't very good and I thought pro bono was Latin for a lot of money, but apparently it's not. It means you don't get paid.' It wasn't quite the truth, as legal aid does pay, but a significantly lesser amount than barristers charge their funded clients.

His comment about a possible adjournment was the wrong time to mention it to the wrong judge and Waterstreet got a very clear message on delays – no. At the time Waterstreet's comment was innocuous, and having spoken to him a few days before it seemed the case preparation still had a way to go. Waterstreet complained he was getting 'missiles incoming daily'.

25

LET THE GAMES BEGIN

The trial began on Monday, 27 July 2015 at Central Criminal Court in the courtroom on the right side of the complex. The crowd was surprisingly light. The media were there in force, along with a smattering of people along to watch the show. Absent were members of the Rogerson and McNamara families and Rogerson's longstanding media contacts he'd been feeding stories and bons mot to over the years. Rogerson's wife Anne told a contact she'd returned to work in order to pay some of the legal bills and wouldn't be coming. The contact reckoned Anne 'hates Roger's guts, but she's a very loyal woman and is terrified she'll have to sell the house to pay for the old bastard's lawyers'. Anne had also told him she 'didn't have a clue' where the initial tranche of money had come from to pay the lawyers.

One rumour was John Ibrahim had contributed to the defence. The two men have a long history, with Roger telling the *Sunday Telegraph* in July 2010 he'd 'known John since he was 14 but we hadn't spoken for a long time, so I gave him a ring'. The call was prompted, according to Rogerson, by reports Ibrahim 'felt persecuted and depressed by police attention on his family'. Rogerson said, 'He is depressed about it all. John is hating the constant publicity but he's having to wear it, and he feels like everybody is all over him.' On helping with Rogerson's predicament following his arrest in the Gao case, he said, 'Look he's a mate and if he or Anne were short of a quid I'd help out like I did with Anne when he was in prison last time. But funding his defence, no.'

At 9.30 a.m. the judge began the task of whittling down the conga line of potential jurors who'd been marched from the jury room through the corridors, out into the car park then across to the courtroom. Selection can be a long task, but by early afternoon 15 jurors had been selected – with the possible duration of the trial three extras to the usual 12 would be sitting in the jury box just in case. The judge wasn't taking any chances.

Roger was seated on the left side of the dock facing the judge. He was dressed like a genial grandfather heading out for a night at the bowling club in a white polo short, camel-coloured sports jacket and brown trousers. His eyes were twinkling, he was smiling when appropriate, and very much on his game. In his right ear was a hearing aid provided by the court to make sure he didn't miss a word. At one point he beckoned to the sketch artist sitting near the media gallery and joked that he could turn to make sure the man caught his best side.

McNamara was in stark contrast. He looked pale, sweaty and pudgy. His thinning hair was dragged over to cover the pink bits, and rather than engage in the proceedings he often had his eyes closed, and kept his head down.

With the jury empanelled and instructed on their duties by Justice Bellew, Maxwell began by outlining the Crown case in painstaking detail. The opening address by the prosecution lays the foundation for the case they will be building. Maxwell took the jury through the events that led to the murder of Jamie Gao, and showed still photos from the CCTV he'd be showing in detail later in the case. He said: 'Something unusual is happening you might think in unit 803 at this time shortly before Jamie Gao meets his death in the unit and it involves both men,' reinforcing his main theme of 'joint criminal enterprise', designed to overcome the 'cutthroat' defence of two defendants laying blame on each other in the hope the jury will be so perplexed they can't make up their minds.

Rogerson was busy with the documents in his folder, examining them, having whispered conversations with his solicitor. McNamara had risen from his earlier torpor and was busily taking notes on his writing pad – he's left-handed – and looking at the jury, perhaps trying to read how they were taking in the enormity of the crime Chris Maxwell QC was alleging he'd been part of.

The first day finished at the usual time of 4 p.m. and court resumed at 10 a.m. the following day, but for the jury the day would be a lot shorter than anticipated. Courts run on a predictable timetable with morning tea around 11 a.m., followed by lunch at 1 p.m. sharp, and by the time the tea and biscuits for the morning break were ready for the jurors, Maxwell had completed his address.

Next up was Waterstreet. Prior to the trial, the three barristers had discussed and agreed on topics that wouldn't be mentioned in the opening or until the groundwork had been laid. Included in those topics were Rogerson's long history both as a corrupt detective and criminal, and his association with members of outlaw motorcycle gangs. If you've stolen three kilograms of ice you need to be able to sell it, and outlaw motorcycle gangs were the ideal clients. Unfortunately the agreement lasted until Waterstreet stood and opened his case, taking aim at Rogerson from the outset. He said McNamara 'saw Roger Rogerson pull out the gun; that he had a discussion with Mr Gao about the drugs and that Mr Rogerson shot Mr Gao in cold blood'. Waterstreet paused, then said, 'Glen McNamara says that he knows nothing about having any gun in the shed or when he came into the shed. He had no idea he would pull a gun on Mr Gao. It was at all times, from beginning to end, the property of Mr Rogerson.'

Moving on to duress, he said Rogerson pointed the gun at McNamara and 'threatened to kill his family. Mr McNamara has two daughters and Mr Rogerson knew that. Mr Rogerson threatened to kill Mr McNamara and threatened to kill his daughters if Mr McNamara did not comply,' and from that point all his client's actions were motivated by duress.

He then set up the defence for McNamara's association with Gao, saying the young man was a member of the Sing Wah Triad – a Hong Kong–based criminal gang – that was deeply involved in the ice trade and McNamara had become involved with him as he was researching a book on ice and the involvement of Triads with the working title *The Ice Age*. Having laid the groundwork, he mentioned Roger's friends in the outlaw motorcycle gangs and Roger being responsible for two killings, but omitted to mentioned they'd been 'in the line of duty' as a police officer.

It was a showstopper. While the jury had their lunch, the barristers and a very angry judge had little time for food. There were discussions in the judge's chambers, corridors, and outside in the weak winter sun. Consensus was that Waterstreet was in strife.

Back in court shortly after 2 p.m. both Thomas and Maxwell agreed with the judge that the opening and in particular the reference to Roger's killings and biker mates had tainted the minds of the jury so greatly that the fairness of the trial was potentially compromised. Unsurprisingly, Waterstreet didn't agree but he was outnumbered. At 2.24 p.m. the judge discharged the jury and announced the next available jury panel was on 18 August. Both defendants had bail refused.

In the usual post-court chats outside, it was obvious that Waterstreet wasn't flavour of the month, and we all speculated as to what the judge might do to him. I chatted to Waterstreet a few days later, who said he couldn't see what all the fuss was about, and on the bright side, he'd just got a 'lick of cash' to keep going. While he wouldn't be drawn on where the 'lick' had come from it was unlikely to have come from McNamara's family members who were either not in a position to fund what was to be an expensive defence that was likely to end with McNamara being released from prison in his dotage, or who had said no.

One extended family member told me they'd been disappointed when Glen had sent his daughters around to plead for money for his defence. The person said, 'It was disgraceful. He sent those two lovely girls around to try and persuade us to mortgage our house. We worked damned hard to get this place and we're not going to squander our future on him. He's just not worth it, but those two poor kids – they're both lovely and dedicated to their father. The reality just hasn't hit them yet.' The person went on, 'When we heard he was involved in drugs, and that awful ice, that was it. That drug ruins lives. So no, Glen won't be getting our help.'

McNamara had funded his defence with his own cash reserves, which had been meagre until his share of the divorce settlement came through shortly before the Gao debacle, but cash burns through lawyers' fingers fast as the hours rack up and by July the cash was gone. McNamara was on the nose with his family and friends and legal aid was the only alternative.

Justice Bellew runs a scrupulously fair trial with a keen eye to any points that might give rise to a legitimate avenue of appeal, and with that in mind, Waterstreet might have been more alert to the potential problems that social media can bring to a contemporary trial. The scheduled second trial was over before it started. On Tuesday, 11 August the cast was back in court for more housekeeping matters, when Bellew announced he was aware of social media posts allegedly by Waterstreet that had been drawn to his attention in an affidavit by Rogerson's solicitor, Peter Katsoolis, and that might have an impact on the fairness of the forthcoming trial. Waterstreet had allegedly posted a photograph on an Instagram account purportedly in his name and allegedly repeated the posting on a Twitter account in the name @charleswaterstreet. The photo was of him standing in front of graffiti on a wall near the courts – the graffiti said 'Blue Murder'. In the picture Waterstreet was his usual smiling self. The judge suppressed reporting of the caption, as he feared it might 'adversely affect the right of one accused to a fair trial'. Waterstreet denied posting the photo.

Early that afternoon we were back in court and Bellew said he had two affidavits. One was from the Crown's instructing solicitor, a Mr Prince, who'd accessed Waterstreet's Twitter account and taken a screenshot of a post made early on the morning of 7 August, containing the caption that had so upset the judge, plus the link to Instagram. The second affidavit was tendered by Thomas and was from a member of Katsoolis's staff. They'd been doing their own cyber sleuthing and found by 11.08 a.m. on 11 August, the photo and caption had been removed from the Instagram account. The judge adjourned the proceedings until the following day to give Waterstreet 'a further opportunity to consider his position and seek such advice he thought appropriate'. The reality was Waterstreet's representation of McNamara was now untenable.

The mood was such that after court had adjourned for the day, even seasoned reporters who like a chat were so struck by the suppression order they declined to talk about what had happened even to each other.

The following morning when everyone re-assembled to sort out what should happen, Waterstreet was notably absent. In his place was Tim Game SC, a senior barrister from the same chambers as Waterstreet, who'd been drafted in to appear for Waterstreet, but not McNamara, whose representation that morning was his solicitor Abdullah Reslan who'd come along with former NSW Attorney General Greg Smith SC who was potentially replacement counsel. It was getting quite crowded at the bar table.

I checked Twitter and noted Waterstreet had posted he was in make-up for a cameo in a film that morning. Game told the court that he'd advised Waterstreet to stand down from the case, but that if he did so it wasn't any admission of any wrongdoing. Both Game and Maxwell agreed Waterstreet's alleged conduct should be investigated and Bellew referred on to the Registrar of the Supreme Court for 'advice of the Crown Solicitor as to whether proceedings for contempt should be taken against Mr Waterstreet'.

Bellew said he had 'no other choice but to vacate the trial scheduled for the next week' and 'to say the vacation of the trial date is unfortunate is a gross understatement'. Smith told the court he would represent McNamara on legal aid, but wasn't available until March 2016, which lit the fuse under Rogerson's barrister George Thomas. Thomas told the court that any senior barrister could pick up the defence case with two weeks' hard work, and any person getting legal aid 'doesn't have the luxury of choosing a barrister' and should take whoever was available, adding his client was suffering. He went on the attack, suggesting McNamara had been responsible for Waterstreet's actions, an allegation quickly dismissed by Bellew who also noted that a barrister would need a lot more than two weeks to come to grips with a few thousand pages of evidence. Of scheduling the trial earlier, he said, 'It would be particularly unfair to place Mr McNamara in that position when the circumstances which have led to it are, as I have said, not of his making.'

The judge adjourned the case so he could sort dates for a new trial.

On 14 September it was back to court to clear the debris of two false starts and set a date for the third and hopefully final attempt. Greg Smith had disappeared from contention and public defender Kara Shead was representing McNamara with Reslan still as solicitor. Shead is a highly experienced criminal lawyer with an early career as a prosecutor with the DPP, and she had the judge smiling within moments because of the precise and careful way she operates.

All parties agreed that an earlier estimate of three months – prompted by Waterstreet's reluctance to agree on which prosecution witnesses needed to be called – was too long, and that six to eight weeks was more likely. Judge Bellew set the trial to commence on 1 February 2016, the first day of the legal year. It was shaping to be a battle between two former friends with the Crown as ringmaster. Roger, the persuasive and 'mesmerising' witness against the man who was once a self-appointed crusader against paedophiles and drugs.

For McNamara the trial was about damage control and he was the key witness for his own defence. George Thomas is a tenacious and experienced advocate and McNamara didn't have the expertise in the witness box of Rogerson. McNamara had confided to family members he was dreading the clash. On the other side, Rogerson was eagerly looking forward to it. He'd told his few remaining friends that he was ready to best Maxwell – 'I've done it before and I'll do it again' – but what was secretly troubling him was McNamara's new team. Roger, a man still stuck with the prejudices of the 1950s, would be cross-examined by a capable and skilled female advocate instructed by a Muslim. The world had changed since the good old days, he'd told one of his visitors.

In early November Roger got some more bad news. Gunshot residue was found on the clothing he'd worn the day of the murder, but it hadn't been found on McNamara's clothes, thus strengthening the integrity of the latter's version of events. And a name from the past was added to the list of Crown witnesses – Flannery – but David, not Christopher.

The late addition of the son of Australia's most notorious hitman Christopher Dale Flannery was perplexing. While his father had had a long association with Rogerson dating back to the wild days with Neddy Smith, that relationship ended in May 1985 when Flannery disappeared. Coroner Glass who presided over the inquest into Flannery's presumed death pointed the finger at Rogerson as being the key to the mystery. The Flannerys had had little to do with Rogerson since, and Christopher's wife, Kath, had accused Rogerson of complicity in her husband's likely murder, but to be fair, Kath accused a number of others as well. Flannery's statement was about Roger taking him out on his boat shortly after Christopher had disappeared – a story of kindness. Pundits speculated the Crown were trying to introduce the notion of Flannery DNA on Roger's boat, a bit of malice by the Crown to wind up Roger over one allegation his boat had been used to dispose of Christopher Flannery, and to remind him of the recurring boating theme in Roger's life. The true situation, as we found out after the trial was mundane. David Flannery had engaged the Rogerson/McNamara team to help with a legitimate debt collection case. He was not called to give evidence.

One other curiosity was police had either reopened their investigations or kick-started an investigation that had gone quiet in the lead-up to the trial. In late August they'd tapped on the doors of Roger's drinking friends from the Crown Hotel, and shown them photographs taken from the CCTV of the Thursday night gathering after the Gao murder. It was odd timing as my mates in the 'New Tricks' team of old detectives, so nicknamed after the UK TV series about retired police returning to the force, reckoned this was something that should have been done prior to trial – 'not like the old days,' we all agreed. The detectives were asking questions about the chaps 'of Middle Eastern appearance' and other observations of incidents that might have been out of place. Over the next few months they returned a few times, and added Bill Duff to their interview list. Smart money had it, based on their questions, that they were trying to glean evidence on who Roger and Glen were planning on selling the drugs to, and the likelihood the buyer may have been among the attendees at the drinks. With Duff eliminated from the list of likely middlemen it was back to square one, and while proving the links from Gao to the buyers would be useful in prosecution, it wasn't essential.

Police were also asking questions about where the gun came from. While in prison, Rogerson had claimed to a captive audience and visitors, that after Gao was slipped over the side of the Quintrex, he 'stood in the bow to celebrate our big win' and 'loosed off a few shots' presumably from the murder weapon. Common sense and experience suggest the gun should have gone overboard shortly after Roger's alleged theatrical outing. The same factors also suggest the gun hadn't been acquired for the outing but rather came from the stock that detectives of Roger's vintage kept for a 'just in case' moment.

However, and the source is likely to be McNamara, the story was Roger acquired the gun from a mate. One prompter for this renewed investigation was earlier on police were chasing the angle it was McNamara who'd got the gun. They were steered down this line by McNamara when they found that on 3 May 2014 he'd been at the Condell Park gun club doing some handgun practice.

Comprehensive searches of Rogerson's homes and cars hadn't yielded any evidence of the gun, and there was speculation he might have boxed it up and given it to a friend for safekeeping. Roger has form for this sort of thing. At the CIB he had a locked cashbox he stored in his next-door neighbour's gun safe – the man was a licensed gun dealer. The precaution was unlikely to be because Roger didn't trust his wife and daughters. The neighbour never saw nor asked what was in the box. Roger would collect the box, take it home, then bring it back soon after. Detectives on Taskforce Omega that investigated Roger said the neighbour was probably entitled to use the 'Sergeant Schultz defence' (from the television series *Hogan's Heroes*) of 'I know nothing'.

The truth, according to sources, rested somewhere in the middle. Roger had allegedly disposed of his stash of guns in the early years of this century, believing quite rightly that he was 'too hot' and since then if he felt the job required a gun he'd source one. For the Gao killing, Roger allegedly got his mate to source a pistol but hadn't told him what it was to be used for and his mate didn't ask, though it's a fair bet he thought they'd be used to back up a threat rather than for murder. The gun was from the man's stock, and if returned unused, the normal charge of a few hundred dollars would be waived. If used, the full price would have to be paid up because the gun was worthless. In the underworld, a gun without a history of use in crimes can be resold for a high price, whereas the moment the trigger is pulled in a crime, the value of the gun plummets and it becomes less of a weapon and more of a liability.

Two days after the murder, Roger allegedly visited his mate and returned the gun, which was inside a rubber glove to avoid fingerprints or DNA. He told his friend it hadn't been used. Roger was calm, cool and persuasive and the man trusted him. It wasn't until police announced Roger was sought for his role in the disappearance of Jamie Gao, that his mate became concerned he'd been misled by a man he considered a friend, but also knew to be an accomplished liar but 'he wouldn't lie to me,' the man thought. When Gao's body was found and examined, the mate knew he'd been done.

It gives an insight into Rogerson that he cold-bloodedly 'stitched up' his mate by lying and in doing so, saved himself the cost of a gun.

26

LET THE GAMES BEGIN — AGAIN

The trial began on Monday, 1 February 2016 at Number 3 Court in King Street – a building designed by convict architect Francis Greenway as a school and constructed between 1820 and 1829. The old pile has been renovated and upgraded over the decades but remains cramped quarters for a large trial, and the comfort of the participants wasn't helped by dodgy air-conditioning in Sydney's sticky February weather – even more unpleasant if you're wearing a wig and gown over civvies.

The day started later than usual, with the lawyers and judges off to church for services to mark the beginning of the legal year and with God out of the way, off to a tribunal of fact. Shortly before 11.30 a.m. the legal teams arrived with barristers flanked by their instructing solicitors and a phalanx of young lawyers lugging files and wheeled airline cabin bags – they're easier to drag up and down the stairs of the old courtroom than the usual file trolleys designed to be moved from a lift to the courtroom. Criminal trials are still driven by mountains of paper rather than contemporary electronic data. After a sharp knock to alert the court, Justice Geoffrey Bellew strode on to the bench and began the trial at 11.30 a.m. sharp. Bellew is a judge who doesn't waste time.

The public and media were removed from their hard wooden seats and sent outside as the jury panels were marched up Elizabeth Street, then into King Street and Court 3 for selection. The procedure, which can be arduous, was mercifully brief and within an hour we were right to go. Outside the courtroom the crowd poked at their smartphones and tablets – a generational change from the last time I'd waited for a Rogerson jury to be empanelled and Chris Maxwell QC to open the Crown case. Thirty years ago we paced, sat and fidgeted after reading the *Daily Telegraph* cover to cover while waiting for the first editions of *The Sun* or *Daily Mirror* to arrive, and drank cups of awful International Roast or Pablo instant coffee served up by the Salvation Army for a few cents a cup, with all profits going to a good cause.

The public and press returned to the courtroom shortly before 2 p.m. Both of the accused were brought up into the dock on the judge's right-hand side, and their view was across the bar table to the jury on the other side. Rogerson, dressed in a white shirt with his oatmeal-coloured jacket, looked straight ahead, aloof and ready for battle, with a pile of papers and notebook at the ready. McNamara was in his court suit, looking sweaty and nervous. His hair had thinned noticeably since the last time I'd seen him, and he'd been left with a Tintin-like tuft sitting alone at the front.

The trial began after the sharp two-tap knock on the door to the judge's bench to indicate he was about to return to the bench. Bellew swept in, in full judicial regalia of gown, sash and wig, bowed slightly at the standing crowd who returned the bow, sat, and called for the jury. Another knock, this time on the door to the jury room, heralded their arrival in court. McNamara rose easily from his seat and Rogerson struggled up as the jury entered.

Fifteen – nine men and six women – had been selected for the jury of 12, with three reserves given the likelihood of a long trial. In age they ranged from around late twenties through to fifties, and with the exception of one of the women who looked to be from Southeast Asia, all were white. No one was expensively dressed, and only two men were in ties – a stark contrast to the wigs, gowns and luxury suits of Sydney's legal precinct. Two men had accessorised with sunglasses perched on their heads. The judge spent the first 30 minutes outlining the jury's duties and giving them a quick guide to their new home. The judge emphasised the importance of their role and real criminal sanctions that would come their way if they strayed from his instructions. High on the list was no investigation work on their own, including the use of Google or social media – the judge was still reminded of the Waterstreet incident. They were to remain impartial and not be amateur sleuths and if they strayed from his concise instructions, getting booted off the jury would be the least of their worries.

Just as in the earlier ill-fated trial, there was no sign of any Rogerson friends or family in the public gallery, but McNamara had two family members in court and they'd loyally be there for the run of the trial, with Glen acknowledging them with a nod each morning. The media seats were full of bright young journalists, some covering their first trial, and there was again the notable lack of any of Roger's old contacts.

Then Chris Maxwell QC rose to begin the case for the Crown. Quietly spoken and with the air of a university don, his opening address was similar to the one he'd given to a different jury a little over six months earlier, a meticulous view of the crime's timetable, supported by CCTV, phone records and shopping dockets. Throughout he came back to them that the two men were acting in 'joint criminal enterprise', and that meant he didn't need to prove who pulled the trigger.

Maxwell began with the drugs followed by a few points not covered in detail in his earlier opening. He told the jury 2.78 kilograms of ice had been found by police in plastic bags in a brown pillowcase under the driver's seat of the white Falcon wagon, and it was likely they'd been pushed under from the foot well of the car's rear seat, and thus concealed. Glen had bought the Homemaker poly-cotton blend pillowcases at Kmart in Sylvania on 22 May at 8.08 a.m., recorded on CCTV as he used the self-service checkouts. After disclosing Glen's shopping habits, Maxwell pointed out that three grams of ice is, by law, a traffickable amount, and one kilogram was a 'large commercial quantity'.

He then moved to the scene of the murder, the Rent a Space unit 803, and told the court the lessee, an old friend of Roger's named Mick Maguire, had signed up for the unit on 21 February 2014 and three days later moved some office furniture in. About two weeks later Rogerson had asked to use the unit and Maguire had given him keys to undo the padlock on the roller door which was the only access to the unit, and access codes to the site, and that Roger had returned the keys two days later. However, Rogerson's silver wagon had been spotted at the unit on 2 April and again two days later, this time along with a blue XR6 Falcon consistent with McNamara's.

On 19 May, McNamara removed his 4.5 metre Quintrex boat from Hunter Self Storage at Taren Point – again recorded on CCTV, and bought some outboard oil on the way to his Cronulla apartment. While he was attending to boating matters, Roger was at the storage unit, and unknown to him, Jamie Gao was outside the gate looking in. The pair had no idea of each other's presence.

Where the address became intriguing was new evidence of the aftermath of the killing. After Maxwell had talked about the day of the murder, and foreshadowed Jessica McNamara's evidence of Roger with an object in his pocket at the McNamara home, he disclosed that on 21 May, CCTV again captured Rogerson and McNamara, this time outside McNamara's apartment. Glen had towed the boat out of the garage with his XR6 at around 7.28 a.m. – the blue tarp wrapped around the surfboard bag were quite obviously in the boat. Four minutes later, the cameras recorded Glen and Roger standing beside the boat, both carrying fishing rods. Maxwell drily added 'it was unlikely they were going fishing'. Maxwell, moving towards a robust finish, told the jury the Crown would not be offering evidence of where the boat was later launched from. (The court later heard they launched from the Grays Point boat ramp, about 11 kilometres from McNamara's home.) Then he came in with a few tantalisers. He said Police had found two compelling pieces of evidence when they searched Rogerson's Padstow home on the Sunday after the murder, while Roger was in Queensland.

In the back of the silver station wagon was rope, and chain 'consistent' with that found wrapped around Jamie's body when pulled from the Tasman Sea, and inside the house they seized four items of clothing to test for gunshot residue. Analysis found residue on the cap, shirt and dark pants but not on the running shoes they found. Maxwell didn't mention the results of testing on McNamara's clothing, but in a tantalising twist, the defence told me they came back negative for residue. In a cutthroat defence, McNamara had drawn first blood. The revelation prompted George Thomas for Rogerson to get to his feet and try to argue the admissibility of the gunshot residue evidence, which prompted Kara Shead for McNamara to stand and tell the court it proved her client wasn't the shooter, which wasn't proven at that point but added some spice to the afternoon. The judge took a dim view of Thomas's interjection, pointing out that he'd had months to bring up the issue during the numerous housekeeping hearings but hadn't. George, a barrister with an air for the theatrical, may have been prepared to take some stick from the judge in order to get the chance to discredit the evidence in front of the jury. But he didn't get his chance that day.

Shead then opened her case, and while not as theatrical as Thomas, she has a fine sense of drama, and got the full attention of the courtroom when she rose, looked squarely at the jury and said, 'Roger Rogerson shot and killed Jamie Gao, and then threatened Glen McNamara's life and that of his two daughters.' The jury and public gallery were rapt, leaning forward in their seats and relishing the change in dynamics from the Crown's precise and undramatic outline.

Glen McNamara, she said, was using Jamie Gao as a 'secret informer' for research on his third book, this one on 'Triads,

Asian gangs, drug people, weapons' and 'how they were all associated and how they worked'. On Rogerson, she said the two had met years before at a book launch and become friendly and began to do some private inquiry work together. As for Gao, McNamara had met him when working as a private inquiry agent for Sydney barrister Charles Moschoudis who was representing Lok Lam, who was charged with serious drug crimes. Gao was acting as his interpreter for their legal conferences. She also alleged Gao was part of a Triad and once a member of a gang called 'Sing Wah' and had ripped off his Triad colleagues by skimming money from their drug deals, and was an occasional informant – though Shead didn't indicate whether it was an informant to police or to other gangs. McNamara wanted Gao's insight into the gangs – only ever for research Shead asserted – and in return Gao wanted counsel from the former copper. The timing was perfect because by January 2014 Jamie was terrified he'd be found out.

Having built up Jamie's need for the wisdom of his elders, Shead again opened the bomb bay doors with Rogerson as her target. Rogerson stopped his frenetic notetaking and apparently feigned disinterest in the proceedings by taking an interest in the timber side of the dock to his left. Unlike Maxwell's quietly spoken and occasionally circuitous delivery, Shead switched to concise dot points driven in like nails. Gao, she alleged, had asked her client to advise him on his predicament and told him he knew of Roger Rogerson and his relationship with McNamara, so would Glen introduce him? Roger could help, and Glen did the introductions, and the pair met on 'multiple times' without McNamara's presence. As that relationship developed, she alleged McNamara had maintained his only interest was in book research and had declined to meet with Gao on a few occasions, but Roger was keen for the pair to keep in contact and Glen did. Their meeting at the Meridian Hotel on 19 May was for research.

On the day of the murder, McNamara had rung Gao in the morning, but was worried, given all the talk of Triads, drugs and skimming, when someone he didn't know answered Jamie's phone. The event prompted McNamara to find a difficult-to-trace public phone to call him again, and this time Jamie answered. Their afternoon meeting was on – and for Glen it was an opportunity to learn more about the Triads and their ice business and Roger had insisted the meeting take place and they'd combine it with repairs Roger needed to make to the roller shutter door on the storage unit, which also made an ideal place for a clandestine meeting. After a stop at McDonald's for a quick bite to eat, the pair arrived at the storage unit, fiddled with the roller door, then drove to Arab Street to collect Jamie Gao.

After Roger executed Gao, Shead alleged, he turned to Glen and made 'immediate multiple threats' which placed Glen in 'genuine fear for his safety and that of his family,' and 'duress under the belief he'd be killed by Roger Rogerson or more importantly the danger posed by Rogerson to his daughters'. Glen was 'terrified'. On that strong closer, Shead sat down. She'd set up the cornerstone of her defence. McNamara was ignorant of Roger's plan for Jamie Gao, and was complicit after the killing because of the threat to himself and his daughters. At this early stage in the case, the lawyers couldn't mention Rogerson's reputation – it was something Waterstreet had tried and that resulted in the earlier trial being aborted. Reputation was something both sides had slated for the future.

One long-time Homicide Squad detective, now retired, said to me, 'I reckon she's right about Roger doing the deed. You can see him now. He's pulled out the gun and told the kid to get to his knees or sitting in one of those crappy old office chairs – he'd need to have been because the bullet trajectory was downward and Gao was much taller than both of them, and if he'd been standing the kid would have been blown backwards by the bullets. For Roger, it made the situation controllable. Then "bang bang, you're dead, cunt". Roger was always a good shot and two in the chest was precisely the way we've been trained.' His words provoked a clear picture in my mind – while there were alternatives, this one made sense.

The final address before the first witness was called was by George Thomas for Rogerson. Thomas, tall, slightly stooped and with a hawk-like face, rose slowly from his chair, adjusted his wig and gown, and using his right hand to emphasise points, told the jury the story of Rogerson's involvement came from 'a very different universe' to the story told by Kara Shead. 'A very different universe' would be his catchcry throughout his opening. Roger maintained his deep interest in the side of the dock, purposely letting Thomas engage the jury. Like any great performer, he knew when it was his time to star and his time to step back. McNamara was the reverse, with his focus on the jury and their reactions to Thomas's statements.

Unsurprisingly, the story was very different. Roger had never met Gao, and, according to Thomas, had entered the storage unit and found the young man had been shot and McNamara in shock. Glen told him Gao had pulled out a gun, whereupon the two men had struggled, the gun went off and Gao was shot twice. Roger, said Thomas, believed what McNamara had told him. Thomas said his client and McNamara had known each other both professionally and socially for a bit over three years, and that in 2014 just a few weeks before the killing, they'd been in the front row of a boxing match. Two days after Gao died, the two were at the Crown Hotel having a beer with Roger's mates. Thomas's comments grabbed my attention, because it looked like he was setting up a storyline to explain his client being in the same place at the same time as a couple of gentlemen who might be called as prosecution witnesses and who, it might later be claimed, were associates of the Rebels and Comanchero outlaw motorcycle gangs. If you've got the contacts and a large pile of drugs that need shifting, who better than the bikers?

Thomas then switched tack. His client was at home on 20 May 2014, pushing the lawn mower to keep his meticulous garden in top condition. At chez Rogerson, you'd never find a blade of grass out of place. Glen turned up and told him he'd arranged a meeting that afternoon with his Triad contacts and was worried that something might go wrong, so would his old pal come with him to watch his back? Roger agreed, concluded his lawn mowing and followed Glen. When Roger followed them back to the storage unit, he did a drive around because he was 'watching out for Glen'. In another unusual move, Thomas referred to a statement by a man called Politis about his alleged witnessing of the pair launching the Quintrex the next day, with Thomas asserting the witness couldn't be correct because of the timing. Glen had put the boat back into storage by 11 a.m. and Politis, according to Thomas, recounted an incident in the afternoon.

It was odd because Maxwell had earlier told the court he wouldn't be introducing evidence of where the boat was launched. It may have been a pre-emptive strike against evidence from

McNamara's team, or just an oddity. Thomas concluded his opening by telling the jury that aside from finding a dead man and his mate with a smoking gun, he knew nothing. It was a reprise of the 'Sergeant Schultz defence', and confirmation the pair would use the cutthroat defence of blaming each other. It's a tactic that doesn't have a great track record of success, particularly when 'joint criminal enterprise' is supported by so much CCTV footage, and the Crown had a couple of particularly telling photographs to show the jury as the trial lumbered ahead.

Maxwell returned to centre stage with Justin Gao, Jamie's cousin and the first witness in the trial. It was near to the end of the second day. In lower courts, police give evidence first followed by civilians, but in a criminal trial the order is reversed. While many witnesses called to give evidence are just like bricks in a wall, Justin was significant because he was the vehicle to introduce the story of his late cousin.

Justin said he and his cousin were friends and Jamie told him he'd been meeting with Glen to put together a deal that would be 'massive' and he would be 'rich soon and wouldn't have to worry about money again' and rubbed his index finger against his thumb. The conversation was two days before Jamie died. During their regular catch-ups at Miss Saigon Vietnamese restaurant in Hurstville Jamie had bragged of 'dropping off ice' and that 'drug dealing was beneath him, unless the deal was big enough'. Justin didn't want to know about Jamie's entrepreneurial activities.

On the day of the killing, he'd had trouble getting through to Jamie's mobile and had tried Facebook with the same result. Around midnight, he was contacted by other friends in Jamie's social group, now all worried because the talkative and readily contactable Jamie hadn't been heard from. They had a rough idea where Jamie had been heading and went out in search of his car, eventually finding it not far from Rent a Space. In the back was Jamie's sports bag with his wallet, phone and passport. Something was definitely wrong. In one of those strange moments that happen in crime, they decided to move the car because it was parked in a loading zone and might get booked in the morning. Moving the car proved problematic because only one of the group had any knowledge of how to drive a manual. The ensuing drive to a quiet – and legal – parking place nearby wasn't smooth.

At 11 a.m. on 21 May, the friends resumed their search, this time heading to Jamie's house in Hurstville to 'look for clues' and using a key they'd found on Jamie's key ring. However, they didn't have much luck, but they did find a machete attached to the underside of the dining room table, which they took – a bad look if Jamie's mother had found it. Shortly after, Jamie's mother, on the hunt for him as well, rang Justin and he'd lied to her. The sad truth about her son would be days away. Later that day they contacted the police, and when asked why it had taken so long, Justin replied it was because 'Jamie might get into trouble,' and he noted the cultural issue of dobbing in his cousin – it wasn't the done thing.

Next witness was Wayne Cai, a friend of Jamie's since Year 8, and also at UTS. Like Justin, Wayne was significant because his evidence fleshed out Jamie Gao and his motivation. It was a glimpse into how a young middle-class man was seduced from a comfortable upbringing into the underworld. Wayne said his friend was a bright and personable young man bored by university who'd been attracted by the crime and believed he could do it better – more money, less risk and the life he wanted.

Like many young men their age, they were enthralled by action films – particularly out of Hong Kong – and video games, but in Jamie's case he took them a little too seriously. The line between fiction and reality blurred. The two men had 'philosophical discussions' about Jamie's uncertainty about staying at university and having a career grounded in his business studies. He didn't want a nine-to-five job.

Wayne believed the catalyst for Jamie's disquiet was in 2012. Jamie had grown close to Bing-Jie Wang, known as BJ, who was among his coterie of friends, but BJ wasn't a hardworking student, BJ was a drug dealer working with the Lam brothers. BJ kept his criminal life secret to the best of Wayne's knowledge, but that secret ended in May 2012 when he was arrested on serious drug charges. The Lam brothers were arrested around 10 days later, on 11 May, at Lok Lam's apartment in Wolli Creek not far from Sydney airport. Police found 2.2 kilograms of ice and the men were charged with 'supply a prohibited drug'.

BJ didn't get bail, but his co-accused Lok Lam, who'd come to Australia in 2008 on a student visa to study business at Macquarie University, was granted bail and was out in October 2012. Jamie introduced him to his circle of university friends, though they kept him at arm's length. Around this time Jamie told Wayne the arrests hadn't deterred him but instead had motivated him to 'do what BJ and Lok were doing' but to use his studies and abilities to do it better. Wayne didn't push him on specifics and he didn't want to know. It was the start of a distancing between the two, and they'd catch up once a fortnight or so when Jamie would 'pop by my house for a cigarette' or they'd meet in Hurstville. It was at these catch-ups that Jamie told him he'd met a former policeman called Glen who was a private investigator who wanted to work with him, but he didn't disclose on what.

In cross-examination by Kara Shead, Wayne reiterated he didn't know that Jamie was a drug dealer, and that he and his mates weren't involved, and the first he had known of BJ's involvement in drugs was after he was arrested. He told her he and his friends didn't ask if Lok was a Triad member, and that Jamie told him he wanted to be a gangster and climb the hierarchy of a crime gang, but wasn't specific about which gang. The perils of social media emerged when Shead asked him about his Facebook posts including one on 2 March 2014, 'fuck that's heavy, I knew I should have bought knives when I went!' It was a joke, and possibly not a funny one Wayne reckoned, and referred to an incident in China when he was visiting his family. Much of his group's humour derived from Hong Kong action films. Wayne also agreed he was worried about the choices Jamie was considering and had posted 'An open letter on fate' on his Facebook page in April 2014. The letter was published on an Australian blog site 'Your Friend's House' by Shane Kang four days before, and described how young men like Jamie were lured into drug dealing.

It said, 'A week after you graduate high school with not a clue in the world what you want to do with your life, that man will invite you to his house in Sydney for the weekend. He'll pay for your flights and everything else. When you get there, he'll show you his Ferrari, his Harley-Davidson, his yacht, his jet skis and his smoking room and poker room. There'll be a moment you'll never forget. It's when he takes you to his used car business. You'll be standing there in the middle of the gravel lot and he'll ask you a question. He'll ask if you really believe that he could be living the way he is by selling cars. You'll say that you don't. He tells you it's because he's in the business of trafficking pills. He says he wants you to go back home to Brisbane and start selling his stuff there.' Later in the piece the writer said, 'every fortnight you'll be making the average annual person's salary in cash, then that morning when the police crash through the door and the dangerous but luxurious life is over – your new home is a prison'.

Jamie's response was 'it's so fierce bro'. But the fate of the fictional drug dealer in the piece didn't deter Jamie Gao.

27

TRIADS EVERYWHERE

The next witness for the prosecution was the recent arrival to the Gao circle of friends, Lok Lam, and he caused more than the usual ripple of interest when he entered the courtroom. In criminal cases, witnesses waiting to give evidence aren't allowed in the courtroom until they're called to give evidence, and once done, they can remain. The reason is to reduce the risk of their evidence being influenced by the testimony of prior witnesses. They wait outside the courtroom, apprehensively pacing, reading or working their smartphones or tablets with one eye cocked to the door. The judge instructs the sheriff's officer in court to call the witness, and the officer, often a retired police officer or from a military background, shuffles through the courtroom to the foyer and calls the name of the witness three times. The witness then enters the courtroom and is escorted to the witness box where they're sworn – either by an oath or affirmation – to tell the truth. The usual witness has dressed for the occasion, and for men it's a coat and tie. Criminals usually have a sharply styled suit in their wardrobe set aside for weddings, funerals and a day in court either as a witness or as the defendant. Lok Lam grabbed the room's attention because he made his entrance up the staircase from the cells, the same entrance Rogerson and McNamara made every morning, and he wasn't wearing a court suit.

Lok Lam, dressed in drab green prison issue T-shirt and shorts, with a pair of white trainers with Velcro fasteners rather than laces, was escorted by two burly officers from the dock stairs, in a lap through the public gallery, then past the jury to the witness box. The shortest distance was behind the bar table, but protocols preclude moving the prisoner through the lawyers' turf. Looking at the faces of the jurors, Lok Lam was probably the first prison inmate they'd seen in the flesh. Lam told the court he lived with his wife in the same apartment complex as his brother Kip, and the pair were involved with BJ Wang in the drug business they operated out of Lok Lam's apartment. He was granted bail on 21 September 2012 and was finally released on 11 October after his family had raised the necessary funds. While on bail BJ introduced him to Jamie Gao, and to Jamie's circle of friends, most of whom didn't want much to do with an alleged drug dealer on bail.

Lam, giving evidence for the Crown, told the court he and his brother had engaged solicitor Adam Ly to represent them and in December 2013 the police had served their brief of evidence on Lam, who'd decided to plead not guilty to the charges – not an easy task given he was caught red-handed in a room with 2.2 kilograms of ice. He admitted that one of the reasons for his current time in prison was that none of his gang – brother and

BJ – were careful on the telephone and had no idea police were on to them and recording their calls.

Reality dawned at the time police kicked in the door to the apartment, and Lam said of their phone habits, 'That's how we got caught.' After deciding to defend the case, barrister Moschoudis was briefed, who suggested using Glen McNamara as a private investigator to get witness statements to help build their defence strategy. In January 2014 Glen met with Lam, Moschoudis and Jamie Gao who'd joined the team as Cantonese interpreter for Lam whose English was still rudimentary. After the conference McNamara, Gao and Lam ate at a cafe where Glen sold his skills to them, explaining he was an ex-copper, well connected to the underworld and drug scene. According to Lam, Glen wanted to know about the drug network he'd been running and who the customers were. It was the first of a couple of very strange alleged conversations in which McNamara did most of the talking.

The three met again a few days later at the Meridian Hotel in Hurstville, the scene of other meetings between McNamara and Gao. Glen opened by telling them his costs for getting statements then quickly segued into pumping both men for an insider's glimpse of the drug business. Lam was worried about being sufficiently prepared for his February court case but thought getting an adjournment would be difficult. However, McNamara had a sure-fire plan to deal with that problem.

Back in the 1980s Christopher Dale Flannery had successfully obtained two adjournments in serious court cases using subterfuge. In one instance he faked chest pains the day before court and took himself to St Vincent's Hospital in Darlinghurst where you could guarantee being admitted and kept under observation for 24 hours. On the second occasion he'd checked himself into a private hospital in Liverpool for a few minor procedures, which, no doubt because of sheer misfortune had a few complications which required him to remain in hospital. His doctor, Geoffrey Edelsten, kindly provided a medical certificate that got Christopher out of his day in court.

McNamara, however, had a far more dramatic idea – he offered to shoot Lam in the leg with a small calibre pistol and assured him the damage would be minor and he wouldn't hit anything vital. Lam didn't share Glen's view of minor, nor was he confident in his marksmanship and declined the bizarre offer. Lam delivered this tasty morsel like all of his evidence – quietly, deadpan, and with an interpreter beside him just in case. When asked again about McNamara's offer he was more animated – Glen, he reckoned, 'was very serious!' The jury and media contingent clustered together in seats in the centre of the courtroom, scribbled on their notepads. Finally, some spice had come into the proceedings.

Lam then told his now very attentive audience that McNamara had offered to use his expertise in surveillance to teach him how to hide from surveillance police and how to safely meet with customers. The three met again the next week at the Meridian and Glen began by asking for cash for his investigative services before returning to his theme of drugs, this time asking Lam about his drug-buying clients and telling him he had access to both drugs and clients. Lam said he'd decided not to trust his investigator.

It was obvious from the evidence that McNamara believed Lam was still in the thick of drug dealing and likely to be a major dealer. Lam said he had no interest in Glen's offer and reiterated that after being arrested he'd given up the drug business. What

I was thinking in the public gallery was that Mr Lam, in spite of his fairly ordinary look and polite demeanour, was a crafty individual. At one level he presented as someone contrite, but at another, he might also be a fine actor and a calculating crook – you don't get your hands on 2.2 kilograms of ice without connections, a comment that could also be directed at Jamie Gao.

For Rogerson, Lam's evidence had little impact, but for McNamara it rattled the assertion of a man researching a book. Kara Shead pounced on Lam, asking him in detail about what the police found when they raided his home. He responded in his usual quiet manner, admitting they'd also found $36 000 seized as proceeds of crime and 694 grams of heroin – a drug making a comeback to the market after years in the doldrums. The highly addictive drug is cheap and plentiful, and marketed heavily by the Mexican drug cartels that were major suppliers of cocaine and ice to the Australian market. He also admitted that Police had found cutting agents that were used to 'stamp' on the drugs – the process where they mixed the high-quality original product with the agent to reduce its potency and make their purchase go a long and highly profitable way.

Shead delved deeper into Lok Lam's drug operation and he said BJ handled the phone calls and faced the customers, and in prison, BJ had 'turned over a new leaf' and found religion. He asserted that though Gao and BJ were very close friends, Jamie had never been to the Wolli Creek apartments, was not involved in their operations and hadn't, to the best of his knowledge, sold drugs. Gao and Lam had only become friendly after the arrests, and they were just friends, enjoying 'chats, drinks and fun'. Lam denied the allegation that Jamie had been involved in their drug business and had skimmed around $130 000 from sales. Shead then switched angles and referred to conversations in social media in which Lam had been referred to as 'big brother'. Was this a type of address used to indicate a person's place in Triad hierarchy, a question that got most of us in the court leaning forward and listening intently.

Lam, until that moment a witness who hadn't made any errors and kept his answers concise and as brief as possible like any skilled witness, made a mistake and answered that it might have been, but that it was also used in his group of friends as a common term of address. His slip suggested he had some Triad knowledge and she asked him if he was a member of a Triad and his response was a very firm no, that he wasn't a member or friendly or familiar with them. To dig himself out of the hole he said he'd got his knowledge from the action movies he loved. The question that hadn't been asked was how he'd managed to get his hands on a large stash of drugs. Lam's credibility had taken a beating. It didn't help that when asked about his assistance to police after Gao's murder in return for a chance at having his sentence reduced, he didn't know police had reported he'd given information on Triads. My thought was whether Lok Lam would still be healthy the next morning. Even a suspicion he'd been ratting out a crime gang like a Triad can be unhealthy.

Lam was followed in the witness box by Jamie's less colourful friends who'd been in the search parties scouring Padstow on 20 and 21 May 2014. Their evidence was like much you hear in a criminal trial, not particularly intriguing but necessary to painstakingly build the case. It was so mundane that at one point, the snoring of a sheriff's officer could be heard above the proceedings of the court. By the close of the second week, the Crown was into its fifth witness. The hopes of a six- to eight-week trial had moved on to hopes the case would be done in three months. Like a legal Stalingrad, winter was looming.

On Wednesday, 17 February, the slog of the trial and the witnesses called to build the Crown case were revved up when Detective Sergeant Aaron Phillips, the officer in charge of the investigation, gave evidence. Phillips was called so he could be sworn as a witness and introduce the CCTV film prior to the jury's tour of Padstow the next day. While the footage of Rent a Space and Micks Meat in Arab Road had been played in news coverage before, there were some new and startling pieces of vision.

Phillips took the jury through footage of the 19 May meeting at the Meridian Hotel between Jamie and Glen, then Glen at the payphone the next morning, then the prelude to the murder and Jamie's corpse covered and manhandled into the back of the station wagon. Phillips moved to the pair at Kennards at 4.20 p.m. on 20 May, buying the two-tonne chain block to help lift Jamie's body into the boat. Both were conspicuous with McNamara in sneakers, shorts and pink shirt and Roger with his stoop and obvious physical impairment in dark trousers and shirt and wearing a baseball cap. The men re-appeared on film the next morning, wearing different outfits, with McNamara in his blue XR6 with boat and trailer attached, driving out of the secure car park under his apartment building at 7.28 a.m. The camera caught a large blue-coloured object in the boat, and a few minutes later Roger and Glen in the building's lift with their fishing rods. Phillips then showed the men on 22 May at the Crown Hotel, sharing what appears to be a pleasant gathering of old mates.

But there was one photograph that stopped both jury and the public gallery in their tracks, and stirred the media pack into a frenzy of scribbling then texting. It was in a series taken around 6.24 p.m. on the day of the murder showing Roger and Glen getting into the lift at the Cote d'Azur apartments, with McNamara offering his right hand to help the stooped Rogerson, and in McNamara's left hand – his dominant hand – is a six-pack of James Boag's beer. The *Daily Telegraph* on 18 February 2016 had the shot in colour on the front page with the headline: 'Thirst Degree Murder'. The need for a cold beer after a busy afternoon torpedoed the credibility of McNamara's claim of duress.

28

THE LONG GRIND

The jury's visit to the Padstow crime scene was a brief respite from the grind of the trial, then it was back to evidence from more of Jamie's friends, with the word 'Triad' appearing regularly and the involvement of that organised crime group always denied. The jury heard from witnesses for the prosecution like the man who'd sold McNamara outboard oil for his boat, and we learned the witness – a Mr Ames – was a 'Ford man'. There was also the grindingly boring but essential detail of the security operations of Rent a Space. The statement of the late Michael Maguire was tendered, with Maxwell making the clear point that Roger had pilfered a key in order to give him access to the storage unit without Maguire finding out.

What was becoming apparent to the audience in the courtroom was how skilfully Rogerson had let McNamara do the hands-on work while he sat back and orchestrated. However, his good times came to an end with the evidence of forensic specialist

Dr Sylvia Hale. She examined clothing found during the police search of Rogerson's home for gunshot residue, and told the court she'd found residue on his hat, shoes and track pants, including the pocket – a piece of evidence that would accord with Jessica McNamara's testimony of seeing something in Roger's pocket.

Following Hale's evidence was Gao's girlfriend, Misaki, who appeared via video link from Tokyo. She was conservatively dressed in a skirt, black top and pearls and sat demurely in a bland room with an interpreter at her side. She told the court how she'd met Jamie and his friends, including the Lam brothers, and much later, a man called Glen. She recalled Jamie and Glen had met regularly in Hurstville, sometimes in the evening, and how, on 17 May, Gao had arrived at her home and asked if she had any small plastic bags. When she asked why, he showed her a parcel of crystals wrapped in newspaper. She said she'd last heard from Jamie around 12.30 p.m. on 20 May when the two had exchanged messages on WeChat. She'd tried calling him during the afternoon without any luck and at around 6.30 p.m. his phone was answered by a male speaking in what she thought was Cantonese. She later received a few text messages including one in English saying, 'I'm his friend. He lost his phone,' and shortly after a message saying Jamie was in the city. Under cross-examination she said Jamie didn't work for Lok Lam, and hadn't mentioned any Triad connections.

Donald Burke, a coalminer who'd launched his boat from Grays Point on 26 May 2014, was planning a pleasant day's fishing. He motored up Port Hacking and around 6.45 a.m. entered the sea and turned northeast. Off Shelly Beach he spotted what he thought was a sail floating in the gentle swell. When he got closer he saw a blue tarpaulin and a silver-coloured bag – then what looked like a human foot in a white trainer. He pulled out his mobile and dialled 000. After the drama of the finding of the body, it was back to routine, broken only by a juror who was struggling to stay awake. His dozing was noticed by the ever-alert Justice Bellew, who dismissed him from the jury. He was the second to go – the first had departed early in the trial after reporting she knew one of the journalists covering the case. By the end of February, the jury was down from 15 to 13.

Jessica McNamara was called as a prosecution witness in early March. Prior to her entering the courtroom, the tall blonde 24-year-old had been waiting outside, supported by her aunt. The witness box is a lonely, difficult place, and even more so when you're giving evidence in a major criminal trial and that evidence is one of the deciders of the fate of the father you love very much. The Crown case took her through the afternoon of the murder and her observations of Rogerson and her father. She told the court she'd seen Roger's right hand touching the right-hand pocket of his track pants in a tapping, rubbing motion, and she noted a 'lump' in the pocket. George Thomas began his cross-examination with a light touch, but that didn't last long, and his manner became aggressive in an attempt to rattle the witness. Just before lunch on 3 March, she broke into tears. On resumption at 2 p.m., Thomas had moved his aggression up a notch and was warned by the judge. Jessica, however, had regained her composure and was stoic, glancing regularly at her father sitting in the dock.

When Thomas flagged he was about to raise the issue of her allegations of duress by Paul Kenny, the jury were sent out. Tapes of phone calls from McNamara to his family in the week following his arrest were played. Jessica gave evidence that Kenny had visited their apartment and checked it for security. During this visit she alleged

Kenny said to her Glen 'was stupid getting in with the big boys' and didn't know what he was doing. She said talking to Kenny was upsetting, but she wasn't pressed on why it took around 10 months for her to report the meeting and her fears. What the court also didn't hear was Kenny's detailed version of the same events.

Kenny is a meticulous notetaker, yet his notes were never called upon. Kenny was contacted by McNamara and asked to visit, which Kenny cleared with his client Rogerson. He said McNamara was a 'good friend' and while he couldn't speak to him on any legal matters, he was concerned for his health and wanted to know if there was anything he could do to help the family. On 30 May 2014 he went to Silverwater prison in which remand prisoners are kept, arriving at 9.45 a.m. McNamara joined him at 9.57 a.m. and Kenny said, 'He looked dreadful, but relieved to see a friendly face. What stunned was the first thing he said – have we got any support outside?' Kenny said they chatted about his health and McNamara alleged he'd been assaulted during the arrest and needed medical help and asked whether he could arrange a transfer to Long Bay.

Kenny recalled Glen asked him to visit his family to see if they were safe and secure because he was 'terrified of the Triads'. Kenny, being careful, had Glen write and sign the request in Kenny's notebook. Kenny met the McNamaras on 1 June at Cronulla, and Jessica instigated the visit. He returned the next day and inspected their home unit to assess its security, noting of the windows that 'someone could get in here'. The unit was on the ground floor so less secure. They talked about Jessica's job at the NSW Crime Commission, and Kenny, who'd interview her father a few days later on 4 June, offered to give her a hand if there was a problem. At one point in the visit, the enormity of what was alleged against his friend McNamara and client Rogerson hit him and he said, 'I broke down for a little bit.' The meeting, at which Cheryl McNamara had been present, ended amicably. He recalled Cheryl was living in Hong Kong but regularly in Sydney and had given him her business card. He believed the 'script' which alleged duress had been written after Glen's visit to the NSW Crime Commission two days later.

McNamara, accompanied by his barrister Ian Lloyd QC and solicitor Hudson Lu, had tried to cut a deal in return for giving evidence on a range of issues, but had been rebuffed. One source told me Glen's evidence was 'unconvincing veering to the improbable' and from the prosecution's perspective, giving up Roger was not only self-serving, but the ample amount of electronic surveillance, the body and the pile of drugs made the case hard to beat. Glen's evidence wasn't necessary.

Then it was back to the grind, with evidence about the purchase of the white Falcon, a moment brightened by evidence from Karl Bonnette, now in his eighties and still looking like he'd stepped out of a *GQ* photoshoot, but Karl denied involvement. By the end of evidence from a few witnesses about the car, it was highly likely Rogerson had orchestrated the deal, and his fingerprints were literally on the invoice for the purchase – later explained unconvincingly by Roger, who reckoned he'd touched the invoice while checking out the wagon to see if it was an ex-taxi.

However, it was Roger's publican friend Stephen Farley whose evidence nearly derailed the trial that had been running for seven weeks. In cross-examination by George Thomas, he'd been asked if he knew McNamara. Farley took the question as an opportunity to try a bombing raid of his own and replied he'd met him when he was working at the Mansions Hotel in Kings Cross. Farley said he'd known McNamara was a detective in Kings Cross at the time and added 'and a drug dealer'. A stunned moment of silence followed, then the judge sent the jury out of the room. Farley's bombshell landed late in the day, so we all went home, wondering if the trial would continue or whether it was over. Justice Bellew took submissions from all the barristers, with McNamara's counsel pushing to have the jury discharged. He returned with a decision the trial should continue and noted he'd instruct the jury to 'hearken to the evidence and obey the direction of the trial judge'. He also believed Farley's comment was 'gratuitous' and if the jury system couldn't take a few knocks along the way then it would never operate effectively. However, the trial was about to take another serious hit.

At the beginning of the tenth week, Chris Maxwell QC was just a few hours from the end of his case, and Kara Shead was poised to call her first defence witness – her client Glen McNamara. Over the weekend his legal team had been preparing him, but had run into a problem. While privilege and ethics preclude them telling what the issue was, it might have been prompted by a discussion over the proof of evidence they'd taken a few days before from Paul Kenny. The probability is that McNamara was changing his story to cast himself in a more favourable light, which creates a massive problem for his ethical team.

The Monday morning 10 a.m. start was delayed at Kara Shead's request, and when court resumed at 10.30 a.m., she stood and announced her client had withdrawn her instructions. She picked up her files and left the courtroom with her solicitor from the Public Defenders in tow. McNamara was now left with his solicitor Abdullah Reslan to represent him. The case resumed at 2.30 p.m. when Reslan, now seated at a less crowded bar table, rose and announced his instructions had also been withdrawn. The judge was a very unhappy man, the court was on tenterhooks, the jury were still outside and unaware of the drama being played out in the courtroom, and McNamara was standing in the dock, white-faced and sweating as Justice Bellew asked him if he was able to proceed or did he want to retain new lawyers, then adjourned the case for a couple of days. Outside, the jury still had no idea and wouldn't until they returned to find new faces at the bar table.

The departure of defence counsel at such a point in the trial offered up the terrible prospect of the trial being aborted. For Rogerson, who was funding his own defence, the prospect was unfair, and on broader issues, millions of dollars and the time of police, lawyers, the court and the jurors would be wasted if the matter ended because of McNamara's decision. The judge ordered everyone back in court at 2 p.m. the following Friday and as I was walking towards the court I saw Charles Waterstreet, gowned up and ready to offer himself as, he quipped, 'counsel of last resort'. He was joined in court by McNamara's new solicitor Ali Abbas who'd once been mistakenly held in the US as a suspected terrorist – until they'd checked his fingerprints and realised they'd got the wrong man and released him.

On 11 April, the court resumed at 10 a.m. and Waterstreet wasn't at the bar table, but Gabriel Wendler – a man with a magnificent nose and author of the 'Wendler on Wine' pieces for the legal magazine *Justinian* – announced he was appearing for McNamara. After legal aid funding was expedited, and haggling over how long it would take for the new team to 'get up to speed', and with the poor jurors in limbo, Justice Bellew adjourned the case until Thursday, 14 April.

29

THE CUTTHROAT DEFENCE

Chris Maxwell finished the prosecution case at 2.50 p.m. on Thursday, 14 April. The forty-ninth day of trial. The seasons had changed, the cast in the courtroom were no longer sitting uncomfortably in pools of perspiration and the first cardigans had appeared. The positions in the dock had changed too, and when the accused were brought up that morning from the cells, Roger had come first, followed by McNamara. When Maxwell sat down, Wendler called for his client to give evidence. McNamara, looking surprisingly confident, stood, crossed the courtroom and took his place in the witness box, where he took the Bible in his hand and looked at the judge while the sheriff's officer administered the oath to tell the truth. The judge then told McNamara to take a seat.

Wendler opened his case dramatically by asking if his client had shot Jamie Gao, and the reply was no surprise – 'No I did not.' As the evidence rolled along McNamara said he'd gone to the storage unit with Rogerson who told him he needed a hand to fix the roller door – an explanation of why the two had been recorded opening and closing the door a few times on their visit earlier on 20 May and McNamara added Rogerson had brought a light with him to assist in their repairs, which also conveniently explained why it wasn't pitch black when the two met Gao there shortly after.

McNamara said Rogerson was supposed to meet Gao at the nearby McDonald's, but instead came to Arab Road, and Jamie appeared to be 'very scared' as he slipped into the back seat of the white station wagon McNamara was driving. After they'd arrived at the storage unit and were inside, Gao told him, 'The Triads have been chasing me all fucking day, they are up at Arab Road,' prompting Glen to ask, 'Why did you come to me?' Gao said, 'Roger told me to.' Glen said, 'Where's Roger? The Triads wouldn't have got him, would they?' and Gao said, 'No, he is supposed to be right behind us.'

Rogerson arrived around three minutes later. McNamara said Gao was sitting on one of the old office chairs with his backpack on his lap. He told the court, 'Rogerson said to Gao, "You were supposed to come to me, you fucking idiot," and Gao said to Rogerson, "It's better to have a witness, where is the money?" Rogerson said to Gao, "Where's the gear?" Gao said to Rogerson, "The two guys I came with are holding it. It will be here in half an hour, but money first."'

McNamara's testimony was clear, concise and had everyone in court riveted. He was performing better than I thought he would. He went on. 'Rogerson said, "Those two idiots who got out of your car? Bullshit. Give me the gear." Gao said, "No, it will be half an hour, money first." Rogerson said, "There's no money for you, fuckwit." Gao said, "Fuck you, I'm going." Rogerson said, "I want the gear," at which point Gao reached into his bag and began to pull out a combat-style knife.'

McNamara said Roger was 'seething with anger, the angriest I've ever seen him', which is a curious observation that makes you wonder what the two had been up to that would stir someone with a reputation for being calm. 'Mr Gao attempted to get up. He was seated on this chair with all the cross brace of wheels on the bottom, it was like a concrete floor and he was a large man, a tall man, so he had to flick himself backwards to move up, if you like, to stop the chair from going backwards. As he moved, I could see that when he stood up he was going to be directly in front of Rogerson's chest with the knife. As he flicked to go up, he moved his body up slightly and Rogerson shot him,' twice. The first shot pushed Jamie back into the chair and his arms splayed. McNamara said he heard the 'tinkle' of the knife falling to the ground, again a curious observation given they were in a tin shed moments after a loud gunshot. He said Jamie was moaning and Rogerson held his aim and didn't move, then fired again. Jamie 'stopped moving, there was no noise, he just killed him instantly'.

McNamara, who'd taken refuge under a table, yelled, 'Why why why?'

Up to this point, McNamara's evidence had been delivered convincingly, and it was a story that made sense. Wendler then stopped the narrative. They'd reached a point at which the jury should leave so the next tranche of evidence could be discussed. Justice Bellew said, 'Ladies and gentlemen, I have been made aware that an issue is about to arise,' and so the jury left the courtroom, unsure of how long the issue would take to resolve.

With McNamara still in the witness box, Wendler told the court the evidence his client would now give, if allowed, was 'Rogerson then turned and approached him pointing the gun directly at his head and said the words "I did Drury" a reference to a person called Michael Drury, a former police officer, "I did Drury, I'll do you too. Get up and fucking help me you weak cunt or I'll leave you on the floor lying next to him." I expect the evidence will be then that Rogerson's rejoinder was, "he pulled the fucking knife first, get up and help me or you'll be as dead as him, then I'll kill your girls".'

The story had the gallery riveted and journalists feverishly taking notes – it was a magnificent piece of theatre. Wendler then moved to conversations McNamara had had with Rogerson in the bar of his Padstow home. McNamara said Roger had agreed to let him write his life story after he was dead, and could include the list of people that Roger either killed or was complicit in their deaths. Rogerson allegedly told him he'd murdered Warren Lanfranchi, was complicit in the murder of Sallie-Anne Huckstepp and Luton Chu, and arranged the murder of Alan Williams. The excitement of the afternoon paused with a note from the jury, still waiting in the jury room, requesting more lever-arch folders and pencils.

Wendler resumed his grisly narration and said Rogerson had told McNamara: 'When I was charged with conspiracy to murder Drury, that cunt, Clive Small, got Alan Williams to give me up. Williams only did three years for pleading guilty to conspiracy with Flannery and me to murder Drury. Williams is dead now. It looked like suicide but it wasn't. I never let anyone get away with giving me up. I couldn't let Williams get away with that, the cunt of a thing.' Wendler paused, then said, 'The rejoinder from

McNamara was, "You arranged his murder?" The response from Rogerson was, "Yeah, I'm connected everywhere. He thought he was living a quiet life after jail, but not so.'"

Wendler said Roger then told his client he'd also despatched Christopher Dale Flannery, who '"was real close to Alan Williams, both Melbourne blokes. As soon as I heard that fucking Small was working on Williams to roll over, I couldn't leave it to chance that Chris wouldn't roll as well. He was a coke fiend. He wasn't as tough as everyone thought. It was the coke. Kath, his missus, used to dose him up before he went out and did a job to hype him up. He was with me when I done Drury, off his head on coke, the useless cunt. If the two of them had been against me I would have been fucked. Chris had the twitches from too much coke so I shot Drury. Chris was just a useless drug addict.'" When McNamara asked about Flannery's fate, Roger told him, '"Chris had run out of mates in Sydney, he's killed most of them. He had to go. I was his only friend. It was easy. I met with him and put two in his chest, then we put him on a boat, went out three miles off Sydney Heads, mate.'"

Wendler said, 'The conversation moved to the circumstances of Mr Lanfranchi. Mr McNamara asked, "What happened with Lanfranchi?" He replied, "I shot Lanfranchi twice, once in the neck and then one in the chest. That was close. The jury said I didn't act in self-defence. Those fucking lefties at the *Herald* and the ABC gave me fucking heaps but I got through it." Mr McNamara said, "Why did you shoot Lanfranchi for a second time?" And Mr Rogerson said, "He had to die, he ripped off Ned's gear which was my gear. Only one thing for a bloke like that. He was wanted for attempted murder of a police motorcyclist so it was easy to justify.'"

With Rogerson's best-known moment on record, Wendler said he moved on to Sallie-Anne Huckstepp and said, '"Fuck me, she had to go. Even after I sued Channel Nine she was still into me, the fucking junkie bitch. It was a problem for Ned as well, one we solved. You know she drowned in a shallow pond. No one puts shit on me, I always win.'" Finally, Luton Chu was a '"heroin dealer, up and down between Australia and Hong Kong. Thought he could outsmart his suppliers. I helped my Chinese friends fix him up as well.'"

Wendler said that was what his client would say, 'in broad terms'. It was an extraordinary end to a memorable afternoon. Roger concluded his bragging by showing Glen the pen set made of bullets and with the names engraved.

It was no surprise when Justice Bellew declined to let McNamara's allegations be given in evidence in front of the jury. McNamara told the court about the origins of the murder weapon. He alleged Roger said to him it came from his mate, and, 'He's a mad gun perv. I've got guns from [him] when I've needed them. My Chinese friends told me what a dangerous little cunt Jamie was and I got a gun. God strike me, he pulled a knife first.' Roger's mate was interviewed by police but not called to give evidence in the trial. McNamara spent 10 days in the witness box, telling the court he had no idea Rogerson had been armed. He talked about his friendship with Gao, who was helping him research a book on ice and organised crime gangs. The two became so close they even had pet names for each other – Glen was 'son' and Jamie was 'mum'. When shown evidence of over 20 meetings and multiple text messages even in the early hours of the morning, McNamara passed this off as research opportunities and his genuine care for Jamie's welfare.

He also talked of the threats by Rogerson and how on the day of the murder he was 'terrified, paralysed, stunned' when Roger demanded his help, saying, 'Do as I tell you or I'll kill your girl'. It was a well-woven tale, which put Glen firmly in the frame as a victim of circumstances, and not a cold-blooded killer and drug dealer. But it wasn't convincing. Glen's skill as a witness deteriorated after his magnificent opening moments, becoming evasive, talking too much and not addressing the question, which resulted in him often being pulled up by the judge.

His testimony also posed one question in my mind. He said while the two were back at Cronulla having finally got Jamie into the boat, that Roger had told him to take the white wagon up to the visitor parking so 'it can't be seen around the garage'. McNamara said he drove to the upper level where the visitor parking was, and saw the caretaker, Herman, whom he engaged in conversation. McNamara said he did so as it meant Herman would recall seeing the car in that spot. McNamara reckoned he was 'laying crumbs' that investigators could later follow. In my mind, his credibility hit a new low. Why didn't he explain to Herman there was a gun-toting homicidal geriatric one level below who'd just put a murder victim into a boat on a trailer and was threatening both him and his daughters, one of whom was in their apartment? If he'd told Herman to call 000 he would have been credible because the coppers would have arrived before Roger could have hobbled into the killing range of the .25 calibre murder weapon. Instead, they exchanged pleasantries, then Roger and Glen went to Glen's apartment to have a cold beer.

Cross-examination by George Thomas was the predictable, 'I put it to you, Mr McNamara, you are lying.' McNamara was an uninspiring witness. Aside from his own testimony, McNamara's defence case was brief. The extensive preparation his previous team had done, looking at the deaths of Luton Chu and Butch Byrne, and the litany of stories about Roger couldn't be used.

As McNamara's defence was coming to an end, Thomas floated the idea the trial might be ending sooner than recent estimates because his client was considering not giving evidence. After howls from the bar table about the unfairness of this surprise move that bordered on ambush, and a further conference with his client, Thomas told the court that the moment we'd all been waiting for would not be denied to us. Roger would be the sole witness for his defence.

On 6 May at 2 p.m., Rogerson, dressed in a black shirt and his usual ill-fitting oatmeal-coloured jacket, entered the witness box, and followed the same routine as McNamara. When seated, his left hand was on the rail of the box, and his right hand, with an obvious tremor, fidgeted about in his lap. He used both hands when sipping from the water glass provided. He turned the charm on the jury, telling them he'd introduced Glen to his mates at the Crown and at the Grandviews Bowling Club, but Glen hadn't reciprocated. He talked about how Glen had told him Gao was assisting with book research, and how on the day before the killing McNamara had said to him 'things are hotting up' with Jamie's alleged problems with the Triads.

On 20 May, Roger said, he was out working in the garden when Glen arrived in the white station wagon and said he was going to meet Gao at the McDonald's on the corner of Davies and Arab Road. Jamie believed the Triads were following him, and the two set up a 'default meeting place' at the storage unit. Roger had given Glen the keys and the code. When he arrived at the unit and saw Gao on the floor, Roger said, 'I was shot to pieces' – a poor choice of words that didn't register with him – and 'the enormity of what happened hit me'. Glen told him '"this arsehole nearly killed me!"' and when Roger inquired if he was okay, Glen said, '"He can't hurt me but his mates can and I'm very worried about my daughters".'

Roger alleged McNamara then said, '"What about giving me a hand getting him into my boat. I'll get rid of him in the morning,"' and '"I've got to distance myself from him. If his body is found with bullets in it, his mates will be after me!"'

Roger went on to tell the court the next morning he'd waited at the boat ramp as Glen sailed off to get rid of Jamie's body.

Throughout his evidence, Roger had been long-winded, off the question and occasionally rambling, causing the judge to repeatedly warn him. Roger was trying to tell his own story the way he wanted to tell it, but he wasn't going to get away with it. This was no longer the persuasive witness I'd seen 30 years before. Roger was shifty, trying to be devious and clever, and failing badly.

In cross-examination by Wendler, Roger made a remarkable statement, telling the barrister he was fearful of the Triads, and thought if they'd caught up with him and Glen there would have been 'a bloody scene, these people are killers,' and that Gao had told McNamara 'he'd ripped these blokes off and was going to piss off'. However, Roger hadn't called the police because he feared there would be 'bloodshed for sure'. Then he said he'd trusted Glen, to which Wendler asked, 'You're effectively saying you're a victim?' Roger replied, 'I have been a victim.' Looking at the faces in the jury box, Roger had just lost any hope of convincing them of his innocence. He quipped that while the day of the murder wasn't a nightmare, 'I've had plenty since,' and that he'd only gone with McNamara as a gesture of friendship and a 'second set of eyes'. He thought 'the whole thing is solvable' and contradicted his earlier testimony by saying it could be explained to the police if they'd been contacted.

Of his relationship with Glen he said, 'I accepted more orders than I have given,' and explained a note in his own handwriting that outlined the opening address to the jury, as 'my sort of humour is a bit strange'.

His frequent response to hard questions in the cross-examination was his old favourite, 'rubbish, absolute rubbish,' or 'complete fantasy'. Unfortunately for Roger, his evidence could be similarly described. He was making comments out of context, rambling, raising his voice to the point where the judge would reprimand him and Roger would not acknowledge the judge. The once-brilliant witness ended his career in the box with a whimper.

The summing up by the three barristers began the next week. Maxwell said the stories of the two accused were 'far-fetched' and, 'Right from the fact Jamie Gao opened that partly opened door on Arab Road, everything was done by both accused to make sure that he disappeared, that he disappeared and would not be found at all.' He outlined 29 reasons why both men should be convicted of murder and drug supply, and ended his address with, 'It will be your solemn obligation to return a verdict of guilty in relation to both counts against both accused.' Thomas followed, then Wendler, with both men raking through details of the case to cast doubt on the 'joint criminal enterprise' and shift the weight of blame on to the other.

Justice Bellew had the last word on the case. His instructions to the jury began on 30 May. He recapped four months' worth of evidence and told them about their responsibilities and the law. On 2 June, the eighty-first day of the trial, they retired to consider their verdict. The thirteenth juror saved the need for a vote to see who would be removed, when one explained to the judge he had both family and business commitments, so Justice Bellew thanked the man and let him go.

In the huddles outside the courtroom, speculation on how long the jury will take dies off quickly. No matter how experienced you might be, guessing what is in the mind of the jury or how long they'll take is futile. However, by the sixth day of deliberations it was getting worrying – was someone holding out, would there be a hung jury and thus another trial, when would the judge bring them back and ask what the problem was? I was overseas when the jury went out, and was waking a few times during the night to check and see if they'd come back with a verdict. After 30 years of Roger-watching, I needed to know. I arrived back in Sydney on Wednesday, 15 June 2016, at 8.30 a.m. after a 22-hour flight, and just as I'd stepped from the shower one of the court watchers rang me – 'Great timing,' she said, 'the jury has just sent a note to the judge saying they have a verdict.' It was 10.15 a.m., and I made it to the courtroom just as the verdict was being read – both men were guilty of murder and supplying of a prohibited drug.

Roger stared malevolently at the jury, and McNamara looked at the railing of the dock. When Justice Bellew thanked the jury for their service in this epic trial, they rose and began to leave the courtroom for the last time. McNamara, in keeping with protocol, stood. Roger, however, remained seated, glowering at their backs.

30

JUSTICE AT LAST

The old court complex in Darlinghurst has been the scene of some of Australia's greatest criminal trials and Rogerson's many victories when he was a serving police officer. On 25 August 2016, court five was the venue for his and McNamara's sentencing hearing. This time, there would be no photoshoots or press conferences afterwards by Rogerson. I'd been told that since the verdict Roger was still defiant, but had sold his precious classic 1950s Dodge car – I've spoken to a few of Roger's acquaintances and no one knows if the name of his choice of collectable had any irony – and told a mate he could have all the tools in his home workshop.

The large and airy courtroom was packed with media and the public, keen to hear the closing moments of what had been a long and dramatic trial. McNamara, wearing a suit and now with a luxuriant white–grey beard, was first up the well-worn steps from the cells beneath the courtroom. As he entered the dock, he smiled at his family in the public gallery, trying to offer them some reassurance.

Rogerson was next. The familiar oversized oatmeal jacket wasn't being worn this morning; instead he was dressed in his dull-green prison pants and sweatshirt. It might have been for comfort, but I reckon it was defiance – an 'up yours' to the judicial system he'd once manipulated, but which for many years after the end of his police career he'd held in contempt. He looked about briefly, and not seeing any familiar faces in the gallery, sat down. There were no quips to the sketch artist in the press gallery about capturing his best side. Just as they had been throughout the trial, both men sat as far away from each other as possible, and avoided even a glance. Both men stood when Justice Bellew entered and took his seat on the Bench.

Chris Maxwell QC outlined the prosecution's submission on penalty, and said the murder of Jamie Gao was 'more serious than just a straight-out killing for the payment of money' and that it entailed gaining the young man's trust and then 'to lure him into unit 803 and there to execute him and steal the drugs'.

George Thomas for Rogerson and Gabriel Wendler for McNamara reprised snippets from the trial, pointing at each other's client as being more culpable than the other. Thomas said there was never 'a plan to murder the deceased, rather the plan was to rip off the drugs'. Thomas didn't have any character references to tender on his client's behalf.

Wendler said it was 'contrary to commonsense that both offenders, former experienced police officers, devised the plan to kill the deceased, during a business day, at a public storage facility covered by CCTV and then in a most incompetent, ludicrous manner, transport the body to the multi-residential complex'. Wendler tendered eleven character references on behalf of McNamara from family members such as his mother, two daughters, ex-wife and his aunt, and from friends. Their opinions were consistent – Glen was a good, caring and honourable family man; virulently anti-drugs, and his crimes were totally out of character. Glen's version of the incidents at Kings Cross in 1989 had been accepted as accurate by almost everyone. Both Thomas and Wendler were arguing their clients should receive sentences commensurate to their complicity in the crimes, and avoid a life sentence for murder.

Maxwell, in his reply, said there was nothing 'ludicrously incompetent' about Rogerson and McNamara's crimes, but 'there is a boldness about [them], particularly, one might think, consistent with Mr Rogerson's general attitude'. Maxwell went on, saying, 'This was a killing to enable both offenders to obtain the drug, the large commercial quantity, almost three kilograms of the drug colloquially known as ice, a drug that results in so much crime itself being committed.' He said, 'It is not just for the money. It's so they can obtain, and then distribute a drug which has been proved to be, amongst others, a scourge of our society.' It was this final ingredient that Maxwell reckoned made their crime 'more serious than just a straight-out killing for the payment of money'. His submission was for a life sentence for each man on the murder.

Justice Bellew then adjourned until Friday 2 September. Roger had sat stony-faced throughout the entire proceedings. Unlike his fervent scribbling during the trial, there were no notes, no paperwork to shuffle. McNamara alternated between looking into the distance, and staring down at his hands on the ledge of the dock. On leaving, he looked at his family and pushed his chin up with his finger and smiled.

On that wet and blustery afternoon, the courtroom was again packed with media and the public. McNamara's family were in the court, but Roger's wife Anne wasn't, and there were few if any supporters for him. However, there were some there to see justice done. Sitting discreetly behind the detectives who worked on the case was Lola Scott, whose police career had been savaged by McNamara. In the public gallery were Warren Lanfranchi's brothers, Lyn Woodward's brother and one of Neddy Smith's sons.

McNamara entered the dock first, still bearded and wearing a suit. He again smiled to reassure his family and friends. Next up was Rogerson, still preferring prison greens. He looked around and noted *Daily Telegraph* crime reporter Mark Morri sitting in the jury box with other reporters. Morri had written extensively on Rogerson since the verdict, talking about other killings in which Roger may have been involved, including Lyn Woodward's disappearance and likely murder. Rogerson wasn't too happy to see Morri, and mouthed the word 'cunt' to him.

Justice Bellew arrived on the Bench at around 2.15 p.m. He read from his written judgement, speaking for nearly two and a half hours. As expected from a judge who'd kept a complex rollercoaster of a trial on track, the judgement was detailed and meticulous, and began with a detailed recounting of all the evidence. Then came his comments on the gravity of Rogerson and McNamara's crimes. Justice Bellew said, 'The joint criminal enterprise to which each offender was a party was extensive in its planning, brutal in its execution, and callous in its aftermath.' He noted it was clear both men acted with a complete disregard for Jamie Gao's life, and that Rogerson had said during cross-examination, '"I had no respect for the deceased as a person. . . . I had no respect for this person as a decent person. As far as I knew he was a drug dealer.' This had caused a stir among those of us in court who knew of Rogerson's long association with the drug trade.

The likelihood of life imprisonment for both men for the murder became more certain when Justice Bellew said, 'This was not just a case where the offending as a whole was motivated by the prospect of financial gain. It was a case in which that financial gain was to be realised by the participation in further serious criminal activity. In my view, on the whole of the evidence, there is nothing at all to materially distinguish the respective roles played by each offender.' He followed with a clinical dissection of the improbability of many of their claims, then moved on to canvassing McNamara's references and past, then on to Rogerson, his medical history, and noting that he had 'no criminal history of violent offending' – which drew loud snorts and sniggers from the gallery. It was a reference to Roger's official criminal history and not what most of us knew he'd gotten away with.

Bellew found there was 'no relevant distinction' between a contract killing and the case before him. Both men hadn't shown any remorse for their actions and McNamara in a pre-sentence report had still 'adamantly espoused his innocence', and that neither man accepted the jury's verdict. Bellew said both remained a danger to the community and 'any sentence to be imposed must be such as to deter the offenders, as well as others who might be minded to engage in acts of this nature for illegal monetary gain'. Justice Bellew told both men to rise. He dealt with Glen Patrick McNamara first – sentence for supplying a prohibited drug to a non-parole period of nine years commencing on 25 May 2014 and expiring on 24 May 2023, with a further three years expiring on 24 May 2026. For the murder of Jamie Gao – life imprisonment starting from 25 May 2014.

Roger Caleb Rogerson received identical sentences to those of McNamara. Justice Bellew paused, and one man in the public gallery stood and cheered. As the Sheriff's Officers moved towards the man, Bellew briskly ordered the two prisoners to be taken down.

Throughout the afternoon's proceedings, McNamara had sat pale-faced and moist around the eyes, wiping an occasional tear. Rogerson was again stony-faced, staring down at his gnarled hands resting on the ledge of the dock and only raising his eyes slightly when Justice Bellew mentioned a point specifically about him. At one stage I thought he may have been dozing. Neither man reacted dramatically when their fates were announced – both looked as though they knew what was coming.

Roger Rogerson, once touted as one of the nation's best coppers, an insatiable media tart with a carefully crafted image of a jovial old rogue, and considered by many – until his arrest for the cold-blooded killing of Jamie Gao – as a good bloke, will die in prison. Over the last forty years, this callous, evil man has ruined the lives of decent honourable coppers, ordinary citizens and more than a few colourful characters who had the temerity to cross him. It's taken a while, but justice has finally caught up with the man who didn't like being called 'The Dodger'.

ACKNOWLEDGEMENTS

My thanks to everyone at Hachette for their terrific support, enthusiasm and professionalism, and to my agent, Lyn Tranter – if it wasn't for her I'd never have written a book. Finally, to the usual suspects – a wonderful mix of ex-coppers and colourful identities whose knowledge, integrity, insight and networks make research both a pleasure and an intriguing journey.

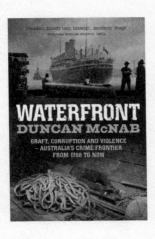

It's been over two centuries since the first crooks arrived on Australia's waterfront. Business is still booming . . .

Ever since the First Fleet dropped anchor, Australia's ports have been a breeding ground for many of Australia's most notorious criminals, and a magnet for local and overseas crime syndicates.

From the rum trade of colonial times to modern-day drug smuggling and alongside the rise and dominance of waterfront unions, a criminal element has always found ways to survive and thrive. After a century of Royal Commissions, reports, denials and crackdowns, crime and wrongdoing in Australia's ports remains organised, entrenched and incredibly profitable.

In *Waterfront*, investigative journalist and former police detective Duncan McNab chronicles the larger-than-life characters who have populated Australia's docks, wharves and ports – and lifts the lid on the crime, politics, violence and corruption that has always been present on Australia's waterfront.

Praise for *Dead Man Running* by Duncan NcNab and Ross Coulthart
'a fine read . . . full of accounts of murder, mayhem and dirty dealing'
Sydney Morning Herald

ASSASSINATION?
CONSPIRACY?

JFK
THE SMOKING GUN

COLIN McLAREN

Evidence of the shocking truth is finally revealed

On 22nd November 1963, the 35th president of the United States, John Fitzgerald Kennedy, and his wife Jackie were taking part in a presidential motorcade through Dallas. Thousands lined the streets cheering; others hung out of windows to catch a glimpse of the much-loved First Lady and President. Suddenly, the unthinkable: three shots – bang ... bang, bang – rang out. In front of the world, JFK was fatally wounded.

Lee Harvey Oswald was caught. But did he fire the fatal bullet? Who *really* killed JFK?

More than fifty years after the tragic events in Dallas, *JFK: The Smoking Gun* solves the ultimate cold case.

With the forensic eye of a highly regarded ex-cop, Colin McLaren gathered the evidence, studied 10,000 pages of transcripts, discovered the witnesses the Warren Commission failed to call, and uncovered the exhibits and testimonies that were hidden until now. What he found is far more outrageous than any fanciful conspiracy theory could ever be.

JFK: The Smoking Gun proves, once and for all,
who did kill the president

**Compelling stories from Australia's dark heart – of catastrophe
and misfortune, intrigue and passion, betrayal and tragedy.**

Australian Tragic ranges across our past and our present: the heartbreaking story of the fire at Luna Park; the unstoppable opportunist
who snatched innocent men and women from Palm Island to be part
of P.T. Barnum's 'Greatest Show on Earth'; a world-class boxer who
lost his battle with alcohol and ended up in an unmarked American
grave; a man who heroically survived a war to find himself crushed
and defeated by events close to home; and a new story – of an echo
from Ned Kelly at Stringybark Creek, in our own time . . .

Heartbreaking and shocking, gothic and bizarre, these fascinating
and true stories tell us of the Australia we don't know, the one that
simmers with love and hate, of hopes raised and futures dashed,
unheralded and unnoticed . . . until now.

'Indecently entertaining and . . .
full of stories that deserve to be more widely known'
Age

hachette
AUSTRALIA

If you would like to find out more about Hachette Australia, our authors, upcoming events and new releases you can visit our website, Facebook or follow us on Twitter:

hachette.com.au
facebook.com/HachetteAustralia
twitter.com/HachetteAus